What people are saying about Rethinking Leadership...

Traditional approaches to leadership may have served us in more settled times but they pull up well short in this new, fast-changing world. It is a well-researched, readable and practical guide to moving from individualistic leadership to harnessing the array of gifts and skills of the group. – **Harvey Collins, Non-executive Director Navitas Limited and Save the Children Australia, Chairman Insitor Impact Asia Fund and executive coach**

Rethinking Leadership makes a compelling case that traditional ideas and ways of thinking about leadership don't work. It provides a range of frameworks and practices to navigate change and complexity, and build a leadership practice that is adaptive, agile and authentic. For anyone interested in making change in the world, in your organisation or community this is a valuable, comprehensive resource to guide you through. – **Liz Skelton, Director Collaboration for Impact and co-author The Australian Leadership Paradox**

The core concepts here have helped me considerably working with companies facing disruptive change, both as a chairman and coach to CEOs. – **Ian Pollard, company chairman, executive coach & writer**

A beautifully thought out, well-designed read that can be easily navigated: a rare example of 'simplicity on the other side of complexity'. A must read for anyone seeking to step into the unknown and play a role in bringing about change in the complex and ever moving world we live in. – **Bessi Graham Co-Founder/CEO The Difference Incubator**

The problem with disruptive change is that a bumper sticker philosophy doesn't work. Rethinking Leadership outlines practical ways for groups to constructively engage such complexity. This book turns the myth of the superhero leader on its head and speaks powerfully to a generation looking for better ways forward. – **Trevor Thomas, Managing Director Ethinvest, Trustee John T Reid Charitable Trusts and Community Impact Foundation**

Not here a shopping-list template or an alpha-leader who rallies a tribe by force of will. "Rethinking Leadership" starts at a different place altogether.
– Steve Collis, workplace and learning environment strategist

We have had first-hand experience in our school of transforming a top down leadership model into a something very different to meet the challenges of contemporary education. It has been incredibly rewarding. This book offers life-giving frameworks for this. It is a must-read manual for developing effective sustained change within your school. It challenges your thinking about your own leadership and can help you stay sane and strong. The ideas here helped us be at our very best in the transformation. **– Doug Thomas and Janelle Ford, Principal and Deputy Principal, Claremont College**

A scholarly yet engaging work with lots of stories and personal/group exercises. I highlighted many many sections that I need to come back to and think about. **– Dr Bruce Robinson AM, Professor of Medicine, Physician, Director of NHMRC Research Centre of Excellence, the multi-award winning Fathering Project and Western Australian of the Year**

For many First Nations leaders, we are continually hindered and frustrated by the speed of social change, and the accompanying complexity of adapting to disruption and rapid change. This book is definitely overdue! The wisdom here could be quite life changing. **– Ray Minniecon, Aboriginal community activist and chaplain**

Emanating trustworthiness with its good solid leadership scholarship the book is full of sound leadership practice. Its format is rather like a virtual coaching experience. If I was teaching leadership to students or recommending books that provide an overview of the field, this would be one. If I think of young emerging leaders I have coached, I am sure that they would find something in it to reassure themselves. And, if I had come home from work as a leader responsible for a thorny leadership problem, I would use the book as a reference and find a way forward! **– Hilary Armstrong, PhD, Director Changeworks, leadership coaching and culture change**

A breath of fresh air. The authors address bullet points we've been staring at for years by looking at them from a new angle, or from a perspective we've somehow lost. This book is worthy of your time and attention and should be prioritised in this year's reading list. **– Julian Dunham, Arrow Leadership, International Development**

A comprehensive primer for all the important change and leadership theories as well as a tool for connecting oneself to the challenges we face in trying to lead in the real world. Probably most importantly, it is grounded in the idea of leadership being about a real contribution to the world. – **Geoff Aigner, Executive Director Social Innovation, Life Without Barriers**

Rethinking Leadership is an insightful and practical guide to the kind of leadership that is required for real change and engagement. If we care about the broader community we live in, then collaborative, engaging and non-traditional leadership practice and models are needed. This book is a template for how to go about it. – **Michael Traill, Chair, Social Ventures Australia and Goodstart Early Learning, Director MH Carnegie and Co. and Author Jumping Ship**

The democratising of leadership will create the change we want to see in our institutions and communities. This book is an outstanding overview of the type of contemporary leadership that can help an individual or organisation take positive steps into this future. – **Doug Taylor, Director Uniting NSW/ACT, Board member Australian Centre for Social Innovation**

Anyone involved in leadership in the social sector will value this book because it is a unique resource that encompasses all the latest research and provides a practical guide about how to be an effective leader in a community setting. – **Jill Reich, Director People and Systems, Uniting NSW/ACT**

An antidote to the toxicity of leadership models that rely on an individualistic, messiah-like vision of leadership. – **Darrell Jackson, Associate Professor Morling College Sydney**

A fantastic approach to reflecting on our own leadership styles and experiences, and how we act in the context of change. – **Maayan Adler, management consultant with PwC**

Published by Thousand Lakes Publishing, Sydney, Australia.
For further information: publishing@thousandlakes.com.au.

National Library of Australia Catalouging-in-Publication entry:

Kaldor, Peter, Nash, Naomi and Paterson, Sophie, authors.
Rethinking leadership: Building capacity for positive change.
ISBN 978-0-6481311-0-6 Paperback
ISBN 978-0-6481311-1-3 Hardback
ISBN 978-0-6481311-2-0 ebook

Subjects:
1. Leadership.
2. Organisational change.
3. Positive psychology.
4. Personal development.

Design by Mezzanine.

*This book is dedicated to three people who
shaped our thinking and our lives:*

Alan Dutton, Dean Drayton and Peter Pereira

With many thanks.

Rethinking

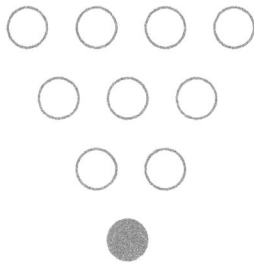

Leadership

Building capacity for positive change

About the authors

Peter Kaldor
With a background in community development and social policy, Peter is a researcher, partnership-builder, innovator and experience-based educator. He has been involved in research into personal and community wellbeing, values, spirituality, social capital, as well as patterns of effective and sustainable leadership, drawing on large-scale survey research and insights from the social sciences. As founding director of research agency NCLS Research and an honorary research fellow with Australian universities he has written many publications including Building Stronger Communities and Lead with your Strengths. He is a Director of New River Leadership, loves team sports and wilderness exploration.

Naomi Nash
Naomi is the Managing Director and lead consultant with New River Leadership. She has worked with social welfare agencies, schools, executives and individuals, and to explore leadership and cultural change. She enjoys listening deeply to organisational story, encouraging individuals, and fostering positivity. Naomi has a passion for entrepreneurship and mentoring start-ups, particularly with young people. She loves playing music and songwriting.

Sophie Paterson
A teacher, coach, team-builder and New River Leadership team member, Sophie has a passion for systems thinking and educational leadership that can equip students, staff and schools to effectively engage change. She has worked in NSW public schools as a teacher, leader, mentor and curriculum coordinator and is an AITSL accredited lead teacher. More broadly, she is passionate about creating learning moments for individuals that unlock potential and purpose to make a difference. She loves walking in the Tasmanian wilderness, building community and creative gluten-free cooking.

Peter, Naomi and Sophie are concerned to support people of all ages and backgrounds to discover their leadership strengths and, alongside others, make a positive and sustainable difference wherever they are. They want to assist organisations across our society navigate complex change, something that requires a different understanding and practice of 'leadership'.

info@newriver.org.au
newriver.org.au

Some of the material in this book was developed as part of Peter's work with NCLS Research between 1996 and 2007, reported in Lead with your Strengths, written with John McLean and the NCLS team.

Contents

Introduction
There has to be a better way

We assume we paddle our organisational canoes on calm lakes, and periodically have to go through some temporary white water. But we never get out of the white water. We think things will settle down after whatever is now upsetting things is over, but things never settle down because some other upset always comes along.

– Peter Vaill[1]

ARE YOU PART of an organisation facing disruptive change? Or wanting to make a positive difference in complex situations? We live in times where swirling change is the norm. Change is often more challenging than we expect. Tossed about by loud voices, competing agendas and options we start to lose traction. Wheels spinning, we dig a deep hole for ourselves and our teams. Researchers commonly suggest 70% of change initiatives fail.[2]

If you are looking at this book you probably already recognise that creating change and contributing leadership in the uncertain, unpredictable and volatile world in which we live is not a simple task.

Perhaps you are in a social sector agency, business, union, church or community group, facing challenges to do with a changing community, changing needs, practices, government expectations, advancing technology, increasingly global markets, increasing competition. You might be experimenting with new possibilities. You might be in a school facing big questions about how to best equip students for a future no-one can yet see. Or involved in community development or social action. You might be trying to support others through consultancy, mentoring or coaching.

Perhaps you face complex challenges at home or in your community. Or, as a parent you might be doing well with one child yet struggling with another due to factors out of your control within the family, school or wider community.

You may have a role where you are responsible for delivering outcomes and generating change. You are struggling to develop ways forward, things are a bit precarious and people are anxious. What might effective leadership look like in your context?

Or you may be in middle management seeing damage being done by people further up the food chain who think they know best but lack detailed understanding of the coalface. How to respond?

Or you may sit at the foot of the table without formal responsibilities, yet have a desire to make a positive difference. Can a pivotal change in an organisation's direction ever come from the bottom up?

You may see yourself as a good leader and want to be a better one. Or maybe you have doubts, even feeling you are an imposter. Or you might want to reject the leadership paradigms you have experienced. You don't want any part of anything that encourages dominating manipulative people wielding power because they can.

We all face a common question: *how can we contribute effectively to making a positive difference amidst the complexity around us?*

If you are passionate about what you do and wish to engage authentically and meaningfully with people, this book might help. If you value honesty, authenticity and personal growth, it might help. If you stay awake at night balancing pressures to achieve strategic outcomes, are distressed about wasted opportunities or ineffectual behaviour, or see the limitations of how things currently are, we believe this book might make a real difference.

The seductive myth of superhero leaders

It is critical that leaders resist assuming the role of saviour, even as people beg for it.

- Margaret Wheatley[3]

WE OFTEN TALK about 'leadership', meaning very different things. Sometimes 'leadership' is about position or formal roles, other times gifted people with particular traits. Sometimes it denotes people who inspire, other times it is about control or management. No wonder we trip up in thinking about it!

So often beneath ideas about leadership is an all-encompassing myth that 'good' leaders are 'special' people with special gifts and powers. In the 1950s cowboys rode in to rescue hapless citizens before riding off into the sunset. Today intergalactic superheroes do something similar, but the message is the same: a hero single-handedly saves the day.

Historically researchers saw leaders as being special people and sought to identify the characteristics of their greatness. While research has moved on, everyday practice too often has not. Must we try to be superheroes with special powers, eventually collapsing disappointed and broken from the effort? Or wait for a superhero to rescue us?

Leadership is a massive growth industry. Amazon lists over 500,000 books with 'leader' as a keyword. Millions are spent on books, superstar presenters and international gurus (nearly always white, male westerners). People flock to hear their secrets, to become the superheroes they feel they need to be. Yet for all this effort and expenditure the cry for 'good leadership' today is louder than ever.

Superficially attractive, heroic thinking is naïve and dangerous. We've all witnessed leaders who, like bulls in china shops, impose radical changes to staffing, systems or priorities in ways that dramatically damage morale, performance and commitment, reducing rather than enhancing organisational capacity to navigate change. Sometimes their egos seem all that survive the toxic cultures they create. Sometimes that doesn't survive either.

We try to be someone we can never be, till we collapse, exhausted and broken, with a disillusioned audience. In New River's consultancy work we hear one horror story after another of such leadership having unfortunate, unintended consequences. What works in movies doesn't translate into the real world. It is what it is: escapist fantasy.

Part of the reason we have lost our way is that we have conflated 'leadership' with positional authority, attacheded notions of greatness and prestige to it, and invested in leadership development for this special few. Like barnacles on the hull of a boat this creates drag on our collective ability to achieve change. Perhaps a focus on producing great leaders - special people able to achieve the impossible - is missing something?

It's time to rewrite the script. Perhaps this book can help.

A better way?

Ring the bells that still can ring. Forget your perfect offering. There is a crack in everything. That's how the light gets in.

- **Leonard Cohen**

THERE ARE MANY books on particular styles or ways of doing leadership, or wisdom from individual experiences in leadership. Here, however, we seek to do something different: to bring together key lessons from a wide range of leadership research and to rethink our notions of leadership right from the very definition we have for it.

From solid foundations we can look more clearly at how to grow leadership, build organisational capacity and navigate complexity. We need these solid foundations around something as important as 'leadership'. It is more than a role, more than management, more than a trait and not just about people in positions of authority.

What if, rather than focusing on leadership as a personal trait some possess, we look at it as something a group needs to which we can contribute? How about this:

Leadership is a critical ingredient in the healthy functioning of a group to enable it to discover and move towards its core purposes.

Once we shift our thinking away from heroic individuals to collective action to achieve group purposes, many things fall into place.

Different kinds of leadership contributions are needed. Those of us in positions of authority need to consider ways of **developing and leveraging leadership capacity**, growing a leadership culture, where leadership flourishes rather than relying on a few louder, more confident or charismatic people.

After stripping away the wealth, authority and status elements from leadership thinking we are left with its most important elements, as explored in this book: the ability to take effective individual and collective action in a complex world to make a positive difference.

What if, rather than reserving leadership development for a special few, a luxury item for those at the top, we gave everyone access to high quality leadership development and the chance to discover how they can contribute to a positive future? Might this unlock greater resources for the task ahead? We believe so.

By rethinking leadership, we can create a positive future.

Four key questions

Rethinking Leadership invites you on a two-step journey: to first rethink your paradigms of leadership, and then to reshape your practices. It explores four critical questions:

1. What are the challenges we face?

2. How can we build effective leadership for complex times?

3. How can we develop agility with ongoing change?

4. How can we each contribute authentically and sustainably?

Why take this journey?

THE BENEFIT OF stepping back and exploring these four questions, is firstly equipping you and your team with a language and lens for naming the realities of your context. Frustration with unpredictable situations, stuck systems and unfocussed teams is a natural consequence of life in complexity. In **Part 1**, we illuminate the dynamics that are at play in most contemporary organisations and offer you fresh ways of looking at your situation. With this perspective and clarity, you can let go of needing to control the impossible and instead discover a different way forward.

Similarly, by shifting your mindset on leadership you will discover that there is more capacity around you than you realise. **Part 2** moves beyond the mythology of heroic, command and control leadership and into a space where there is room for a multidimensional understanding. This broader view can unlock possibility and potential in your team, as well as increasing their engagement in the foundational purposes of your organisation. These are critical assets if you are seeking to move forward and even flourish amidst complexity.

There is increasing pressure on organisations to be innovative, step out into the unknown and stay ahead of the shifting sands. A loss of traction and impact can be the result of failing to adjust the ways we are working in light of these pressures. The alternative we explore in **Part 3** is the opportunity teams have to change the ways they work, to become more agile and collaborative. The rewards of such a shift can be huge, developing teams that can move safely through uncertainty, work creatively and purposefully, and organisations capable of learning.

In some contexts, there is so much toxicity or brokenness in the system that it is difficult to make any real impact. Turning the tide begins with individuals who have the courage to change themselves, considering both how they act and what they choose to act on.

Part 4 steps through a process of discovering your leadership strengths, exploring your core purposes and how to authentically bring them to the table alongside others. The result will be greater energy, imagination and hopefulness about facing the challenges before you and stronger personal foundations for when things get tough.

The value of reading this book will be in the changes you make to your own practice and to that of others with whom you work.

A solid base for thinking

THERE ARE MANY "how to" books numbering key principles for effective leadership, written largely from anecdotal experience, suggesting success comes from following formulaic answers. This is NOT one of those books. Drawing widely on thinking from across different schools can enrich leadership practice (*see Figure I.1 overleaf*).

We bring together here a wide range of thinking about leadership and change. Built on robust theoretical foundations it provides a positive model for unlocking capacity and developing authentic practice. We explore leadership thinking over the last century, from great man models of leadership (to the 1950s), transformational leadership (1970s and 1980s), adaptive leadership (since the 1990s), leadership as contribution (servant leadership) and notions of strengths-based capacity building and collaborative leadership.

We also engage systems theory, organisational dynamics, community development and community organising, personality theory and positive psychology. And, because leadership is not just about what we do but also who we are, we look at authentic leadership, personal development and growing self-awareness.

Peter was involved for decades in systematic quantitative research into effective and sustainable leadership, wellbeing and social capital with NCLS Research, a collaborative research organisation he was involved in founding in 1991. These research findings are included where relevant. Detailed references are included so you can follow up any ideas that spark your curiosity.

Two crews, one island, opposite outcomes

IN THE FACE of complex disruptive change, how people think about leadership often places limits on teams and organisations. We will explore the experiences of two shipwrecked crews stranded at the same time on a remote island, their ultimate fates strongly linked to their leadership paradigms. Similarly for us today, amid swirling change many established companies lose their way. Kodak and Blackberry broke up on uncharted reefs, while Amazon and Apple could reorient themselves and thrive.

In this book we will meet many people, groups and organisations facing various challenges:
- The principal of a prestigious school with a burning desire to create educational opportunities for Indigenous children, who did, indeed make a positive contribution but in a very different way to what was initially conceived.
- Two development workers in Zambia, concerned by preventable diarrhoea-related child mortality, who developed an ingenious award-winning solution that was both critical and totally irrelevant.
- Facing a shock financial disaster, the CEO of a community organisation stepped up to make hard decisions to save it. Or did he limit it?
- The power plant down the road from the well-known Fukushima nuclear power that also faced the wrath of the 2011 tsunami.
- A team of remote area fire-fighters facing an on-rushing wildfire who discovered the potential of creative genius, and the limits of a poor team culture.

- A chemical engineer who, leaving a multinational where the most important conversations happened in the car park, set out to create a company encouraging serial innovation and quality communication. You may make use of this company's rain jackets, guitar strings, electrical cables or dental floss, but are less likely to be using the space suits to which they contributed.

What can we learn from them and others? We have used pseudonyms where appropriate. In each case, assumptions about leadership significantly affected outcomes. Like seismic forces deep below the earth's surface, leadership assumptions can affect things dramatically.

The research basis for this book

Aspect	Chapters	Key idea
1. Leadership and complex change		
Systems theory	1, 7-11	Leadership involves engaging complex human systems.
Adaptive leadership	2, 7-11	Moving people beyond work avoidance.
2. Rethinking leadership		
Classical 'greatman' thinking	3	Leadership is about particular people with special traits.
Leadership and positional authority – Community organising	4	Leadership can be exercised with or without formal authority. Leadership is about listening and collective action.
Leadership as multi-dimensional	5	Healthy groups need many different types of leadership contributions.
Task and people dimensions	5	Leadership includes both relational and task aspects.
Purpose focussed – Transformational leadership	5	Leadership includes both growing shared directions and sound management.
Personality theory	12	We bring different capacities depending on our personalities.
3. Leadership as a collaborative endeavour		
Shared or distributed leadership	6	Groups need interlocking collaborative contributions from many.
Positive organisations	6	Positive cultures build productivity, motivation and personal satisfaction.

4. Engaging complex change and developing organisational agility

Change management	7	Complex challenges require adaptive responses: traditional approaches may be inadequate.
Learning organisations	7	Organisations need to learn and grow from experiences.
Personal transitions	8	Change typically involves anxiety and deep personal transitions.
Experimentation and innovation	9	Organisations need to foster group genius and safe-to-fail experimentation.
Unpredictable systems	10	Iterative practices will minimise risk.
Organisational agility	11	Organisational agility is foundational to navigating change.

5. Leadership from a Strengths-based Perspective

Strengths-based thinking and positive psychology	12, 14	Working with our strengths is a pathway to both personal effectiveness and well-being.

6. Not just what we do, but who we are

Authentic leadership	13	Leadership is not just about what we do, but who we are.
Burnout/emotional exhaustion	13	Sustainability is vital to long term effectiveness.
Personal foundations	14	Strong personal foundations can hold us in challenging times.
Toxic leadership dynamics	15	Internal drivers that lead us into unhealthy practices.
Personal development strategies	15	Self-awareness is a lifelong path to effective leadership.

Figure I.1 The research basis for this book

How to best use this book

THIS BOOK COVERS a lot of territory. Take your time. Don't rush. Create space to get a bird's eye view of your work and life, asking yourself: '*What is this saying to me*'? Use the reflective questions at the end of each chapter to help.

Ideally don't read this book alone! Growing shared understanding and language for leadership in a team is an invaluable investment. Step through chapter by chapter together, exploring both ideas and your situation. What questions, possibilities or priorities emerge?

Why we wrote this book

Peter

As a young adult, I longed to help change many aspects of the society I was part of. Three experiences had an impact on me.

In the 1970s and 1980s I became involved in a movement to protect threatened Tasmanian wilderness around the Franklin River. Starting with just a few concerned individuals, it grew into an international movement marshalling tens of thousands, each contributing what they could. Collectively, their hard-won victory has ripple effects to this day.

In a poor area where I worked, an agency closed a community centre with little notice after 150 years. Our team spent 12 months re-establishing the range of services we believed vital, achieving outcomes we scarcely believed possible.

In the 1990s, I put in place such models of leadership as director of a small team implementing a large research project. By identifying core purposes and iteratively exploring ways to achieve them, it was a wild ride for people whose combined strengths became more than the sum of their parts.

These experiences generated in me a lifelong belief in purposeful, collective leadership. How we offer leadership and shape organisational culture can make all the difference.

Naomi

Leadership and I have had a difficult relationship.

In Year 4 I was made the director in a week-long film project. On day three the class 'fired' me for being bossy.

Leadership felt risky.

At 12, I was 'tapped on the shoulder' to join the local youth council. We held meetings, ran events and represented our peers. After a year, I realised our work was tokenistic; we lacked permission to do anything real.

Leadership felt fruitless.

At 20, I started work connecting with young adults in regional NSW. After a while I came to see how community-level dysfunction was the source of many of their individual struggles.

Leadership felt complex.

By 24 I pushed myself to exhaustion, had to take stress leave, needing the team around me to step up and carry the project. And they did. Leadership wasn't about what I could achieve alone, I needed to build the capacity of those around me.

Leadership can break your heart.

So, why write about something that has personally generated so many mixed feelings?

Because I know I am not alone in experiencing the tension between a desire to make a difference, and facing the difficult realities of doing so.

I want to encourage others to wrestle honestly with the personal and systemic challenges they face. And help teams large and small discover how our hopes for change in any sphere can come alive with a collective practice of leadership.

Sophie

I first came to this book to help structure its ideas, but this quickly spiralled into a desire to be more involved as I recognised in it so many of my own experiences and struggles. Having been empowered by rethinking my own leadership practice I am passionate about encouraging others to do likewise.

As a teacher, I tried to do everything myself, seeking to hide my limitations. I readily embraced the latest developments in education but struggled bringing others along with me. I would jump ship for the next adventure leaving behind me burnt bridges and distrusting colleagues. I kept separate my personal and work life out of fear of being vulnerable. I sought to create the illusion that I could do everything. Finally, this all caught up with me.

Rethinking leadership as a collaborative contribution has been a great release. I found new ways of using my strengths alongside others, allowing me to accept both my strengths and limitations. I have learned to slow down, listen and connect deeply with others, learning, growing and innovating together. Together the shared workload is lighter, and shared successes richer.

I hope you will gain many insights through experimenting with the ideas here, that the book is provocative and helpful, an encouragement to you and those around you.

This book is written with a belief that, though seldom easy and usually challenging, change IS possible. Traditional models of leadership and management of change are broken, but there can be better ways. We have sweated over this book, alongside many readers, supporters and perspective givers, to encourage those very ways.

Peter Kaldor
Naomi Nash
Sophie Paterson

Acknowledgements

WE WOULD LIKE to thank so many who contributed to this collaborative effort. Over 50 readers gave us critical perspectives at different stages of a challenging journey. Thanks to various editors and typists for massive work polishing an initially very rough gem, particularly Ann Harth, Jenny Godfrey, Deborah Singerman, Felicity Baker and Margaret Robinson. Thanks also to the team at Mezzanine for their design and to Jennifer Crooks for her line drawings.

In developing our thinking Robbie MacPherson, Paul Porteous and Geoff Aigner, then with Social Leadership Australia provided seminal ideas around adaptive leadership. Peter's research with NCLS Research and John McLean also laid an important foundation, as did critical reflection with Paige Williams on positive psychology and authentic leadership.

Thanks to Ben Weir, Paula Taylor and Jess Pollard, colleagues within New River Leadership, for massive support. Ben developed the reflective questions for each chapter. Thanks to Sue Kaldor for her involvement with each of us in different ways, for her understanding, support and encouragement. Finally, we would like to acknowledge the influence of three key people in shaping our thinking through the example of their lives: **Alan Dutton** and **Dean Drayton** modelled alternative ways of offering leadership that opened Peter's eyes to new possibilities; and **Peter Pereira**, a dedicated colleague and friend who deepened our understandings and helped us grow.

Part 1

The Challenges
We Face

Introduction

What are the challenges we face?

THE CHALLENGES WE face in the world today are becoming increasingly complex. Change is also faster than ever. For each of us as individuals, and for organisations, it is so easy to lose our way or get bogged down.

On urban rail networks the world over we are reminded to "Mind the gap". In our work and personal lives, and in society at large, there is so often a gap between our hopes and purposes and where things, in fact, are.

Reducing the gap between aspirations and reality is seldom straightforward or pain free. We often long for stability and certainty, yet are regularly tossed about in turbulence.

Understanding the complexity of what lies in front of us is an important first step in responding more constructively to what is going on around us.

That is the focus of Part 1.

Finding your way around Part 1

IN CHAPTERS 1 and 2, we explore the context in which leadership is to be offered in our rapidly changing world. Understanding our context, and being clear on our purposes, can provide a starting point for exploring models of effective leadership.

Chapter 3 engages deeply entrenched myths and mis-thinking about leadership as being about special people with special characteristics and purposes, pointing to a critical need to rethink our ways of thinking about change.

Chapter one

The times we are in

Where do we begin?

OUR WORLD IS changing at a faster rate than ever before. Each day brings complex challenges and our ability to understand these challenges is critical.

Some months before the US invasion of Iraq in 2003 Kurdish leader, Masoud Barzani was sceptical: "Getting rid of Saddam is the easy bit, it's what happens afterwards that is the problem."[1]. On May 1 2003, after a meticulously planned and executed operation, President George W. Bush delivered his "mission accomplished" speech announcing: "Iraq is free"[2]. The invasion of Iraq with its meticulous timing, use of technology and firepower was an amazing demonstration of the capacities of a massive war machine, mounted with seemingly flawless precision with little doubt about the outcome.

Yet more than a decade after the President announced victory in Iraq, peace and stability are perhaps further away than ever.

Creating a positive future after this conflict has been a different kind of challenge. There is diversity in the region's politics, historical hostility between cultures and ethnic groups, together with the international interests in the region and its oil. Those responsible for establishing peace were soon outplayed by local power brokers, religious leadership and sectional interests. Masoud Barzani was right: stability is a challenge of a different order.

And a second question: what were the purposes of the Iraq invasion? In his speech Bush suggested it was about making Iraq 'free'. That is a very complex purpose, and one that is potentially vague and ill-defined. No doubt the various parties in the region had many different agendas.

In this chapter, we will look at the different kinds of challenges and situations we may face. We also identify the critical importance of shared purpose.

Simple, complicated and complex systems

SOCIAL RESEARCHERS COMMONLY draw a distinction between *simple, complicated* and *complex systems*[3].

Simple systems are relatively easy to work with. A simple system might be cooking a meal by following a recipe. Follow the instructions and things will go well.

Complicated systems are bigger. They might be multidimensional, involving many people and much effort, but they are still predictable and largely reproducible. There are a finite number of variables affecting the system. Because they retain a clear structure, problems can be solved using detailed blueprints, step-by-step formulae or flow charts, together with well trained staff, quality technological support and efficient teamwork. A carefully developed machine can achieve amazing outcomes in complicated situations. Consider robotic surgery or online taxation systems. Though there might be occasional hiccups, once established, processes can be refined and reproduced.

Complex systems are multidimensional and do not have fixed boundaries. They involve many people and groups where each element or sub-system is interdependent, intertwined with the others. They interact with, and influence, each other in intricate and often unpredictable ways that we may not (or cannot) fully understand.[4] Everything affects everything else, like a massive hanging mobile. Start one part moving and the others will follow in sometimes unusual ways.

In complex systems, small changes can have very disruptive consequences. Natural ecosystems provide a good example: removing one element in the food chain or introducing new species can have catastrophic consequences. What was finely balanced is now inherently unstable, as we have seen in many spectacular environmental disasters. Likewise, the human body is a collection of systems generally in balance. When one is destabilised it

Context:	What it might be like?
Simple systems	Straightforward tasks sometimes requiring particular skills.
Complicated systems	Might involve many people, different skills and much coordinated effort, teamwork and commitment, but is still fairly predictable and reproducible.
Complex systems	Each element interacts with the others in sometimes surprising or disruptive ways.

Figure 1.1 Different types of contexts in which to contribute

can dramatically affect others. Systems theory explores the functioning of complex systems and has important applications in the natural environment, urban planning, organisational change, as well as in leadership, management and family therapy. People and organisations exist together in many interrelated systems that impact on each other. In complicated situations we can explore interactions, develop plans and then roll them out at scale because things are essentially predictable. Complex situations require a different leadership response to those that are merely complicated.[5]

In times of complex change, effective leadership will look at the situation as a system, consider how to intervene and evaluate the likely impact of that intervention on each component part. Those with positional authority need to recognise that they do not stand outside the system, but are participants and are impacted by changes to it.

Characteristics of complex systems

IN THIS BOOK, we are interested in the processes of change in complex systems, and the leadership needed to effectively engage these systems. Complex systems are all around us, in business, government, community development, welfare, environmental care, social justice, and in our families. Sub-parts of complex systems exist as entities but are also part of larger systems. The family unit is a good example of this. Every child is unique, as is the context and environment in which they grow up, but a family is also part of a community, which is part of a wider society and part of all humanity. Interactions at one level can affect interactions at other levels.

Here are some key characteristics of *complex* systems:

- All elements are *interconnected* like a web. A family is a sub-system interconnected with others: schools, neighbours, friends, local communities and workplaces. There are many elements with a level of independent action, but which are also interdependent.
- System behaviour is often *unpredictable*. Small changes can generate cascading consequences.[6] New friends at school may have a positive or negative impact on children; a work redundancy will affect finances and the rhythm of life for a family. A birth, marriage or divorce in one family can impact relationships within the greater family unit. Components interact in seemingly unpredictable, nonlinear ways.
- Systems have their own *inherent* sense of order, but are not centrally controlled. That order comes from the multifaceted interplay of each element. Each family has their standard operating procedure for meal times, communicating and leisure activities. These are not set down with a single policy or by one person yet all members know how to behave in ways that maintain order.
- Systems are held together by a *few rules* that govern interaction and create the discernible patterns in the system. These rules often go unspoken and evolve from people doing things in a particular way in line with others. An addition to a family through marriage or having a visitor will make people more aware of the patterns of operating, many of which are self-reinforcing, deeply embedded and very hard to change.
- Living systems have the *capacity to learn* and adapt to change or feedback. One family member's illness can affect other member's attitudes or behaviours towards their own health. Family members can learn to live differently, which can then affect how others relate to them.

Complex systems are the stuff of everyday life, in organisations, communities and families. We need to become agile in navigating continuous change.

Dangers of treating the complex as complicated

ROSABETH KANTER LIKENS leadership within complex systems to the game of croquet that is depicted in "Alice in Wonderland".[7] Instead of hitting a ball through hoops with a mallet, Alice's mallet becomes a flamingo and the ball becomes a hedgehog. With a mind of its own it unrolls and moves to another part of the court whenever the mood strikes. In complex situations, as in Alice's game of croquet, nothing is constant and things can be wildly unpredictable.

Sometimes things that appear simple or even complicated are actually complex. There are grave dangers in treating the complex as simply complicated. The graphic in Figure 1.2 was part of a 2009 US military slide presentation to map the situation in Afghanistan at the time. It shows the massive intricacy of a complex system, but also the folly of attempting to treat a complex system as merely a complicated one.

"When we understand that slide, we'll have won the war", the head of American and NATO forces in Afghanistan, General McChrystal dryly remarked. One of his advisors recalled that the room erupted in laughter. Sometime later another general (Brigadier General H.R. McMaster) sought to explain: "It's dangerous because it can create the illusion of understanding and the illusion of control. Some problems in the world are not bullet-izable."[8]

There can be great complexity even in seemingly simple organisations. Consider local community groups or workplaces where everything is interconnected and people's interests are often in tension. What about bringing a new idea or product into the marketplace? Or funding competing initiatives that support disadvantaged communities?

Recognising complexity is a first step to responding more appropriately.

Disruptive change

GLOBALISATION AND NEW technology have made once-stable aspects of life more volatile. Many of them are being transformed by 'disruptive' change, to borrow a term coined by Clayton Christensen[9], who raised eyebrows claiming it is possible for companies to go out of business even though they made good, logical decisions every step of the way.[10]

Early personal computers are an example of what Christensen called a 'disruptive innovation', upturning an entire industry's way of doing things. Manufacturers of mainframe computers made sound decisions about the design and marketing of their product but in pleasing those customers, they did not see the emerging market for personal computers and, over time, lost an entire industry.

Disruptive change can reap havoc: larger or less agile organisations ignore these changes, thwarted by their unwieldy structures and processes. Short term it may appear unprofitable to respond. For others, disruptive changes provide opportunities to address an issue, situation or market that previously couldn't be served. Think Sony Walkman, Apple iPad, or in sport: high jump athlete Dick Fosbury as the first person to clear the bar backwards rather than forwards, breaking records and creating a new approach to high jumping.

Ongoing disruption requires us to rethink leadership and traditional approaches to 'managing' change. Convoluted plans can be outdated before they are enacted as organisations respond more slowly than the change around them.

Attempting to map a complex system

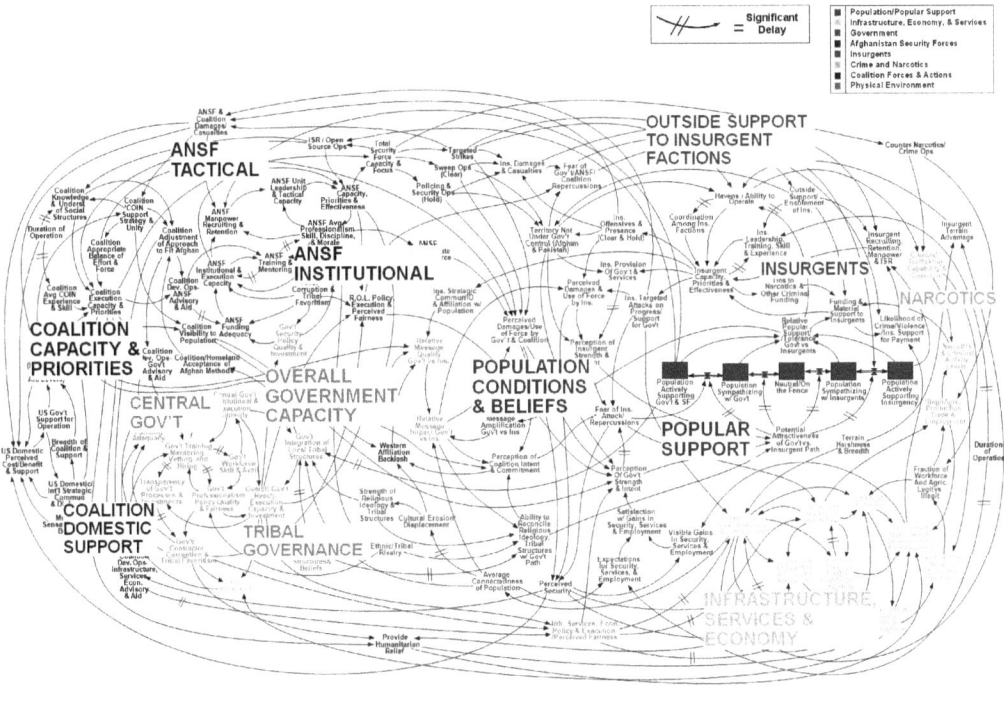

Figure 1.2 Powerpoint slide used in 2009 by military to describe Afghanistan conflict

Failure to respond to change

PEOPLE IN THE west generally have lower confidence in, and loyalty to, organisations than they did 30 years ago. There is less trust in government, media, police, legal systems, large organisations and people in positions of authority.[11]

It is easy for organisations to degenerate from being alive, innovative and relevant in one era, to being disconnected, institutionalised and irrelevant in another. Natural processes can encourage ossification. A team with vision, insights and dreams creates *movement*, and movements held together by a common vision over time become more like well-oiled *machines*. But a machine is not easily adaptable to new circumstances. There is the danger it will become obsolete, a *monument*, which may have important traditions and history, but whose time has passed.

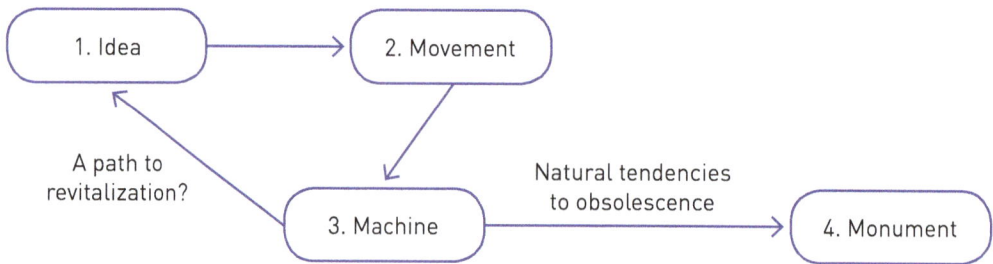

Figure 1.3 An inevitable path?

Community groups, successful in one context, struggle or fail in another as members, values or practices change. Organisations fail to adapt, continuing with a plan that doesn't work anymore. By the time they realise what is happening, it is too late.

New products or contexts may leave organisations battling to catch up. Many products have limited lifespans. An introductory phase is followed by rapid growth that plateaus as the market matures, then declines as consumers drop off. Smart companies will carefully monitor this, always developing new products.

Many organisations struggle to retain the flexibility enjoyed by a movement. Others, now nearly monuments, have an even greater challenge.

The maze of increasing choice and connectivity

IN THE WEST, we have more and more choice, increasing complexity in our lives. Compared with previous generations, our values and beliefs are more of a personal project than an inheritance from our family or background. Those from cultures emphasising collective values can find it difficult to navigate this individualism. Even those of us brought up valuing individualism can be overwhelmed by choices.

Indeed, our society often manufactures uncertainty. Supermarket aisles are packed with choices of cheese, shampoo, pasta and tea. 'New and improved' products are released with little difference from previous models. Just when we think we have decided on the best phone plan or computer program, we are presented with yet another range of options.

Increasing choice also comes from escalating global interconnectedness. Social networking, telecommunications and the 24-hour news cycle have 'flattened' the world: anyone can reach out to connect with like-minded others across the planet.

Overwhelming choice can lead to what psychologists call *'learned helplessness'*, an idea developed by American psychologist Martin Seligman. Studies with both people and animals show that having overwhelming choice can ultimately make us give up due to a feeling of powerlessness. How many of us abandon checking the myriad of available insurance plans? Exploring all the choices just isn't worth the potential savings.

How can we move past such helplessness and discover life-giving priorities and directions?

Equipping ourselves for the future is not simply about learning what we need to know. What we need to know in the future might well change. Rather, **we need to learn how to learn** so, when faced with a challenge, we can constructively develop a positive future in our family, workplace, community or planet.

Never straightforward

NO ORGANISATION IS immune to change. Many of the top 100 companies in one decade become forgotten failures in the next.[12] Not-for-profit or community organisations established in one era become irrelevant as the world changes. Business-as-usual can lead to fossilisation and irrelevance. Meaningful patterns of parenting at one stage in life can quickly become a liability as children grow and develop. We regularly need to re-examine ways of doing things at each stage, often challenged by our partners or children. Continuing to treat teenagers as children quickly leads to trouble!

Change is never easy, even when it is important. Why, for instance, do people with health reasons for losing weight, often find it challenging to do so? We develop patterns of behaviour that are comfortable and help us avoid facing the challenge.

What makes change so difficult?

1. Personal uncertainty: Change often generates personal uncertainty, anxiety and other emotional responses. So often when faced with challenging complex situations we either freeze or act in knee jerk ways, which have more to do with fear or self-justification than finding real ways forward.

Because we are all wired differently we may respond differently to the unexpected. We each have natural modes for dealing with a crisis – panic, paranoia, mistrust, fight, flight or freeze. Risk will generate many emotions and reactions: anxiety, fear, grief, excitement, scapegoating, withdrawal, and controlling or coercive behaviour. Under pressure we may even respond irrationally or dangerously!

The risk in change is that things might get worse.[13] People are being asked to forego stability, to take a risk. Ignoring a challenge seems safer; it might even go away. Fear of change can paralyse, creating inertia that somehow feels safer. Understanding and managing fear in ourselves and in others is vital. Our reactions can affect everyone else. Anxiety can be contagious.

Leadership that invites people to move towards a different future can expect to generate uncertainty, anxiety and a desire to hang onto what is comfortable. Those in positions of responsibility may want to push people through transitions, but it cannot be rushed or sugar-coated with false certainty. People need space to grieve or let go before they can start to embrace ways forward.

2. Unknown territory: Change involves travelling through unknown territory, which can be scary, a strange country with no maps. We leave behind the safety and comfort of the known. Yet change is so rapid there is just no other way. We engage the unknown effectively, or join the dinosaurs.

In the early 1980s some respected management consultants studied excellence in business, scrutinising 40 top companies to unlock their secrets to success. Two years later, Business Week ran a cover story: *Oops, who is excellent now?* [14] Over a third of these companies were in serious financial trouble. It is hard to imagine the Apple or Google giants of today failing, yet history shows how temporary their success might be if they do not continually explore the unknown, unfolding territory of an unimaginable future (think Blockbuster or Motorola). One decade's dominant player is the next decade's corporate basket case. [15]

3. System unpredictability: Change can also be difficult because it is unpredictable. Sometimes we think we understand what is happening around us and then surprising things occur. We discover unanticipated consequences of our actions; grand plans can quickly fall apart due to 'unforeseen circumstances'.

In human systems, everything affects everything else. Often unpredictable responses occur because we have not seen the complexity of a system and only have a limited view of things. Organisations may have clear structure diagrams, protocols and procedures, but there are also the more subtle 'actual ways we do things around here' that need to be understood. Because our understanding of them may be incomplete, interfering with them is fraught with danger and the possibility of unexpected unintended consequences.

Context:	What it might be like?
Personal uncertainty	Perceived risk and potential loss generates anxiety and deep emotions that can result in surprising reactions.
Unknown territory	There is not the safety of a map or past experience as people seek to discover a way forward.
System unpredictability	It is hard to anticipate the consequences of our actions, sometimes generating unexpected responses or disruption.

Figure 1.4 Causes of complexity

The importance of clear purposes

HAVE YOU EVER sat through a presentation where the images were out of focus? It's disturbing, frustrating and ultimately results with people disengaging. [16] Surrounded by so much change and complexity, organisations need to regularly revisit the central question: What is our vision and purpose at this time, and how can we live this out? Many organisations lack focus, being pre-occupied with urgent or short-term demands rather than critical future directions. Exercising leadership involves developing shared purpose and clear priorities. In the 1970s and 1980s, leadership thinking increasingly focused on purpose and vision rather than just good management of what exists. Stephen Covey summarised this: management is efficiency in climbing the ladder of success; leadership determines whether the ladder is leaning against the right wall.[17] James McGregor Burns, Bernard Bass and others distinguish between transformational and more traditional transactional modes of leadership.[18] Transactional leadership is based on a performance/rewards system: do this well and you will be rewarded (a pay rise, a privilege). Under-performance may also have consequences.

Unexpected consequences

A new principal re-structured his school in what seemed like an efficient and cost-effective way. He appointed new heads of department and removed middle management positions. What he didn't consider was the displacing effect on the individuals of moving from one department to another, severing key relationships between staff that had previously fuelled their collaborative work. He was shocked when his attempt to change things from the top fell apart, was swept well out of his depth in the turbulence, losing key staff and diminishing morale and motivation in the rest.

By contrast, transformational leadership invites groups to focus on broader questions of purpose, to help people to identify their ideal future and how to journey towards it together.[19] It motivates by generating commitment to a group's purposes, and by building stronger shared values.[20] Transformational leadership is critical in many situations: in changing a company's culture to become more environmentally responsible, developing a campaign or movement to change society, or in seeking to connect with a changing community or context.

Responding adaptively to a complex challenge requires careful evaluation of purpose. Communities and organisations develop best when they have a clear, owned vision that binds people together. Research, including some with which Peter was involved, shows that directions need to be owned and incorporate the aspirations of as many as possible. This can be one of the most powerful predictors of the overall vitality of an organisation.[21] We will explore purpose further throughout the book, in Chapter 5 looking at leadership contributions focused on purpose and in Chapter 10 and 11 on ways to involve people widely in the process.

Living systems are complex systems

ORGANISATIONS, COMMUNITIES AND families are not machines, but complex living systems. At any time, they may enter unknown territory and face personal uncertainty and unpredictability. Any real-world system is likely to include elements from all three types of systems: simple, complicated and complex. Being able to successfully navigate them with human rather than machine-like responses is critical. Consider the following example.

Grasping their nature and dynamics is a key starting point to effectively engaging them And, at every moment, clarity of purpose is critical.

A deadly disaster creates a complex system

ONE FATEFUL NIGHT, three people drinking together are ejected from a bar. One drives them to the next suburb to find another bar. In her alcohol-impaired state, she veers off the road hitting a teenage girl walking down the street. The pedestrian is killed instantly.

Her death is the consequence of poor judgement by many: the driver obviously, her passengers, the publican and their duty of care, the families and the communities that encouraged a culture of drinking. The result is a heart-breaking disaster, but also the creation of a highly complex system.

The police are involved, charges will be laid to be heard later in court, involving both driver's and victim's families in a long, painful process. There may be appeals, a prison sentence and the involvement of corrective services. Insurance agencies will be involved in relation to vehicles and victim, requiring another round of intricacies for the victim's family. Traffic authorities will review the incident and determine any regulatory changes to do with pedestrian safety. Decisions at the pub will be investigated, causing pain for several people. The driver will live with the consequences for the rest of her life. She will spend time in jail, carrying guilt and anger, wondering why nobody – family, friends, publican – had prevented the situation. She will need counselling and will have to deal with her many friends and acquaintances who may, in various ways, change their attitudes towards her.

Then there are the relatives, family and friends of the teenage girl: grieving, angry and needing to deal with loss. They too will involve counsellors and support. Their struggles might significantly affect their families. Tragedies can bring people together, or split families. The various dimensions of this new situation will test family members and friends. One action can create a highly complex system of causes and effects that will play themselves out over decades.

Within this, many individuals and organisations will have to make adaptive leadership contributions, and be very clear on their purposes as they do so. Various counsellors will consider how to effectively "help" people to adjust and discover ways forward, carefully reflecting on the purposes of their contributions. Parents and family will need to consider how to respond, how to balance anger and forgiveness, how to turn anger into something constructive. Some may retreat into bitterness, while others may step out and engage in community education to try to avoid a repetition. Within the legal system people will need to ask challenging questions about justice and rehabilitation as part of their roles.

For the publican, there is that niggling question: could we have avoided this by acting differently? One poor decision created massive complexity, requiring various purposeful leadership contributions from many.

Summary

Where do we begin?

Distinguish between simple, complicated or complex challenges and be clear on your purposes

WE LIVE IN a rapidly changing and unpredictable world. It is critical that we learn to effectively cope with complex challenges. We may be faced with simple, complicated or complex systems. Recognising each will help us to treat them appropriately. While simple and complicated systems are predictable and reproducible, complex systems are not. It can be dangerous to treat a complex system as a simple or complicated one.

Effectively dealing with complex change requires clarity about our purpose and a sound understanding of the nature of change itself. Once we have this understanding, we can build capacity for navigating in unknown territory, engaging personal uncertainty and system unpredictability.

Reshaping practice 1

Actions for you

Think about a challenge in your personal or work life. To what extent is this a product of a complex system? What are some of the characteristics that make it so?

How do you generally feel about change? What changes have been helpful or meaningful in your life? And what changes have scarred you?

How might your responses to change support or limit what you seek to do in life, personally and professionally?

Actions for your team

What is your purpose? What are the priorities you need to adhere to in order to acheive it? To what extent is this purpose shared across your team? To what extent does everyone see clearly how their work contributes to the overall direction?

What issues are you facing? To what extent are current responses to this challenge limited by failing to recognise the complexity of the situation? *Map the system:* What are some of the components of complexity in your context? How do they interact? Draw a map of the main people, ideas, pressures and dynamics. Talk about it with others to help gain clarity and perspective.

Chapter two

Responding to complexity

What can make the difference?

BEFORE TACKLING A particular challenge, we need to examine its nature to determine how best to approach it. Leadership writers Ron Heifetz with Marty Linsky have made an important contribution to thinking about leadership in times of change, challenge or uncertainty by identifying the different types of problems we might encounter.[1]

Varying degrees of difficulty

THOSE CANOEING OR rafting wild rivers describe six grades of rapids from Grade 1, the simplest, smoothest water to Grade 6, the most dangerous and unpredictable. Similarly, our personal and professional lives also require us to navigate different grades of rapids, depending on the complexity of the systems in which we are working.

Figure 2.1 Three challenges of very different natures

Simple systems tend to present only Grade 1 or 2 problems. Ways forward and available solutions are clear, requiring someone with adequate expertise or skills to provide what Heifetz describes as a *technical* leadership response. Refining a budget process may require better software, improving a sound system more technical advice,

CHAPTER TWO

Chapter two – Responding to complexity | **27**

or improving after-school safety the employment of a local road safety officer. It is a matter of finding people with expertise.

More complicated challenges, like tricky sections of Grade 3 or 4 white-water, require not just expertise, but careful scouting, navigation, organisation and maximum effort from a quality team, with everyone contributing to the fullest. To support and smoothly integrate an influx of students into a school, for instance would require specialist skills, processes and the commitment of all staff.

Grade 5 or 6 white-water is something else again. Its complex systems require what Heifetz calls *adaptive* leadership responses (some other writers talk about *wicked* problems[2]). These run much deeper. Not only is it difficult to achieve a positive outcome, but the specifics of that outcome and the means to get there are unclear. They require careful reflection, and even a questioning of a group's core purposes.[3]

An organisation or group that becomes disconnected from its purposes, clients or the community faces difficult questions. 'How did we get to this place?' 'How can we change?'

Refining core purposes

By 1914 Rolls Royce had been producing cars for eight years but had never built an engine for an aeroplane. With the outbreak of war they initially decided to stick with cars as they thought the war would be brief. But it became clear that while no-one would be buying a car during this time aircraft engines were badly needed. So, Rolls Royce rapidly changed their entire production line from producing cars to producing aircraft engines, supplying more than half the engines in planes used. After the war, they continued both lines of production.

'What will we have to lose, to move forward?' Addressing these pivotal questions will need to involve everyone with a stake in the issue.

Adaptive responses to complex challenges commonly involve changing directions, responding to changing circumstances or to seemingly intractable dynamics. They mean journeying into the unknown, with its personal uncertainty and system unpredictability. They need everybody to engage the challenges and contribute to the solutions, to be open to both collective learning and personal transformation.

No one person has the solution to climate change: not a politician, mining company executive or member of the population. It will require everyone making significant contributions to generating a quality collective response, and potentially changing lifestyle expectations.

Likewise, to alleviate traffic congestion, it is not enough to build a new freeway that will just increase car usage. Real improvement requires politicians, pedestrians, motorists and transport groups to understand the underlying issues that cause congestion and together find fresh ways forward.

Examples of challenges requiring adaptive responses:

- A CD/DVD production company faces increasing market preference for digital downloads. How might they refine their core purposes, creating a new business model?
- A factory employing hundreds of workers shuts down, with major repercussions for the entire town as the families of workers move out of the area. How might the local school respond to a dramatic drop in student population?
- Several service organisations merge, becoming a larger regional entity. How can they create a new culture from the best of all traditions or will one culture just dominate?
- A long-established business has a new competitor offering the same end-product at lower cost through direct distribution. How can the first business respond?
- How can residents respond to rises in alcohol related violence in their town?
- A new principal finds that her staff have low morale, and do as little work as possible. How can she shift the culture and performance of the team?
- A family keeps criticising each other, causing hurt, frustration and hopelessness. How might they find a way out of the cycle?

Work avoidance[4]

REAL CHANGE INVOLVES external adjustments in behaviour, but also internal reorientation that may be just as challenging. Individuals and groups develop patterns of behaviour that are comfortable or meet their needs. We tend to maintain these patterns and preserve the status quo because it feels safer.

These responses are types of *work avoidance*. We seek cost-free solutions to avoid the hard work that we ourselves might need to do[5]. Work avoidance is part of human nature, of not facing up to real and serious issues that may affect our lives because, right now, they seem too hard to deal with. A short-term focus is more comfortable. Any alternative requiring deep change will create anxiety, so we stick with what we know, even if it is unsustainable and may have catastrophic consequences.

Personal work avoidance

FINDING ADAPTIVE RESPONSES can be tough. We are asking people to leave behind the safety and security of calm water to engage the hazards and uncertainties of white water. To find a way forward together, we all have work to do and changes to make. Sometimes we have to cope with our own internal challenges. Avoiding personal work comes in many forms:

- *Denial*: We say growth is important, but retreat to safety so we don't have to face it. Questions of personal growth seem too hard or scary because we may need to own (to ourselves or others) that we are not the person we aspire to be.
- *Taking the easy way out*: It is easier to put things off or seek quick- fix solutions that we imagine will deliver pain-free solutions, at no cost to ourselves.
- *Losing motivation*: We have ideas but lack the will, or our intentions get lost in the mounting pressures of life.
- *Fear*: We are not sure what to do, feel paralysed by choice and so flee the question.
- *Losing confidence*: We are tossed about by loud voices, competing agendas or opposition we never knew existed. It seems easier to retreat when challenged.

- *Postponing*: We listen to unhelpful voices in our heads that can undo: 'I've failed before, I don't want to again' or 'I'll get everything completely stable first'.
- *Blaming others*: If it is someone else's fault, then it's not our work to fix it.
- *Looking to authority to fix things*: We get frustrated when they don't.

Recognising personal work avoidance is the first step towards overcoming it.

When washing hands is more than washing hands[6]

In 1846 at a major hospital in Vienna there were two maternity wards, one with doctors and the other overseen by midwives. Many women and children were dying during childbirth in the doctor's ward. Why?

Doctors and students commonly learnt through dissection of cadavers before going straight into delivery rooms. One doctor, Ignaz Semmelweis, started to wonder whether a lack of cleanliness was causing those deaths. So, he persuaded doctors to wash more thoroughly before delivery. The result: a dramatic decline in deaths during childbirth.

This sounds simple, but it wasn't. Though the change worked, resistance came from doctors who challenged Semmelweis to explain the connection between hand washing and the saving of lives (which he couldn't). Their scepticism was fuelled by a belief that "a doctor's hands couldn't possibly carry disease because doctors are gentlemen and a gentleman's hands are clean".

Once the medical community rejected Semmelwies' ideas, his morale and work declined. He went from being a rising star to losing his job, started showing signs of mental illness, and died shortly afterwards. Few attended his funeral.

Doctors at the hospital stopped washing their hands and the mortality rates rose again. Even life-saving ideas encounter resistance. Embedding change and bringing others along with you is always an adaptive challenge. The rejection of new ideas because of their conflict with accepted beliefs is often named the Semmelweis Reflex.

Collective work avoidance

CONSIDER A TEAM that reinvents their brand over and again, without noticing that their product is not valued in the marketplace. By focusing on branding they manage to avoid the deeper questions of how relevant their product is…for a while. Think about conversations that revolve around the idea of 'not in my backyard'. Sure, that prison, halfway house or petrol station is important, but not in my neighbourhood. Work avoidance is often collective.

As a team or society we may put off difficult choices critical to our long-term well-being because the cost, now, is too high. We set up a committee, deal with technical matters and carry out research or feasibility studies. We collude to avoid dealing with something.

In our families, we might discuss trivial matters rather than dealing with deeper concerns.

Collective work avoidance does not lead to progress: real discussion is diminished as the issue gets put on the back burner or buried, and we hear comments like:

- Let's not rush into hasty decisions.
- We're burned out or too busy.
- Let's find a quick solution to feel we've done something.
- We've never done it that way before.
- We've only just settled after the last change.
- If it ain't broke, don't fix it.
- Let's form a subcommittee.

Playing happy team

Several members of a team were struggling with one individual, resulting in mounting frustration. People started sharing their frustrations in private, after meetings. While potentially healthy to debrief, they became a 'team within the team', developing a code to signal when there were issues with the difficult person and leaving him out of decision-making when possible.

This reduced tension in the short-term but created deep divisions overall. The lack of honesty resulted in muddied communication and wasted energy. Everyone could feel something was not quite right and it affected their quality of the work. The project was completed but integrity and trust was lost.

Work avoidance in action

SOMETIMES WORK AVOIDANCE is about **not** asking important or challenging questions. Management writer Jerry Harvey tells the story of an extended family who decides to travel a few hours to the town of Abilene for a meal. Neither the food nor journey is a positive experience. Towards the end, one by one, they each own up to the fact that they never wanted to go, but thought they were doing it for the others. The result of a range of attempts at caring and avoiding offence was that they went somewhere nobody wanted to go![7]

One by one they chose not to take the risk to share their real feelings about the trip until it was over. The costs of honesty seemed too great. Do we ever 'go to Abilene'?

Work avoidance in action

Naomi was part of a community project that received a donation to purchase a new property. Volunteers, staff and management gathered data, explored options and articulated ways forward. A wide range of excited voices weighed in, and it was decided to move to a new property on the edge of town.

Yet within four years the project closed-down, the move proving disastrous. What happened? Here are some perspectives in hindsight:

A volunteer: "I had concerns about being further from town, but didn't share my thoughts, I was worried I might be wrong."

A staff member: "I was anxious about leaving the original site that worked for so long. Why move just because of the money? But I didn't feel I could say anything."

Regional manager: "It was not my decision but theirs: those on the ground needed to make the decision. They were taking so long. We wanted to get it done."

Each person's hesitance to raise their voice kept all voices silent.

Work avoidance can show itself in many guises. If a group's purpose is to face difficult issues and move toward change, sometimes it is important to slow down processes, listen to a wide variety of people or set up committees to deal with issues. At every step, we need to ask ourselves: 'what is the real purpose of a committee, report or decision? Is it taking us towards or away from addressing important, though difficult, questions?'

Again, recognising collective work avoidance is a first step to overcoming it. Any of the following may be a sign of collective work avoidance:

- *The presence of a scapegoat or common enemy.* If one person or group can be blamed for everything, it shifts the spotlight from us.
- *Pressure not to deal with deeper issues because they might cause too much pain.* Care is important but, if an excuse for not dealing with deeper issues, may multiply the problems.
- *The feeling that there is too much invested in how things are currently done to consider changing them.* The costs in investing in new possibilities provide a reason for not moving forward that may be a work avoidance strategy.
- *Trying to find a strong leader who offers pain-free solutions.* The never-ending search for a superhero. Just maybe there is an expert out there…
- *Avoiding difficult conversations.* Interactions that cause anxiety or create conflict can be replaced by pleasant, less productive talk.

- *An overflowing 'too hard basket'.* When things are difficult, committees form, reports are prepared and lengthy meetings result in little constructive progress.
- *Fear about what may be lost.* We don't resist change if we think we stand to benefit from it. A fear of possible loss stops us moving forward.

Work avoidance can be highly costly. By taking manageable risks and growing capacity we are growing our personal or professional capital. Over time this may compound and make a sizeable difference to our personal or organisational agility. Engaging in work avoidance is a bad investment providing short-term comfort at the expense of long-term capacity.[8]

Adaptive responses are critical

OUR DESIRE TO avoid the deeper challenge in complex situations can lead us into a subtle but devastating trap: organisations (and individuals) stagnate or get into major difficulty because they seek to solve complex challenges with technical fixes.

Understanding the nature of the challenge is critical. If it is a *simple* problem, it can be solved with a *technical* solution: find someone with the appropriate expertise to do the job.

A more *complicated* situation, one involving people in a multifaceted but predicable challenge, requires an *organisational* approach. Building a balanced team who bring the range of leadership strengths needed, as will be explored in Part 2.

If it is a *complex* situation where the outcomes or ways to achieve them are unclear, one that involves the interplay of a range of different systems (within an organisation or in the context in which it operates) then a more *adaptive* approach is critical.

How often do people and organisations mistake the complex for being merely complicated or technical? Consider this example from our recent experience in a school. The principal sought to connect with students and families from more diverse backgrounds and, having convinced her board, implemented a new initiative that mirrored her personal concerns. With no prior consultation, she announced it to the staff. Some were positive, some questioning, and many remained silent. Staff who had not been involved in the original decision-making responded with passive aggression and resentment, unwilling to go the extra mile when things got tough: "It's not our problem, it's hers". Nothing could change the attitudes of staff who hadn't felt included, ultimately hastening the principal's decision to move on.

Further, the new direction had many more dimensions than expected: an adaptive challenge. The initiative had unexpected outcomes in terms of how the school was seen in the community, reducing enrolment, with consequent financial ramifications. Perhaps with wider involvement in the design by the staff and board, these issues might have been foreseen and ways forward found. What was learnt about leadership from the experience?

With limited information, the board again decided a change was needed and instructed the new principal to implement it. He dutifully obliged, again pushing new directions without adequate sensitivity, insisting on compliance. Disengagement increased, senior staff left and the financial and other problems simply compounded. Two principals sought to address complex challenges with top-down technical responses, treating staff like chess pieces. The school board, well distanced from staff and other input, simply took advice from one person. In a situation like this the merry-go-round continues in a disempowering downward spiral. Then, when it is all far too late, they bring in a consultant to solve their problems!

In uncertain times, it is tempting to import a quick-fix program, or seek an expert 'leader' who appears to be able to provide simple, cost-free, pain-free and risk-free solutions. Organisations that face deep challenges might employ a bright new director, hoping for the desired changes at little or no cost, seeking to solve a complex challenge with a technical solution. A couple or family with relationship concerns might look to a counsellor to solve their problems, becoming disappointed when the counsellor hands work back to them.

Rarely can one expert solve our complex challenges at no cost to ourselves. There will be work we all need to do. Trying to solve a complex challenge with a technical fix will only add another layer to the challenge, increasing the struggle and hardship.

There must be a better way!

Effective adaptive leadership will minimise work avoidance and invite individuals or groups to face challenging realities, think deeply about why things are as they are, identify the work they need to do, and uncover resources people possess to move forward.

The leadership contributions needed to generate adaptive responses are distinctly different from those required when facing something that is merely complicated, because change and readjustment is needed at many levels. Team members will need to explore direction, priorities[9] and even core purposes. It will require the perspectives and contributions of many – potentially of everyone – to find constructive ways forward. Each of us needs to take on the necessary work as part of the bigger picture.

These are ideas we will explore in more detail throughout this book. Those who can contribute to adaptive leadership are more likely to navigate effectively the white-water of life.

Nature of the situation	Type of response needed:	Clarity of goals	Key priorities
Simple situations	Technical	Goals are clear.	Find someone with appropriate expertise.
Complicated situations	Organisational	Goals are clear, but it will require high commitment, teamwork and a wide range of leadership contributions.	Grow a balanced team with a suitable blend of strengths and build teamwork. Maximise the use of available gifts and skills.
Complex situations	Adaptive	Goals are difficult to define or achieve and the means to get there are unclear.	Develop clarity of core purpose, growing wide ownership of directions. Hand work back to everybody with a stake in outcomes. Work together using the strengths, skills and insights of the team to discover and refine directions, one step at a time.

Figure 2.2 Different types of challenges to be faced

Summary

What can make the difference?
Move through work avoidance to face the deeper challenge

AS CHANGE IS difficult, it is often avoided either individually or collectively. Recognising personal or collective work avoidance in ourselves or in others is a first step to addressing it and moving forward, embracing change in ways that may lead to positive outcomes.

At different times, we might face three different types of challenges: technical, organisational and complex. It's important to recognise the nature of the challenge, as each requires a different kind of response. Misunderstanding and treating the complex as simply complicated can be very dangerous as the underlying problem will remain and even grow.

Reshaping practice 2

Actions for you

Make a list: No one knows you better than you. What are your favourite work avoidance strategies? What warning signs can help you recognise you are avoiding important work?

Think of a time when you faced something difficult: what enabled you to do this? What learning from this experience might help you stay on task in future?

We often frame complex challenges as simple or complicated problems: where are you doing this in your life?

Actions for your team

To what extent is your team or organisation responding to complex challenges as though they can be solved by technical or organisational responses?

In what ways is this providing short term relief? What might be the long term costs?

Chapter three

Beyond superheroes
Can one leader do it all?

More has been written and less is known about leadership than any other topic in the behavioural sciences.

– Warren Bennis[1]

WHEN THINGS GET difficult up goes the call for strong leadership. The 'L' word can be heard whenever a group or community is in trouble: "Someone please get us out of this mess!" And, in a whisper "at no cost to ourselves". Familiar models of leadership place one strong, multi-talented person in charge of fixing challenging problems. Although comforting, for complicated or complex problems, this model doesn't work in the long term. It is both dangerous and broken.

The 'white-water' image of continuous change quickly conjures up a picture of a fearless, rugged individual who can conquer everything. Is this what we need?

Peter was once part of an outdoor adventure camp for teenagers. One of its directors was Rick, a highly resourceful, creative individualist. Yet his processes and communication about what was happening could let him down. On a canoe trip down a flooded river, Rick's skill took him past serious rapids and submerged trees. But, without adequate explanation of how to deal with these dangers, the rest of the group were not so lucky. Their canoes capsized with lost gear and team members spread along the gorge, out of communication with each other. It was a disaster, resulting in a loss of trust. Such experiences are seldom forgotten.

Superhero leadership can bring dangers. We need a more inclusive model.

This chapter explores the heroic leadership models that are prevalent in our history, why they don't work, and the benefits of moving beyond this thinking to a more dynamic vision of leadership.

Heroic leadership models

HEROIC MODELS OF leadership are ingrained in our culture and history. 'Great-man' models dominated thinking until well after World War II. The term 'great man' was used because leadership was primarily a male domain, related to formal position and social class.[2] After the war, leadership emerged as a research area, which investigated characteristics of the various heroes of the conflict.[3]

Great-man theories sought to identify the characteristics of great leaders in military, government or social settings – people like Winston Churchill, Abraham Lincoln and Gandhi. If these characteristics could be found, it might be possible to identify, and then groom for greatness, people who had them. Personal qualities highlighted included:

- physical attributes like height and masculinity;
- personality characteristics such as extroversion;
- specific abilities like public speaking; and
- virtues such as intelligence, wisdom, dominance, initiative, self-confidence, tolerance, sociability and broad-mindedness.

But there was a problem. Over time it became clear there was no one systematic set of traits defining a 'leader'. People who might contribute great leadership in one context were not suited to another situation. Winston Churchill was a great wartime leader but was rejected in peacetime. Some politicians are considered better in opposition than in government. Trait-based research into great men failed to crack the code for effective leadership and by the mid-20th century researchers started questioning the model.

Hugh

Tall, handsome, intelligent and articulate, even in his school days Hugh was singled out as a future leader. With this ingrained confidence and his own convictions about the need to make the world a better place, he set out to create significant, lasting change doing development work in South America setting up micro-financing projects.

Ill-conceived plans, poor support and lack of understanding of complex situations quickly dashed his hopes. People's motivations for involvement were more multilayered than he had understood, and community values and ways of operating were far more elaborate. The project failed and the aid agency pulled out.

For Hugh, it was a tough and disillusioning learning experience about leadership in complex situations. It caused him to rethink his understandings of leadership and the dynamics of change, as well as his sense of self.

The longing for a heroic leader

Our longing for a hero leader is both ancient as well as being completely part of contemporary life.

– Carl Jung[4]

IT IS A pervasive myth, central to so many movies, television series and cartoons: special heroes see something about to collapse and use their special powers to come to the rescue. In Hollywood, they nearly always succeed, to everyone's relief.[5] We can admire these people, but we cannot emulate them.

We've all fantasised about the strong leader. If only we had a dictator – a nice dictator – just briefly, to sort out this mess. Then, when the crisis is over, the dictator will renounce power and gracefully leave the scene. Management consultant Colm O'Regan nails it: "Now that's a fairy story!"[6]

Psychologists tell us that the heroic leader has long been a part of the human psyche. For Freud, hero leaders were the primal fathers that groups longed for. Jung described a heroic stereotypical leader who reappears throughout human history.[7]

While we hope that one expert will save the day, this is rarely the case. Superhero leadership, by definition, is limiting, because it assumes all wisdom and capacity for discernment lie with one person.

A few years ago, a large social sector organisation was in financial crisis. Major cutbacks were necessary so the chief executive decided to take control and downsize significantly, making some staff redundant. He retained administrative, IT and systems staff to keep running the organisation, but he removed many of the creative program staff who might have contributed to innovation and fresh thinking.

A well-intentioned and committed person, the CEO worked alone, feeling responsibile for solutions. He did not involve anyone else in the downsizing, nor did he invite others to provide ideas or lateral solutions for the challenges they faced.

In letting program staff go, the organisation lost its best chance of developing new and innovative ideas. The remaining staff were excellent at maintaining the systems, but limited in their capacity to adapt or find creative ways forward. While the staff cuts generated short-term savings, they prevented the system from responding effectively to change.[8]

This organisation's future might have been different had it not adopted the top-down command and control leadership model.

Heroic leadership as collusion

COLLUSION LIES AT the heart of this. People seek to be heroic leaders for many reasons: for reward, to prove themselves, out of a desire for power, a need to control, or because of a feeling of inadequacy. You probably know someone who likes to act out of a desire to be larger than themselves and more important, or because they passionately believe in the hoped-for outcome, and in their own capacities.

Heroic leaders emerge because this model meets their needs, but those who follow can be equally to blame. We encourage the heroic whenever we look for somebody else to solve our problems for us, cost-free.

This might reflect a lack of self-belief, or be a form of laziness. It might arise from a desire for certainty as we experience grief, anxiety and fear. We may be happy to sit back and watch as a 'do-it-himself' leader struggles and drowns. Then, after all, it's their fault they didn't succeed.

For whatever reasons, we often invite heroic leaders in, colluding together to generate this kind of toxic leadership because it meets the needs of both would-be heroes and followers, at least in the short term.

The downward spiral

IN THE REAL-WORLD, superheroes take the unquestioning (or blindly loyal) on a precarious journey. Like those following Rick in his canoe, there's a good chance that there will be casualties. How does such a toxic situation spiral downwards? What goes wrong?

Initially, those of us watching or supporting superheroes feel anxious about our own capacities. We feel disempowered compared to the superhero, maybe experiencing performance anxiety.

Then, over time, would-be superhero leaders come under increasing pressure as they fail to meet impossible expectations. They feel they need to provide all the answers, yet things aren't going as they hoped. Their wheels are spinning and they are losing traction. Unpredictable obstacles may appear, or people may not act as expected. Everything starts to bog down.

As a result, superhero leaders try to do more, faster and better. They try to be who they are not. They run and run, until they collapse, disempowered and broken. Eventually the wheels fall off.

The leader taking on impossible problems without asking for help disappoints the group when he or she fails. At that point, we step in and let our human heroes know that they are not up to scratch. We blame them and question their competency and adequacy. We make them scapegoats, assassinating them with our words, at the ballot box, in the boardroom, in conversation behind their backs. We blame them for failing. We do not recognise that change requires us all to be participants.

When broken by their failure, superhero leaders also lose a lot of self-confidence. The easy way out is to find someone else to blame. And then the fireworks start!

Top-down heroic command and control strategies might look like easy, attractive solutions but, except with the simplest technical problems, they generally don't work, leaving all those involved broken and disillusioned. Reality seldom lends itself to such strategies. Complex change is more uncertain, unknown and unpredictable.

Two things are deeply wrong with the superhero model. First, would-be superheroes will fail to meet impossible expectations, disappointing everyone. The second problem is more sinister. Being passively rescued is disempowering for those who follow. Whenever Batman rescues Gotham City, he renders it even more powerless than before. Increasingly citizens of Gotham feel ill-equipped to solve any problem themselves, reducing their capacity to handle their challenges together.

You're on the inside until you ask questions

Here is a sadly not uncommon example of one of our colleagues who had to recover herself from the damage that superhero leadership caused in her workplace where a 'strong', charismatic CEO created a toxic culture of fear. Those with different ideas were afraid to speak up, learnt to bite their tongues and remain silent. Potentially useful contributions were lost, along with honesty. High staff turnover resulted from people who didn't fall into line leaving rather than confronting the status quo. The CEO acted out of his own needs for power, control, and security, and avoided interpersonal relationships. At every point, he resorted to legislation, using the rulebook, rather than conversation, to pull people into line.

Our colleague was promoted within the system while she said 'yes' and then was suddenly demoted and on the outer when she had some ideas that were different. She now sees that she had colluded with a toxic boss by never speaking up, at great cost, until she finally did speak and, as a result, was accused of disloyalty and pressured to leave.

Dangers of heroic leadership

DESPITE DEVELOPMENTS IN leadership research, 'heroic leadership' thinking is still prevalent in many aspects of everyday life. There is something very attractive about the heroic rescuer role. We often have huge expectations of people in positions of authority. At every election politicians promise the world and then, if successful, talk about how they are going to lead 'for everyone'. This is an impossible ambition generated by our equally impossible expectations.[9] When a would-be superhero steps up to take an organisation through complex challenges, it is bound to lead to disappointment and pain.

So why do we continue to believe in such leadership? Despite contemporary research and knowledge, why do so many still cling to it?

Margaret Wheatley argues that people with power consistently choose to maintain power and control rather than to focus on productivity or effectiveness. She observes that, when risk runs high, groups tend to concentrate power in just a few people rather than growing capacity more broadly.[10]

Women and leadership

IS HEROIC LEADERSHIP just a symptom of the historical reality that leadership has traditionally been a male preserve and remains so in many cultures?

While the percentage of women holding positions of responsibility in organisations has increased in recent decades, there is still a significant disparity. Early hopes that gender imbalances in senior roles might disappear by simply educating and equipping women to take on such responsibilities have not been realised. The challenge is more complex.[11]

Research suggests women taking on senior roles face additional challenges. They are seen as competent but are less well liked than equally successful men. They face more trade-offs between competence and likeability, particularly in organisations where they are breaking new ground. What appears self-confident or entrepreneurial in men is often seen as 'pushy' and 'unfeminine' in women.[12] We still struggle to accept people on merit for their contributions regardless of gender.

Over time there are changes taking place. Women are broadening their career aspirations, and are more willing to take on stereotypically male leadership models.

Being dangled over the ledge

In a large not-for-profit a senior staffer described his CEO's style as hanging people (figuratively) over the top-floor ledge and telling them he was considering firing them; he would let them know in a few months. Not surprisingly, there was a gap between the CEO and the team.

In situations such as these, people are made to feel afraid to keep them compliant. They follow through fear, but are seldom committed. They contribute what they must, but don't go the extra mile, particularly when things get strained. The organisational culture becomes one of fear and anxiety, with staff having absolutely no respect for their boss. It is difficult for them to know how to contribute constructively, or to even want to.

At the same time notions of effective leadership have changed, with contemporary thinking increasingly stressing the importance of emotional intelligence, encouraging participation, and working collaboratively. Interpersonal qualities such as cooperation and sensitivity are being valued. Though leadership research remains uncertain about the extent to which there are gender-based leadership styles, these are qualities commonly attributed to women who may therefore be better predisposed to lead in complex circumstances.[13]

Such thinking has been assisted by the increasing number of woman writing and thinking in the field: Margaret Wheatley, Barbara Kellerman, Amanda Sinclair, Jennifer Garvey Berger and Liz Skelton to name a few. They are broadening and deepening leadership thinking well beyond the narrow 'top-down' command and control models and, alongside their male counterparts, challenging the idea that alpha male stereotypes are the right, or only, way to exercise leadership.

Of course, there are men who also possess emotional intelligence and promote collaboration. Narrow thinking and gender stereotypes can be dangerous. Pointing once again to the need to rethink leadership, regardless of the gender of those occupying roles.

Building leadership capacity

HEROIC LEADERSHIP THINKING comes in many shapes and forms. Models of organisational leadership commonly assume high levels of command and control from above. Thinking about change management has often been quite mechanistic: someone uses data to identify key issues, then generates plans and implements them. When looking for innovation, organisations look for a single creative genius to think up a new idea. The nature of disruptive change in our world challenges such thinking.

The truth is complex situations will need a range of leadership contributions from many people. Yet people still write prolifically about leadership with the individual as the focus. The more we understand the complexity of change, the clearer it is that leadership will involve the contributions of many.

Initiatives such as these may start with an individual action:

- In the 1970s, Kenyan Mwangi Maathai planted a single tree to found the Green Belt Movement, an environmental non-governmental organisation focused on the planting of trees, environmental conservation and women's rights.
- Bob Brown rafted down the Franklin River in Tasmania in the 1970s and was moved to commit his life to protecting the Franklin and wilderness areas across Australia.
- A father lost his son to a drug overdose and went on to create a supportive network for families in need.
- A counsellor visiting an elderly Turkish immigrant traumatised by teenagers vandalising a public housing estate, chose to do something more about it than offer counselling.

These people made critical contributions, but only in the context of many others:

- The Green Belt Movement involved thousands of disadvantaged women in the work.
- The fight to protect the Franklin River involved tens of thousands working together at a community, national and international level.
- The father who lost his son was inundated with calls from families in similar situations and called a public meeting to establish a key support group.
- The counsellor involved with the frightened Turkish immigrant brought together concerned others from across the estate and built a residents' support group that then lobbied housing department and police officials around victimisation, safety and many other issues.

Leadership is fundamentally cooperative: the individuals starting these movements offered critical leadership, but also needed the support of many to make a difference.

When we examine historical movements, we begin to see the interplay of a wide range of contributions from many people. Names we associate with significant moments in history act as one symbol for what was, in fact, the result of aspiration and actions from many. The often-untold story behind these heroes is the support network that underpins their work. Martin Luther King Jnr would never have made his pivotal *I have a dream* speech were it not for long-term friend Mahalia Jackson calling from the crowd, 'Tell 'em about the dream, Martin'. At this, King put aside his prepared speech and spoke from his heart.[14]

Summary

Can one leader do it all?

Positive change requires leadership from many

HEROIC LEADERSHIP MAY superficially meet our needs, yet the likely result is a toxic system: those in positions of responsibility trying to be who they are not, and followers seeking an easy way forward. Such collusion can be damaging, creating broken leadership and disillusioned followers.

Can there be a better way?

Every day we encounter opportunities to exercise leadership: in senior positions of responsibility in organisations or as a staff member in a workplace, as a parent who wants to improve childcare options or safety in our community, as a teacher striving to make a difference in the classroom, or as a young adult longing to contribute to creating a better world. We all have opportunities to make a difference. We will do so most effectively if these contributions are offered as part of a collaborative effort, not as a solo act.

Reshaping practice 3

Actions for you

Leadership Life Story: take a page, and draw a line across it. The left end represents your birth, the right end represents today. Think back, and mark out events that have shaped your view of leadership. It may include people who had positive and negative impacts, experiences, global circumstances, life events you grew through. Use your life story, and the questions below, to consider the way you view leadership.

Think of people you know who are in roles requiring them to be the traditional heroic leader. How did they get there? What keeps them in that position? Who benefits? Who loses?

We are often complicit in seeking heroic leadership to solve our problems with no cost to ourselves. Where in your life have you sought this from someone?

When have you worn the mantle of the heroic leader (by choice or circumstance)? What seduced you into this role? What were the impacts on you? What have you learnt from the experience?

How could you personally benefit from letting go of impossible models of leadership? How might your team benefit?

Actions for your team

What narratives about leadership are prized in your workplace? How is 'success' defined? What are the consequences, good and bad, of these cultural norms?

What circumstances in your context generate a 'command and control' mentality in you or in your colleagues? How appropriate is it?

Are you seeing 'leaders' or leadership in a way that may be limiting your own contribution or that of others?

Part 1

Epilogue

Surviving shipwrecks:
Looking deeply at the challenges we face

What are the challenges we face?

1 Distinguish between simple, complicated and complex challenges, and be clear on your purposes.
2 Move through work avoidance to face the deeper challenge.
3 Positive change requires leadership from many.

Figure E1.1 Rethinking leadership – What are the challenges we face?

COME WITH US to the Auckland Islands. But be warned – they are no tropical paradise: sub-Antarctic islands 400km south of New Zealand dominated by towering cliffs and shrouded in fog and rain. In the 1800s many ships met their end here, not helped by some key navigation charts misplacing the islands 56km to the south of their true position, creating unexpected challenges with potentially serious consequences.[1]

Around midnight on 10 May 1864, the *Invercauld*, a state-of-the-art square rigger with a crew of 25, was wrecked on the northwest coast of the Aucklands. In charge was Captain Dalgarno, who held rigid notions of top down command and control leadership, typical of the times. He held the positional authority and expected the status and control that came with it. A few weeks earlier he sailed the *Invercauld* from London with five regular crew and casuals and then with a few senior offsiders picked up a whole new crew in Melbourne for the next leg of their journey. It was hardly a team; people did not even know each others names. This crew and their captain would soon discover the limits of their leadership structure. A hierarchical leader with followers doing his bidding wasn't enough when faced with the complex adaptive challenge in which they would soon find themselves, both in the storm and after the shipwreck.

A few days out in dark and deteriorating weather the watch suddenly saw glimpses of cliffs and rocks where cliffs and rocks were not meant to be. There was immediate panic and, in the hours after the sighting of the cliffs, the more challenging the situation became the more chaos became the rule. Despite decades of experience, Captain George Dalgarno quickly lost control of his crew. As the situation deteriorated, he and his officers ran around shouting impossible and contradictory orders.

A seaman recounted:

The officers had apparently lost all hope and also their heads, for the mate was crying, the Captain giving orders that could not be obeyed…while the second mate was bullying the man at the wheel. Is it then any wonder we were drifting nearly broadside on.[2]

All up, the time between first sighting the cliffs and the eventual shipwreck on the rugged coastal cliffs was perhaps two and a half hours. In that time frenzied action meant little thinking went into understanding their situation. Looking back a seaman observed that if the ship had been turned just a little bit further she might well have made headway.[3]

Nor in their panic did they look at the deeper challenges of the situation before it was too late. No thought seems to have been given to preparing for an evacuation, or to taking away provisions or resources for survival once on land. No concerted effort was made to launch the lifeboat or even issue a command to abandon ship. It quickly became every man for himself. The able-bodied fled the ship, leaving the others to drown.[4] All up it is a story of uncontrolled panic, confusion, ineptitude and tragedy.

The structured hierarchical model of leadership was not conducive to meeting this unpredictable situation. The few officers could not direct a positive outcome in the midst of growing panic. Trust was not in place; nor did the crew know anything of the skills or capacities they each might bring. Rigid command and control by a few was no match for the complex challenge that was suddenly thrust before them.

What are the challenges we face?

THE EXPERIENCE ON the *Invercauld* highlights the importance of looking carefully at the challenges we face and developing leadership appropriate to the situation. In this part some key priories have emerged, as was summarised in Figure E1.1.

1. Understand clearly the challenge, simple, complicated or complex: Effectively dealing with ongoing complex change requires a sound understanding of the nature of that change. To achieve change and quality outcomes we first need to understand well our situation and its complexities. How well we understand it will affect how we respond, and can drastically affect outcomes.

We need to keep checking we understand the full extent of the challenge and the leadership that might be needed to face it. Careful reflection rather than blind panic needs to drive our actions.

2. Identify the deepest challenges to be faced: A critical starting point for generating adaptive responses is to identify the deepest challenges to be faced and the work we each need to do, encouraging other individuals or groups to do likewise.

On the *Invercauld* for over two hours it was evident the boat might well founder. More effective leadership and a quality team might have retrieved key survival stores from the vessel or possibly set the course of the ship differently. The result was lives and resources lost, and reduced resources and people capacity for the challenges that would lie ahead.

3. Positive change requires leadership from many: Let go of impossible models of leadership. In challenging situations, we need to rethink our notions of leadership. Too much was expected of a few officers and an unknown crew in such circumstances.

In unknown territory or uncertain unpredictable situations we can neither expect a would-be superhero to deliver solutions to us at no cost to ourselves, or that we can or must be that superhero, contributing all the required leadership. If we are to grow teams or organisations more able to navigate change and uncertainty, we need to begin by rethinking our approaches to leadership, developing better paradigms for action.

.

Part 2

Rethinking Leadership For Complex Times

Introduction

How can we build effective leadership for complex times?

Leadership is one of the most observed and least understood phenomena on earth.
– James MacGregor Burns[1]

'WHO, ME? I could never be a leader. That is for others with special talents or qualifications.'

'What we need around here is strong leadership – someone to make hard decisions and give directions. That's me!'

Between these two perspectives lie many understandings of the word 'leadership'. To explore what it means to exercise effective leadership we need a clear understanding of an overused and ill-defined concept. What do you mean when you use the word? What might quality leadership look like?

In this part we invite you to re-examine your assumptions about leadership, to rethink your paradigms and mindsets about it.

What do we mean by 'leadership'?

A 1991 STUDY suggested that in the previous 50 years at least 65 different leadership classification systems were developed[2], a number that has no doubt multiplied since. No surprise then that there are a lot of anxious people trying to improve something they call 'leadership' that is so poorly defined. Consider the perspectives on leadership shown overleaf.

A leader is a man who has the ability to get other people to do what they don't want to do and like it. – **Harry Truman**

Leadership is influence - nothing more, nothing less. – **John Maxwell**

Leadership gets people to confront reality and change values, habits, practices and priorities to deal with what they face. – **Dean Williams**

The function of leadership is to produce more leaders, not more followers.
– **Ralph Nader**

Leadership is about creating conditions where people can do their most courageous thinking together. – **Margaret Heffernan**

Leadership is…the collective capacity to create something useful. – **Peter Senge**

The first responsibility of a leader is to define reality. The last to say thank you. In between the leader must become a servant. – **Max Du Pree**

People are often led to causes and…great ideas through persons who personify those ideas. – **Martin Luther King**

Why does it matter?

In exploring how can we build effective leadership for complex times, let's return to the Auckland Islands and the *Invercauld* survivors. How did they engage the challenges they faced?

In Part 1 we identified the importance of exploring the challenges to be faced, and noted how little those in leadership on the *Invercauld* looked at the situation they were in. Not much changed once onshore. Survivors lived amid chaos and lack of direction, the captain and senior crew were overwhelmed by events, without even fully understanding what was happening around them.

The morning after the shipwreck, freezing survivors found themselves on a stony beach surrounded by cliffs with little fresh water. Neglecting to take supplies when abandoning ship, they only had the provisions drifting ashore. The cook had a wet box of matches in his pocket, but while drying them set them all on fire. The steward also had a damp box that nearly met the same fate until a seaman grabbed them and rationed them for the rest of their ordeal.[3]

Onshore, they were a collection of individuals acting in their own, immediate self-interest. On the first night the group ate half of the washed-up food. Five days on, one man climbed a hill and spotted two harbours: a small one close by and a larger one further away. The group split up to explore them. One group failed to reach the larger harbour and returned. Lacking resolve, the other group gave up on the closer harbour, returning to base claiming they had reached it but that it was useless and had no food.

Figure I2.1 The perils of the Auckland Islands[4]

In fact, that harbour was sheltered, with shellfish, seals and abundant firewood. Had they explored the cove as agreed, many lives might have been saved.[5] In the following days, people wandered aimlessly. The sick were neglected and several died. Finally, one member tried again for the closer harbour and found plenty of food. Returning a week later, he persuaded everyone to move there; it was a month after the shipwreck. Once there, they discovered the remnants of a settlement, houses with roofs, fireplaces, implements and a freshwater creek.

Yet over the following weeks they continued to be aimless, lacking teamwork with people feeling threatened by each other. Many perished in the cold through inactivity or from more treacherous behaviour. Captain Dalgarno and officers did not appear to actively encourage wider leadership contributions, and often appeared threatened by them. They did little to motivate the survivors into action, and demonstrated little capacity themselves to shape outcomes.

Indeed, they appeared limited in their own survival skills. When using a simple boat someone else had made, they left it untethered and it drifted away. A senior officer burnt the roof off a shelter. When attempting to cross some water in another primitive boat, Dalgarno and the First Mate insisted on wearing all their heavy warm clothing, impeding their movement. Ten metres out they capsized and, unable to move, needed rescuing.[6]

Twelve months on, salvation came when a passing ship arrived to repair a leak. All but three of the 25 men had perished: Captain Dalgarno, First Mate Smith and 23-year-old junior naval seaman Robert Holding. Each reported their experiences, but more about these three later.

What might have made a difference?

ONLY A FEW survived starvation on the island, despite reaching dry land and finding a safe harbour. A lack of effective leadership (or a leadership vacuum) clearly didn't help. What kinds of leadership might have made a positive difference?

Finding your way around Part 2

IN THIS PART we explore developments in leadership thinking to build a positive framework for growing capacity to face challenges or make the most of possibilities. This will take us into, and well beyond, mainstream leadership writing into wisdom from positive psychology, personality theory and studies of community development and social action.

Chapter 4 explores the difference between leadership and positional authority, and the notion of leadership as service. Leadership is not just about positional authority. People with or without formal roles can contribute to the aspirations and purposes of the group.'

Indeed, a healthy group needs many different types of leadership contributions and Chapter 5 explores the multi-faceted nature of leadership. Leadership is not just about completing tasks. There is an important *people dimension* to listening and building the right teams or collaborations to take something forward. There is also a critical *purpose dimension* about developing shared directions, and a *safety dimension* about creating an environment where people have the confidence to step forward in new directions. There is also a *strategic dimension*, about knowing when to move to action, when to keep going or stop to learn from experience.

Chapter 6 describes effective leadership teams. Those in positions of responsibility need to grow a group's collective leadership capacity. Leadership starts to look less like one person and more like a collection of people offering various contributions. Rethinking leadership is an important task. Inclusive, effective, collaborative leadership matters. It affects the future of our families, organisations, communities, nations and the entire planet.

Chapter four

Separating 'leadership' from 'leaders'

Leadership: where do we find it?

WHILE WE HAVE seen that the superhero model of leadership is flawed, groups without some kind of leadership can descend into chaos. If we can no longer turn to one person to solve our problems and take us forward, how might we find leadership?

Leadership is neither automatic nor linked to a role or title. It can come from either the head or the foot of the table[1]. This chapter looks at how change requires contributions not only from people in positions of authority, but also from an entire group.

George Orwell tells a fascinating story of an experience he had as a police officer stationed in Burma during British rule[2]. He was told about a normally tame elephant that had briefly gone wild, ravaged a bazaar and killed a person. Orwell was expected to kill the animal. Yet, on arrival, he found a calm elephant grazing happily, its temporary rage completely dissipated.

With 'perfect certainty' Orwell knew, in that moment, that he shouldn't kill it. In his view, the elephant was now 'no more dangerous than a cow'. The crowd however, gathered around him looking for satisfaction and immediately started to pressure Orwell to kill it.

Orwell's positional authority lost out to this crowd whose influential authority won the day. Orwell took his rifle and shot the beast, forcing it to endure a slow, dreadful death. In this he also went against his beliefs and values.

We commonly assume that leadership is for people in positions of formal authority but, as Orwell found out, one can have positional authority and not be able to exercise leadership. Conversely, one can exercise leadership without positional authority. **Both matter greatly to the healthy functioning of a group, but they are different concepts**. Indeed, in complex situations, outcomes are the result of the often-multidimensional interplay of contributions from those with formal authority and those with informal influence.

Change from the bottom up

SINCE THE 1960s our attitudes to people in authority have altered[3]: international research has documented substantial declines in respect for people in authority,[4] so it is no surprise that leadership thinking also started to change. From being largely about people in positions of authority it has broadened to include people contributing leadership *upwards*.[5]

Massive changes have taken place that 30 years ago were unimaginable. People across the former Eastern European Soviet bloc countries contributed significant grassroots leadership that hastened the fall of the Soviet Union. The movement to end Apartheid gathered momentum and was sustained by grassroots contributions of many, including those in prison, and from across the planet.

Closer to home, in the 1970s and 1980s the movement to protect the Franklin River in Tasmania from hydroelectric development started with a small group of ordinary people and grew to a mass movement which was instrumental in unseating several Tasmanian Premiers and an Australian Prime Minister.

Technological change has given us dramatically more access to the world. A larger number of people can connect and contribute to a global conversation, through blogs, crowd-funding and social media. We can use this level playing field to have a voice and make a difference.

Sometimes we underestimate the level of influence we may have. Even without positional authority we have opportunities to bring experience, maturity, skills, ideas, or reputation. Grasping this potential influence is important.

At the same time, exercising leadership from the foot of the table needs to be done carefully, especially if it involves being a dissident voice. We need to be mindful of the constraints others are under, or risk becoming an aggravation, a lightning rod that does attract lightning[6]!

Social action and grassroots community development

We are not people anxiously awaiting a charismatic leader, a saviour who will lead us to a political Promised Land.

– **Community organiser George Lummis**[7]

WHILE THE FOCUS of earlier thinking had been on producing senior leadership for organisations, the turbulent 1960s and 1970s were very concerned about social change, spawning the Civil Rights movement, 'wars' on poverty, action against the Vietnam War and Apartheid, and concerns around issues such as gender equality and the environment. This period also saw the rise of community development and community-organising practices focused on empowering struggling groups and communities.

Locality development models sought to build the capacity of struggling communities, drawing people together around common interests or pursuits, and building trust and mutual support. Rather than focusing on problems or needs, in asset-based community development an agent brings people together to identify strengths and shared passions, supporting them to achieve outcomes together.

Social action and *community-organising* strategies bring individuals and organisations together to work for outcomes where there is an identifiable obstacle: governments, industry or company. These various forms of grassroots engagement all seek to empower ordinary people in communities to identify common goals or aspirations and achieve them together.

Saul Alinsky and the Back of the Yards Council

Saul Alinsky, activist and author of *Rules for Radicals*,[8] was a criminologist working in Illinois who concluded that one of the major causes of crime was poverty. In the late 1930s he organised his first community campaign, the Back of the Yards Council, to rid impoverished areas in Chicago of crime and neglect. For over 30 years he worked with community organisations encouraging people to take hold of their lives and contribute grassroots leadership. Alinsky's legacy lives on in the work of the Industrial Areas Foundation (IAF). His work was sometimes criticised for allowing the ends to justify the means, but the results generally have influenced the development of many people, including Barack Obama.

The IAF strategy is to develop broad-based coalitions of organisations - unions, community groups, religious organisations – and build relationships and trust between them. It emphasises the importance of relational meetings: one-on-one conversations, active listening to identify issues and common goals, understand hopes and aspirations, and to build trust and willingness to collaborate.

Unlike some social welfare programs that reduce people and communities to problems or client status, grassroots community engagement seeks to build power and people's capacity to shape their own destinies by working together, doing what they can for themselves. Unlike many professional management or organisational roles, a community development worker/organiser doesn't seek to be an expert or boss, but rather to be an initiator of conversations and builder of relationships, listening deeply, asking provocative questions and engaging with the deeper complexities of situations.

Through ongoing cycles of action and reflection - listening and building relationships, discerning common goals, acting and then evaluating – we can achieve positive outcomes.

The difference between leadership and positional authority

The key to successful leadership is influence not authority.

– Kenneth Blanchard[9]

ALTHOUGH WE OFTEN think of leadership as being about the person visibly at the front, this isn't necessarily true. In football the goal scorer completes the work of a strong, disciplined defence and creative midfield. Evening sports shows replay the scorers' feats, but they are by no means the sole actors.

We remember Sir Edmund Hillary and Tenzing Norgay for first climbing Mount Everest, but they were not in charge of the expedition. Expedition leader, Sir John Hunt, was one step behind making critical logistics, relational and strategic contributions. He navigated the complex dynamics of personalities and cultural differences (between Englishmen, New Zealanders and Sherpas). Hunt had to make the hardest call: not everybody could reach the summit. He had to ensure all climbers knew that to get anyone to the top, it would take strong commitment to team goals over personal aspirations.

The person with positional authority may not be the person in the spotlight, but they can harness capacity in their organisations towards common purposes.

Ask people which leaders most inspire them and they will mention those with little or no positional authority, like Martin Luther King Jnr and Mother Theresa, as frequently as John F. Kennedy, Winston Churchill or others who held the authority positions. Spiritual figures have influenced the world without significant positional authority: Jesus, Buddha, Confucius, significant maharishis.

Other people have brought about significant societal changes without (or before) holding high office, exercising grass-roots leadership within their group then increasing their influence into wider constituencies.[10] Think, for example, of Lech Walesa in Poland, or Nelson Mandela in South Africa.

In situations requiring adaptive responses, positional authority is rarely enough on its own. Those with such authority need to earn respect and gain commitment. In teams, voluntary organisations, movements, community groups or families, people may choose to participate or to move elsewhere or drop out. Even in the military or large corporate organisations where those with positional authority have coercive powers, it has become increasingly evident that earning respect and gaining commitment are equally critical. People are more likely to act in a committed way if their personal aspirations are aligning with shared group goals. This has major implications for leadership as this book will explore.

Leadership as an action not a position

GREAT DANGER LIES in using the word 'leader' to describe someone as it confuses concepts of exercising leadership with notions of positional authority. *Am I cut out to be a leader?* and *Have I leadership to contribute?* are completely different questions that may have different answers, and it is important not to confuse them.

IT IS LIBERATING to separate out these ideas. Hence throughout this book we have chosen not to talk about people with roles or formal responsibilities as 'leaders' but as people with 'positional authority'.

We can then talk about exercising leadership as something we do – an action or contribution - rather than a role, position or trait. Regardless of our position, we all have leadership capacities to offer in our lives or roles.

A lack of formal authority shouldn't stop us contributing constructive leadership where it is needed. Those with positional authority need to recognise that challenging situations require the fullest leadership from everybody, empowering one and all to contribute to the group, increasing its potency and possibility.

Positional authority matters

SEPARATING NOTIONS OF leadership from positional authority is not to suggest that formal authority is irrelevant or unimportant. A civil society is based on order and delegated authority. It is crucial to the functioning of our lives, even if we are unaware of it.[11] As children we are subject to parental authority. As we become adults, we renegotiate those relationships and the discipline of laws and people with appointed authority takes over.

The presence of authority can encourage people to pay attention. It can help direct resources to best support what is being done.[12] The way people exercise authority is important, and is amplified by the authority of their position.

Every system needs clear patterns of authority to work well: organisations, nations, communities, cultures, families. Authority is in our lives from the moment we are born, primarily from our family of origin. Parents, hopefully, will provide us with direction, advice and protection, and create order within which we can live and grow to maturity. Such authority plays a key role in our growth, just as authority is key in groups, teams, organisations, sport and emergency situations.[13]

Unclear authority structures undermine an organisation. A group without patterns of authority quickly becomes uncomfortable. In a crisis or uncertain times, people will quickly search for, or create, lines of accountability or decision-making through which they can function safely. Immediately after a car accident people mill around nervously, doing what they can. Then police, ambulance or rescue personnel arrive, or maybe a concerned bystander directs others. In the chaos people start to take on roles to enable things to move forward.[14] Similarly, countries without a strong rule of law or judicial system are unlikely to function well as safe societies.

The contributions of many can be more easily harnessed when there are clear systems and lines of authority. People with formal roles and responsibilities will have critical functions in this. If everyone is responsible for everything, it is difficult to notice when something is forgotten. The choice to act or delegate responsibility often lies with those in positional authority and the result of that choice can greatly impact outcomes.

In daily life, the best interventions from people with positional authority may be to create order and promote efficiency. Yet, during serious complex challenges, adaptive leadership might need to be quite different: it might be critical to surface challenges, or uncomfortable questions and encourage people to look deeply at them. Far from creating order these actions may be destabilising as people are faced with the work they need to do. Constructive conflict can promote deeper discovery and experimentation.[15]

Leadership as service

Leaders we admire do not place themselves at the centre; they place others there. They do not seek the attention of people; they give it to others. They do not focus on satisfying their own aims and desires; they look for ways to respond to the needs and interests of their constituents. (Such people) have the interests of the institution and its constituents at heart.

– James Kouzes & Barry Posner[16]

WHETHER CONTRIBUTING FROM a position of authority or the foot of the table, our motivations matter. Some people who achieve higher office or responsibility are driven by the desire for power and authority. Others, however, end up in such positions out of a desire to serve, putting group needs above their own. Of course, this is a complex issue and we are often propelled by many different motivations, some of which we may not even be aware of.

Compare this pair. In the second half of the 20th century the majority black populations of two neighbouring African countries sought to achieve freedom from oppressive regimes. In South Africa, the challenge was to unlock the chains of Apartheid. Nelson Mandela and others spent several decades in jail in the long journey to freedom. In Rhodesia (modern day Zimbabwe), the challenge was to attain independence from British colonial rule. Robert Mugabe and others with the Zanu PF Party led this fight.

Fast-forward several decades to the 2000s. In one country, the former president is revered as a saint, in the other the president is feared, and accused of many atrocities. While both have a long way to go, there is something different in the feel of these countries as you cross the border between them.

What is the difference?

With Nelson Mandela and his colleagues, at critical points they chose to act in the interests of ALL the people they served. President Mandela ruled for all South Africans, seeking to live out forgiveness and service. In contrast, Mugabe and his colleagues in Zimbabwe have a history of backstabbing and self-serving political intrigue. This model of operation, when taken into government, became part of the country's culture.

Both Mandela and Mugabe achieved the outcome of independence, but the result is countries that are on completely different trajectories. Although both face many struggles, one generally journeys forward, while the other is subject to sanctions and vilification.

The truth is that motivation matters. Mandela was committed to the ultimate purposes of the cause, Mugabe to maintaining his own power.[17] Dietrich Bonhoeffer, a pastor in Nazi Germany who lost his life for opposing Adolph Hitler, warned that heroic leadership springing from the need for admiration and power can poison an entire community.[18]

The paradox of servant leadership

The best test is: do those served, grow as persons; do they, while being served, become healthier, wiser, freer, more autonomous, more likely themselves to become servants?

– Robert Greenleaf [19]

POSITIVE PSYCHOLOGY SUGGESTS that greater wellbeing will come from using our strengths to make a difference to things beyond ourselves that matter to us. In doing so, we will find deeper meaning in our lives. Decades earlier, in the 1970s, retired executive and writer Robert Greenleaf explored similar ideas. Concerned about the growing distrust of authority and institutions, he felt people needed a better leadership paradigm. *In The Servant as Leader*,[20] he pointed out the importance of contributing to purposes beyond ourselves; this turned thinking about leadership on its head. While the words 'servant' and 'leader' in the title are often seen as opposites, in Greenleaf's thinking they hold together in creative tension.[21]

His central idea was that leadership must be about service, a contribution to a group or organisation that begins with a desire to serve, not to lead. We contribute because we believe the change or outcome truly matters. We offer a servant contribution to the group; it is not about us, but the bigger purpose.

Servanthood is not about a person in positional authority performing menial chores (though this may happen). Nor is it about being weak. What distinguishes those exercising servant leadership is their deepest motivations. They do not take on roles for honour, status or personal rewards but from believing in a cause or mission they want to support.[22]

While sometimes superficial rhetoric, servant leadership is an important, often-cited concept across the social sector, and is the subject of contemporary empirical research.[23] And since the global financial crisis, there has been more emphasis on values-focused leadership that engages broader social agendas beyond financial bottom-lines.[24]

What does this look like in practice?

IN SOUTH AFRICA after 27 years in prison, Nelson Mandela had every right to be bitter towards his captors. Yet as President, he resisted pressures for retribution and sought to bring people from diverse backgrounds together around a new vision for South Africa.

What about on a mountainside? A surprising choice to lead the 1953 Everest expedition, John Hunt was chosen for his people skills, team-building, ability to grow shared purpose and detailed planning capacities. In selecting the climbing team, he emphasised two seemingly conflicting characteristics: first, candidates had to want to get to the top themselves but second, they had to be even more committed to getting someone to the top, whoever that might be. Only a couple of climbers would form the final summit team. For the rest, there 'might be thankless, even frustrating, jobs during the most critical phase of the expedition'.[25] Individuals needed personal passion but, paramount, was their willingness to serve the team. While some in the team were initially quite upset at Hunt's appointment, his commitment to team goals soon won them people over.[26]

What does this mean in an organisation? One of us came to know Bronwyn, the CEO of a large renewable-energy resource company. Soft-spoken, forthright and courteous, she came to the organisation when it was at a low ebb due to changes in government regulations, redundancies, loss of vision and lowered staff morale. Her attitude and concern for the organisation and everyone involved drew the best out of staff, allowing the development of better practices and ways forward. Staff described her as approachable, authentic, able to laugh at her mistakes and admit them publicly, often putting staff needs above her own, and finding personal reward in seeing the organisation achieving its goals.

According to Greenleaf, directions may occasionally need to be imposed by a person with positional authority but, more commonly, an organisation will discover its purpose through wide and genuine participation. This generates higher commitment to values, higher levels of performance and greater concern for the community in which the organisation operates.[27] Our motivations can make all the difference, something we explore further in Part 4.

A better definition of leadership

GREENLEAF'S THINKING CAN help us redefine leadership. If it is about serving the purposes of a group rather than meeting our individual needs, then its definition is best to focus on the aspirations of the whole group or organisation.

We need leadership to help a group discover shared objectives and move towards them, key for any group. They need to be helped to function in healthy ways, navigating well the complexities of their situation. We need to start to think about leadership as an activity and contribution rather than a position. Consider this definition:

Leadership is a critical ingredient in the healthy functioning of a group to enable it to discover and move towards its core purposes.

Once we shift our thinking from heroic individuals towards collective action, many things fall into place. Leadership is something a group needs, not a special quality some of us have. Individuals can make a range of leadership *contributions* to a group, drawing on their particular strengths.

This increases the group's leadership resources and takes us beyond the confining narrative of one heroic leader. It unlocks capacity that would otherwise remain shrouded in the shadows. Instead, everyone can help make a positive difference.

Individuals may choose to contribute leadership because, for the good of the group, they are moved to reduce the gap between what is and what could be. Our colleague, Craig Bailey, puts it well. The desire to contribute leadership is *born in the heart of a person who sees what is, sees what could be, and is consumed with the tension between the two.*[28]

A critical role of those with positional authority is to develop and leverage leadership contributions in ways that build group capacity. To grow a culture where leadership multiplies rather than residing in a few louder, confident or charismatic people. Aigner and Skelton speak of mobilising people to face their new realities and solve their own problems.[29] Margaret Heffernan talks of creating conditions where people can do their most courageous thinking together.[30] Kouzes and Posner are concerned about the art of motivating others to want to struggle for shared aspirations'.[31]

Summary

Leadership: where do we find it?

Look for leadership capacity right across your organisation.

LEADERSHIP IS NOT a position, but a contribution, a critical ingredient of a healthy, functioning group. We can find it anywhere and everywhere. Sometimes hidden, it needs to be drawn out and applied towards group purposes.

Sometimes people don't believe they have anything to offer. Those in positions of authority can enable constructive, forward progress by helping group members discover the best in themselves, and the courage and self-belief to contribute. They need to model the way, creating a climate encouraging such contributions.

In making their contributions, everyone needs to be driven not by desires for honour, status or reward but by conviction and belief in the cause or outcomes for the group.

Reshaping practice 4

Actions for you

Think of the people who have made a difference in your life, who transformed your practice in some way. To what extent was their role in this a product of positional authority or something different?

Watch and listen: Scan our culture and society for a week (via the news, meetings, politics, movies, TV – anything!). Watch how easy it is for leadership to be placed in one person (the leader). What contributions were required in the whole story or scenario? Did the Leader supply all of them?

Positional authority is useful in a range of circumstances. When have you experienced this?

Leadership can emerge from unlikely sources, often where there is no positional authority. When have you experienced this?

Experiment: Try to eradicate the word 'leader' from your vocabulary for a week and use replacement words like 'leadership' or 'people with roles'. How does this affect your thinking?

Are you clear on why you are offering leadership? What matters to you? What difference would you like to make in your world – family, team, organisation?

Actions for your team

To what extent are the lines of positional authority clear and useful in your team?

Watch and listen: notice when the call for leadership goes out in your context. What is really being asked for? Is the call a sign of work avoidance? Is it ignoring what the organisation might already have?

Motivation matters. Do the people you work with know what motivates you and each other? If not, why not? How can you help include this topic in conversations?

How can you grow a culture of generosity, of service in your work team? What is the one thing you could do, in the next hour, which might be a step towards building a culture of service in your organisation?

Chapter five

The leadership mosaic
What leadership contributions does a healthy group need?

IF LEADERSHIP ISN'T up to one person but a curated collective contribution, what kind of contributions might be needed?

Research has recognised that many different types of contributions will be needed, something highlighted for Peter in 15 years of research as Director and Senior Researcher with NCLS Research, an agency working with universities, community organisations and churches. NCLS explored issues around wellbeing, social capital and personal meaning systems, as well as effective and sustainable leadership, using samples of 6,000-10,000 church communities across Australia surveyed every five years (plus samples from England, New Zealand and the US - see Appendix 1).

This leadership research revealed four distinct dimensions of leadership also found in research more widely:

- *People* **contributions:** how we engage constructively with others
- *Purpose* **contributions:** how we develop shared directions
- *Safety* **contributions:** how we create a secure base
- *Strategic* **contributions:** how we move to action, pacing the journey well.

The *People* dimension: How we engage with others

POST WORLD WAR II thinking recognised that leadership involved both *task focused* and *people focused* aspects: how to complete a job, and the personal support needed for successful completion. The social action and community development movements of the 1960s and 1970s, explored in Chapter 4, highlighted the importance of relationships and community building. *Situational Leadership*, popularised by Paul Hersey and Kenneth Blanchard, argued that no one leadership style is universally appropriate in every context[1]. Rather, people need to find the right blend of task and relational emphases depending on both the task and a person's readiness for that task. Somebody new to a role may need lots of practical help with a task. As they grow in competence, direct instruction will be increasingly replaced by encouragement. Indeed, an experienced person might resent over-direction.

Hersey and Blanchard also noted that we all have a preferred leadership style depending on our personalities that may be more or less appropriate in any given situation. This was an early recognition that leadership contributions are personality-dependent, something to which we will return later.

The importance of relationships

REGARDLESS OF WHERE you wish to contribute leadership, or what your dreams for change are, you will be dealing with people. Building relationships, social capital and discovering critical human assets in groups is critical.[2] Whether in families, organisations or communities, it is important to be available, listening, building connections and gaining insights.

NCLS research identifies two key aspects here: the need to **listen deeply** and to **build connections** (see Figure 5.1).[3]

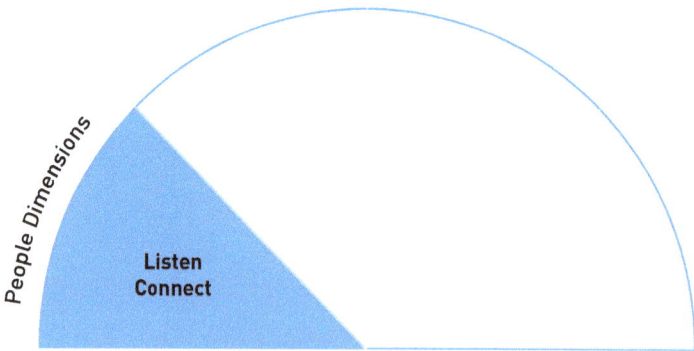

Mapping Leadership

*Figure 5.1 Leadership contributions in the **people** dimension*

1. Listen deeply: is about seeking to understand the perspective of others, sensitively and empathically. Good listeners ask questions more than make statements and ensure they have heard correctly. It is tempting to jump in with a solution, or a decision without really listening but it can have highly damaging consequences. There is immense power in a grounded, constructively provocative question that can take people deeper in their exploration of a situation.[4] From such questions new possibilities and insights can emerge.

'Leadership' is often seen as being about persuading, motivating and action. In reality it is often more about listening. People go through many emotions as they deal with change. The benefits of taking time to listen are greater understanding, trust and respect, and the space to consider alternatives before taking action. It may reveal issues below the surface before they become larger. The more responsibility we have, the more important it is to listen well.

2. Build mutual connections: People with common interests need to come together, discover shared purposes and act collectively to live them out. Connectors can bridge different worlds, enable communication and uncover new possibilities, thereby building trust and mutual respect. This is always important, but especially when starting out or when beginning a new initiative, or when creating strong foundations for new directions.

In a new role, seek to learn and build relationships by walking the corridors of your organisation and visiting other groups or constituencies. Those seeking to impress can build walls rather than bridges. A desire to learn and build relationships can create strong foundations for the future.[5] Impact can be multiplied when action is collective.

Ask the consumer

Listening and getting perspective from those on the ground is critical.

An IT department developing new software found that initial users were not giving it the acclaim they hoped for. When given feedback, the department wrote it off as uninformed criticism. Then the team was taken to a testing lab and from behind one-way glass watched users struggle with their software. Immediately, ways of improving the software became apparent.

The *Purpose* dimension:
How we develop shared directions

IN CHAPTER 1 the notion of transformational leadership was introduced: leadership that invites a group to reflect on and refine its purposes, to help people to identify their ideal future and journey towards it together.[6] One of the dangers of such purpose-based leadership is that its focus can still be on heroic leaders, albeit with slightly different superpowers. Literature sometimes over-emphasises the importance of one person in positional authority as the vision definer: a strong, charismatic person with a total belief in the rightness of their vision and their ability to make it happen. Think politics: people are elected based on overblown promises, then they become disillusioned when much of it proves unachievable.

Over time, transformational leadership thinking has become more inclusive - recognising the importance of teams, participation and collaboration - with increasing emphasis on widely owned directions. Research, including that done by Peter, identifies the importance of ownership of group purposes as a critical litmus test of the overall vitality of an organisation.[7] Imposing vision and expecting ownership can be counter-productive. It will diminish commitment, reducing the likelihood of achieving outcomes. Alignment of purpose is a critical prerequisite for committed action: while it may take longer than imposing directions, longer term it builds motivation and effort, and the chances of success. If overall organisational purposes are not clear, it is difficult to determine meaningful priorities.

When quicker may not be better

The principal of a tertiary training institution had innovative ideas about how his team could work together but, recognising the importance of ownership, opened-up questions for the group to explore, with an outside consultant helping them. Their plan for how to work together was quite similar to what the principal himself envisaged. However, the collaborative decision-making made an enormous difference difference to the team's commitment to it.

Teams can be swept along reacting to urgent pressures, not considering how their work fits into the bigger picture. Where there are owned purposes, people can evaluate how their actions might align with those purposes. In contemporary society, there is a loss of commitment to organisations per se;[8] instead those responsible for organisations or teams often need to bind groups together through commitment to a shared vision.

Figure 5.2 outlines some of the key aspects of growing shared purpose. Mobilising people to move forward will require helping them ***envision together*** shared directions, ***explore options creatively*** and ***inspire heart commitment*** to those directions. It will ***empower people to contribute***, to discover what they have to offer.

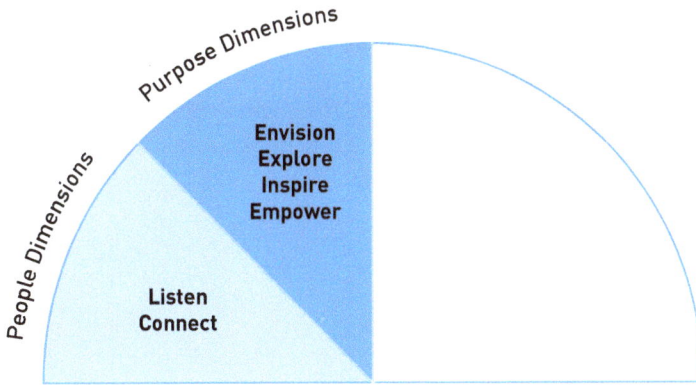

Mapping Leadership

*Figure 5.2 Leadership contributions in the **purpose** dimension*

3. Envision together: Effective leadership contributions include an intentional focus on the future, beyond issues of maintenance, inviting people to imagine a positive future, together discovering meaningful ways forward that are owned by as many people as possible. This involves giving oxygen and legitimacy to interesting ideas and checking progress regularly. Just as in building a stone bridge or cathedral window, all the blocks matter, but developing a shared sense of direction is the keystone that locks the other blocks in place. People who have an orientation to the future are often energising to be around: they are hopeful and focussed on possibility rather than problems, generating enthusiasm, contribution and alignment.

4. Explore options creatively: Research suggests people move forward in new directions when they develop both head and heart commitment. This is the head aspect: those with responsibilities need to help others understand the situation, see the challenges from various perspectives, explore options creatively, seeing things in new ways.

Create space for everyone to share perspectives, invite creative suggestions about ways forward, be slow to dismiss or put boundaries around what seem like crazy or irrelevant ideas. Maybe they are wide of the mark, or maybe our view is too narrow.

5. Inspire heart commitment: an emotionally appealing vision for the future needs to be articulated that connect with people's passions. We often assume rational argument is what moves people, overwhelming them with graphs, tables and rationales for change. People then just try to poke holes in the reasoning. Heart commitment is vital even where compliance can be insisted on. Without motivation, hostility and passive aggression can destroy forward progress. People need to recognise their own hopes in the shared vision to adopt the shared goals as their own. Resist the temptation to cut corners, but equally don't allow the process to be never-ending or people lose interest.

6. Empower people to contribute: Groups need leadership that empowers people to contribute, helping them understand their place in the bigger picture. Capacity builders will equip people to use their gifts and skills, coaching them to harness energy and build contributions. An old adage is: do not do for others what they can do for themselves. By handing the work back to people, we invite them to contribute to shared purposes, in turn growing the capacity to achieve those purposes.

Shaping purpose and culture

A school with which Naomi was involved developed some clear educational and wellbeing outcomes for students. Every part of the school had to articulate how they were enacting this. It became a primary reference point for staff's decision-making, the consistent application of an overall purpose helping everyone make positive decisions every day without cumbersome processes. This also made it easier to face new situations.

The *Safety* dimension:
How we create a secure base

HUMANS NEED ORDER amid uncertainty. In major South-East Asian cities, characterised by chaotically busy streets and a lot of rubbish, street sellers often work hard to keep their spaces clean, tidy, attractive and even spiritually protected. In the wider chaos, they seek order and safety in the space they can control. Engaging with others and developing shared directions can be destabilising: if change were risk-free it would happen of its own accord. Because of this, there is a third critical dimension: safety. Since the 1990s leadership thinkers like Ron Heifetz and Marty Linsky have increasingly recognised the importance of strategically balancing risk and safety.[9] People need a secure environment and stability to take risks within uncertainty and healthy groups need good management.

Think of someone crossing a deep river on a slippery log. Encouraging them to go forward is inviting risk. If they get across safely it will build self-confidence and ability. But if the log is too slippery and they slip off, the result will be a cold swim, lower self-confidence and less capacity to take a risk next time.

There is always tension between the need to step out in new directions and the desire for safety. Managing that uncertainty, allowing it to be a creative crucible for growth, is an important contribution. Ron Heifetz urges people with positional authority to keep the heat on, but not too hot: encouraging manageable risk-taking rather than foolhardiness.

Safety contributions create an efficient and secure day-to-day environment. They produce order, efficiency and consistency within an organisation. Including establishing detailed steps and timetables for achieving results, allocating resources and responsibilities, generating policies and procedures, monitoring progress and developing an ordered environment.

NCLS research identified three key safety aspects of creating a secure base: the need to create **clear positive structures,** develop **reliable communication** and build a **culture of optimism** (see Figure 5.3).[10] Alongside the people dimensions discussed earlier, these safety-focused contributions will provide strong foundations for new directions, a secure base from which to step forward.

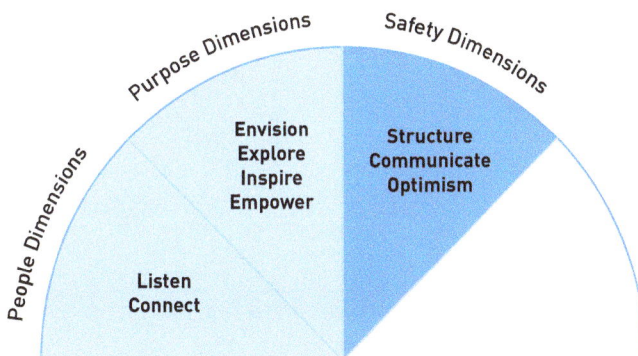

Mapping Leadership

*Figure 5.3 Leadership contributions in the **safety** dimension*

7. Create clear positive structures: are critical for a safe environment, creating clear standards, safe foundations and operational guidelines. Effective day-to-day management must underpin the development of new directions. Everybody needs to understand what is expected of them, receive timely feedback and have their accomplishments recognised (and poor performance constructively addressed).

Everyone needs some structure to ensure a stable group environment, clear boundaries and expectations. It provides the context in which people can contribute.

8. Develop reliable communication: this is a foundation for safety. Information-sharing and ensuring everyone can contribute must be a priority. George Bernard Shaw commented: "The single biggest problem in communication is the illusion that it has taken place". There are many formal and informal relationships across organisations: we may have previously worked with someone, still catch the train with them, or have family connections. An empowered learning organisation will use all relationships to enhance communication.

We often assume that because we have said something, others have heard and understood the intentions of our message. Yet this is rarely how it works. Communication is more circular than linear requiring listening as well as speaking, especially to what is being said below the words. Reliable communication will bring conflict to the surface and then carefully manage it, neither hiding nor exacerbating it. It is critical to create environments that will hold people's attention, keeping them at the table exploring difference, when they are tempted to run away.

9. Build a culture of optimism: We've all seen documentaries about people surviving ordeals through their enormous will to live, or watched sporting events where one team wants victory more than another. Attitude counts. An optimistic attitude affects every aspect of our lives. Many traditional planning processes are problem-focused, which reduces hopeful feelings. Yet an optimistic environment can build up a team in ways that rub off on others, inviting people to consolidate what they have, exploring potential rather than limitations. While we need a clear picture of the realities of our situation, focusing on strengths and hopes rather than weaknesses or problems is more effective. Appreciative Inquiry is a good example of this, focussing on the best of 'what is' to discover 'what could be'.

An exercise in risk or safety?

To many of us jumping off a bridge attached to an oversized rubber band seems crazy, yet bungee jumping has been one of the highest profile innovations in adventure tourism in recent decades. Is the story of the development of bungee jumping about danger and risk takers?

No. Rather it is a story about safety. Young New Zealand rock climber and surfer A.J. Hackett was interested in experiences, but as an experienced rock climber safety was paramount.

Whereas others would say to themselves, 'I wonder what is going to happen if I jump off this bridge?' the question for me was always, 'how do I jump off this bridge safely'? [11]

After his first jump, Hackett spent years exploring the parameters of bungee jumping looking for safety and predictability. He and a colleague worked with researchers at Auckland University to understand the mechanics and trialled the predictability of ropes using weights, testing the elastic capacities of cords, incrementally increasing height and testing for variability by weight.

They were also willing to learn from their mistakes. On one occasion a group of onlookers wanted to jump and Hackett and a friend obliged. In the heat of the moment they became careless and a serious accident nearly resulted. Learning from this, clear jumping systems and procedures became a priority. A jump master is responsible for safety, with a double-check person alongside. The checkers have expertise with knots and in gauging a customer's weight. Through engaging with them, jump masters read their client's personalities to ensure reliable communication, keep the clients at ease and positive enough to jump. The team can thus plan for a wide range of people and jump styles. [12]

Safe systems, communication and trust, can make anxious customers more confident. Hackett wrote in 2006: *"No one has ever died on an A.J. Hackett Bungy site. I am immensely proud of that fact. More than two million people have jumped, but we have never had a death".* [13]

Alongside quality relationships, good systems provide safety for people to leap out into the unknown!

The *Strategic* dimension: Moving to action

IN A REMOTE gorge the water is flowing fast and furious through rocks and rapids before it reaches the next, still pool. Canoeists are standing on the edge, contemplating the currents and potential dangers. Strategies and contingency plans are discussed and decided upon in case things go wrong. The time has come to act. Conscious of the moment, the person responsible for the group cuts in: "we know what to do to make it through. And we know what to do if we don't. Let's give it a go!" Having spent time preparing the group, collaborating and consulting, the time is right for the group to get going.

There is constant tension between developing new directions and creating safety, requiring strategic sensitivity at every step. At each stage in the implementation of something it is important to assess the right time to step out and try something even though it may feel risky. Such strategic contributions are vital to a team seeking to implement adaptive responses.

As is knowing when it is time to curb risk-taking. When faced with unexpected cloud cover or delays, an aeroplane pilot's instinctive response is often to keep pushing on to get to their destination, even if they aren't trained to fly in low visibilty. Such get-home-itis causes many fatal accidents; turning back before it is too late can be critical. Managing delicate risk/safety balances demands wisdom and self-discipline.

A system needs pressure to adapt or there is no incentive to change.[14] Sometimes it is important to inject tension into a system, provoking anxiety that invites people to step forward. Tough questions can raise the heat, encouraging engagement and naming of worries.

Failure to grasp moments for action will eventually diminish momentum. In the words of Canadian hockey player Wayne Gretsky: "You miss 100 per cent of the shots you don't take".[15] The way ahead may be uncertain but the outcome is known if you do *not* act.

Yet, at other times, it is important to seek safe shelter in a harbour, to tend wounds, regain energy and perspective, strengthen relationships and create firm foundations for the future. A system can only tolerate so much stress or overload before it breaks.[16] We can lower the temperature by finding easier aspects to deal with, or by breaking a bigger problem into smaller units.

Carefully balancing risk and safety is about having enough heat to encourage people to keep working but not be so hot to panic or destabilise. We need to ensure change neither stalls through complacency nor paralyses through its speed. In between these two extremes lies what Ron Heifetz calls the "zone of productive disequilibrium", where there is enough heat to engage the real issues, but not so much that things get out of control. This is where people can do constructive work facing and progressing through complexity.[17] Balancing the risk/safety tension to be a creative crucible for growth is a critical leadership contribution.

Healthy groups need various strategic contributions to manage the pace of change, as outlined in Figure 5.4. They include knowing the time to **move to action**, being able to **act with resolve** and **learning and growing from experience**.

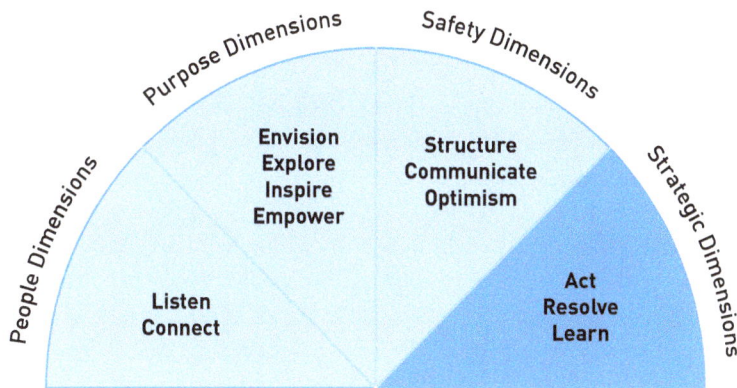

Mapping Leadership

*Figure 5.4 Leadership contributions in the **strategic** dimension*

10. Move to action: A group's ability to act with purpose depends on sensitive discernment of when best to move to action. Some people may relish exploration and, therefore, want to move too soon. Others may value security and never want to step forward into the unknown. Most of us lie in between these two extremes. Knowing the right time to move forward is vital. Getting the balance right is never easy. We often hear people in the union movement say they feel they are good at acting, but not so good at learning and creating safety. On the other hand, those involved with churches often wish some action would follow interminable discussion! There is a difference between taking your time and picking your time. Knowing the right time or season for action is vital.

11. Maintain resolve: There will always be many pressures on us to deviate from our central purposes. Determination and resolve will be important, especially when things get difficult. Persistent people can be powerful role models.

12. Learn and grow from experience: Organisations that are agile in navigating change can learn from both successes and failures; groups need to develop natural ways to do this. People who can contribute this are comfortable with complexity and are open to growth. Expecting others to grow and change, they must be willing to do so themselves! Modelling this can help with the development of a learning culture in a team.

Balancing action and reflection

TRADITIONAL LEADERSHIP THINKING assumes the person with positional authority is all knowledgable, with followers relying on him or her for wisdom about how to act. This is a version of heroic leadership, where the expert delivers wisdom to an empty vessel and it is very limiting. Action/reflection models of learning draw on the work of Brazilian educator Paolo Freire, best known for his work *Pedagogy of the Oppressed*. A campaigner for the poor who experienced poverty during the 1930s depression, Freire saw the empty vessel model of education as dangerous and disempowering. Freire believed everyone brings wisdom from life experiences, that fundamental cycles of action and reflection enable us to learn and adapt.[18] We don't grow or develop resilience without taking some risks creatively exploring our edges.[19]

Effective leadership requires time on the balcony as well as on the dance floor.[20] While the dance floor is about action, time on the balcony is about getting perspective: who is dancing with whom, what are the patterns of the dance? We can learn from such a broader, birds-eye perspective, enabling us to act more intentionally. This concept of balcony time is one to which we will return at various points. In complex challenges where the stakes are high, we too easily get caught up in frenetic activity and lose perspective. For most of us, the more pressing a situation, the less likely we are to take time out. In our experience, one of the most powerful contributions you can make to anyone's leadership is to simply make space for them to get perspective. A change of scene, reflective conversation over coffee, an afternoon away as a team, or 20 minutes mindfulness before starting the day costs little but might change everything, moving people from reacting to responding.

The leadership contributions needed in a quality team

IN 1949, A party of firefighters parachuted into Mann Gulch in Montana under the supervision of Wagner Dodge, a quiet man, who had the team start a firebreak.[21] A sudden wind change turned the fire and it rushed straight at them creating a massive crisis. The men ran for their lives, the fire rapidly gaining on them. There seemed only one possible outcome.

At the last moment, Dodge did something surprising: he grabbed a box of matches and lit a fire in the grass around him. Beckoning others to join him, he lay on the burnt ground with protective clothing over him. The fire-front rushed through and around the burnt patch, leaving him essentially unscathed. It was a brilliant, creative act of adaptive leadership, one so effective it remains an essential part of fire-fighting strategy.

The rest of his team, however, took one look at what Dodge was doing, thought he was crazy and ignored his orders, running even faster. All but a couple perished. There had not been adequate trust built between Dodge and his team. His communication skills were not great. His innate shyness, and too little time spent on team building prior to the event, was the difference between a creative triumph and a disaster. The traditional question to ask would be: was Dodge a good or a bad leader?

Yet this is the wrong question. In truth, he brought some amazing leadership strengths to the team but clearly lacked others. A gifted innovator, he was not supported by others with strengths in communication or empowering others. As inquiries later showed, the system had simply thrown people together on the day without any team-building, further compounding the problem. Knowing our strengths can make all the difference. We need to encourage everyone to identify and develop their leadership strengths, something to which we shall turn in Chapter 12. The challenge is to find others whose strengths complement ours. A quality team can account for deficiencies or weakness in individual team members. Fifty years of research has demonstrated the multifaceted nature of leadership. Figure 5.5 summarises the various contributions described in this chapter.

Leadership contributions needed in a healthy group

People contributions: Engage with others

1. **Listen deeply:** step beyond your own agendas and be fully present for others; see things from their point-of-view and understand what is going on for them.

2. **Build mutual connections:** work alongside others, grow networks of trust around common interests or hopes, a platform from which new possibilities can emerge.

Purpose contributions: Develop shared directions

3. **Envision together:** focus on purpose and future direction, not just on immediate issues or matters of maintenance.

4. **Explore options creatively:** help people understand the importance of moving in new directions and encourage fresh ideas about ways forward.

5. **Inspire heart commitment:** grow ownership and excitement about group purposes.

6. **Empower people to contribute:** help people find their place within the overall plan.

Safety contributions: Create a secure base

7. **Create clear, positive structures:** ensure people know how things operate and what is expected.

8. **Develop reliable communication:** ensure communication is trustable and clear.

9. **Build a culture of optimism:** build on what you have, focus on potential and hopes.

Strategic contributions: Make things happen

10. **Move to action:** know the moment to step out and give something a go.

11. **Maintain resolve:** stay focussed when things get difficult, or there are competing demands.

12. **Learn and grow from experience:** be open to learn and be changed, possibly in significant ways.

Figure 5.5 Various leadership contributions

Case Study: Fukushima

THE 2011 FUKUSHIMA nuclear power plant disaster, after a tsunami, captured worldwide attention. The disaster at the Fukushima Daiichi plant is well known. Less reported was the experience at Fukushima Daini, another plant 10 kilometres south, which also felt the tsunami's wrath.[22] The tsunami was much larger than predicted (10 m rather than 3 m waves), and much bigger than what the plant had been built to withstand (5 m waves). Many different contributions prevented a catastrophe, as seen in Figure 5.6.

Daini's 400 employees had to instantly shift to crisis mode, operating in unknown, unpredictable territory with outcomes beyond imagination.

On March 11 at 2:46 pm the earthquake hit and the team assembled to prepare for the tsunami, which surged in at 3:22 pm. Reactors shut down and cooling them was a top priority. However by 6:43 pm people at the plant realised that the water surge had knocked out power to three out of the four reactors. In a few days, they would have to lay nine kilometres of cable, weighing a ton per 200 m, to get power to cool them, something that would normally take a month. Radiation from the crippled Daiichi plant was also threatening them. Against their natural survival instincts and amid fears for their families, teams needed to go out into the chaos to assess the situation in detail. To deal with their anxiety, teams had to repeat back instructions, sentence by sentence, as they were given.

Recovery plans were redrawn regularly as new information came to hand. Some paths proved to be wrong. Initially the plan was to power Unit 2 first as it seemed most in danger, but reconnaissance then suggested Unit 1 was the priority, requiring the exhausted, sleep-deprived crew to start again. Senior leadership regularly brought coordinators together, updating everyone via a whiteboard, offering people a chance to process things for themselves. Doing this helped to redefine their shared reality. Two and a half days later, at 1:24 am on March 14, close to the impending melt down, Unit 1 was cooled down, followed in the next 14 hours by Unit 2 then Unit 4.

Drawing people together, listening, collecting intelligence and exploring options enabled learning, reprioritising and moving to more effective, purposeful experimentation and action.

People became more optimistic as clear communication and dealing with anxiety increased their hope, resolve and commitment to the risky journey. The various leadership contributions of many made this possible: 400 committed, informed, engaged and purposeful people had successfully worked together in unpredictable and excruciating circumstances to avert a tragedy.

Can you recall a time when you were part of a team or organisation that was really going places, where people were excited and positive, felt included, and their contributions valued? Can you map the leadership contributions made, as we did for Fukushima Daini?

Fukushima leadership contributions map

Listen deeply	Senior leadership needed to listen well to those going out to assess the situation.
Build mutual connections	The response teams were regularly assembled to connect with each other and what they were learning.
Envision together	When together, new priorities were the focus of interactions.
Explore options creatively	Possibilities were explored and new priorities identified each time the situation became better understood.
Inspire heart commitment	Heart commitment was critical to helping the teams get on with their tasks while facing huge uncertainty about their own safety and that of their families.
Empower people to contribute	The teams were well-drilled to know what they had to offer, and those contributions marshalled well.
Create clear positive structures	Good and practised systems were in place and trust built to enable action in such an uncertain situation.
Develop reliable communication	Clear communication was a priority, instructions repeated back and, in a rapidly changing situation, up-to-date information shared.
Build a culture of optimism	Team meetings were designed to build hope and a positive, optimistic environment.
Move to action	In a deteriorating environment, timing and moving to action effectively was critical. To pace this, updates and revised priorities wereregularly communicated, enabling decisive action.
Maintain resolve	Persistence and resolve were hallmarks of the response.
Learn and grow from experience	Prioritising rapid learning was an overriding concern. Everybody brought their own perspectives on an unknown, uncertain, unpredictable situation.

Figure 5.6 The leadership contributions needed - Fukushima Daini

Summary

What leadership contributions does a healthy group need?

Uncover the various *People, Purpose, Safety* and *Strategic* leadership contributions needed

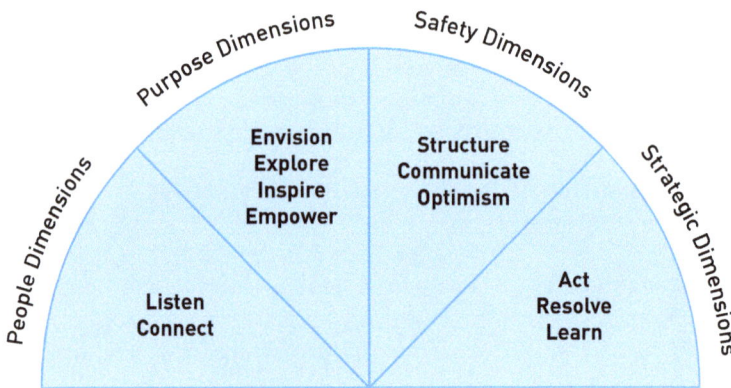

Mapping Leadership

Figure 5.7 The leadership contributions needed in a healthy group

"GRAND DREAMS DON'T become significant realities through the actions of a single person. Leadership is a team effort."[23] Many contributions are needed in a group to effectively engage complicated or complex situations. Understanding the range of contributions needed - people, purpose, safety and strategic - in a healthy group is critical if we are to develop organisations able to respond constructively to their changing environments. These contributions are important to create a solid trusting base, clear purposes, a safe environment and a well-paced journey balancing risk and safety, action and reflection.

These contributions interact with each other in various ways at different stages of a journey. Just as members of a football or basketball team contribute as if a single organism, quality teams will need to be able to do this as well.

As we shall see in Part 4, nobody is likely to bring all these leadership contributions, as they are connected with our personalities and makeup. It needs a team. And that team will be at its best with as many people as possible contributing from their strengths.

For those responsible for teams the challenge is to uncover the leadership capacities and contributions available to them in their teams, to develop teams of people that together bring the range of leadership contributions needed. Chapter 12 helps each of us look more carefully at the leadership contributions we might have to offer.

When we get this right, heightened commitment intensifies the energy flowing around us. Small and larger contributions, combined well, create something special. Rather than wearing us out, they generate more energy and we find meaning in being involved in something bigger than ourselves. Such experiences provide hope and inspiration for when things are hard. What might such teams look like?

Reshaping practice 5

Actions for you

Reflect and map: Have you experienced being part of a group that was going somewhere, where something rich was happening, generating energy, action and increased commitment and trust? How did it feel? What kinds of leadership contributions helped make things happen? Can you map those leadership contributions?

What aspects of leadership do you get the most energy from contributing? What aspects in other people complement your own?

Actions for your team

What aspects of leadership are different members of your team great at contributing? Which dimensions activate different people in your team?

Are people working in roles where they can contribute what they are best at?

Do people in your team know what contributions energise each of the other members?

Chapter six

Leadership: it's a collective effort

How can our collective efforts create impact?

LEADERSHIP IS MULTIFACETED. To be effective it needs to work in, and with, teams; it's a team thing. Here we look at creating teams of people who together bring the range of leadership strengths needed. How do we build quality teams that are more than the sum of their parts?

A football team consists of players with different skills chosen to complement each other. A football game is a collection of sequential acts of leadership as, one by one, different players seek to create opportunities, build on what has gone before and pass the ball (and leadership) to another. A quality team will pass leadership from person to person in a way that is second nature to the players. Even though some may be higher profile than others, all the players are critical to the game.

While each player has individual aspirations, in a quality team people will subordinate those hopes for the good of the whole team. The goal-scorer knows that the goal could not be scored without creative work in the midfield and solid, disciplined defence.

Firefighters, emergency crews and surgical teams know the individual roles they play and the capacities they bring. They will also recognise the need to work together towards shared purposes. Being part of the team is the best way to achieve individual aspirations.

So, instead of seeking a superhero cape, those with positional authority will need perspective from the balcony, to grow leadership capacity within the group and facilitate those contributions as is appropriate to the situation and the season.

Shared or distributed leadership

Individual executives don't have the personal capacity to sense and make sense of all the change swirling around them. They need to distribute leadership responsibility, replacing hierarchy and formal authority with organisational bandwidth, which draws on collective intelligence. Executives need to relax their sense of obligation to be all and do all and instead become comfortable sharing their burden with people operating in diverse functions and locations throughout the organisation. By pushing responsibility for adaptive work down into the organisation, you clear space for yourself to think, probe, and identify the next challenge on the horizon.

– Ron Heifetz[1]

IN THE 1960s academics Daniel Katz and Robert Kahn explored 'shared' or 'distributed' leadership where all members of an organisation lead by using their personal resources towards the purposes of their organisations.[2] Edgar Schein predicted in 1996 that the most salient aspect of leadership in the future would be that it was not present in a few people all of the time but in many people some of the time as circumstances change.[3]

Shared or distributed leadership thinking examines the contributions of *all* people, not just those with specific roles or functions.[4] Leadership is 'stretched' across an organisation,[5] including not just top down *vertical leadership* but also peer influence (*horizontal leadership*) and *upward influence*,[6] bringing many benefits:

- *Reduced pressure on just a few:* No one person is likely to possess all the leadership capacities needed in equal proportion. It is unreasonable and unfair to expect that of one person. We need the contributions of many.
- *Multiplied capacity:* More capacity is available if we integrate the abilities and perspectives of the whole group and distribute work across an organisation. We will be more likely to succeed if we have a wide base of commitment.

     If a family is to identify its core purposes or engage change it will need to hear everybody's voices, not just the adults'. A community group developing priorities will need to hear all the voices, as will any social sector agency, school or business.
- *Shared responsibility:* People with a problem may be best placed to identify solutions. While outsiders can provide perspective or support, those in a group need to take on the adaptive work of shifting group direction or priorities. Psychologists suggest we will lead richer and more fulfilling lives if we share core purposes and work towards them together.
- *Fresh perspectives from the edges:* An organisation's capacity to discover ways forward will be enhanced by the contribution of many rather than leaving it to a few. Newcomers and those more on the fringe of a group can often provide fresh perspectives.
- *Growing commitment to the group:* Collaborative models have the potential to generate increased commitment to an organisation and its collective goals.[7]
- *A shared burden:* While the buck still stops with them, it can be liberating for those with positional authority to feel they are not alone, reducing their isolation and anxiety.

Turning leadership upside down

COMMUNITY ORGANISING WRITERS contrast 'power-over' with 'power-with'. Exercising power-over can restrict capacity and action, as there are only a few active players while the rest just watch. Developing power-with invites more people to become involved, expanding the overall capacity of the team, organisation or movement to respond. In complex change, we can't expect one person to have the resources to deal with everything.

Consider the diagram below in Figure 6.1. At the top of the people triangle is someone with positional authority. If this person has a controlling style of leadership that alienates those underneath it will diminish their commitment, limiting overall leadership within the group.

But what if we turn this concept upside down?

In this triangle, the person with responsibility is at the bottom. He/she is supporting and encouraging the team to contribute their own leadership towards the cause. Each, in turn, offers support to the others, and so on, growing overall leadership capacity.

We often think about power as a limited commodity: *If I empower you, I will lose power.* Many people in positions of authority feel a need to control a group to maintain their power. Any emerging leadership in others is threatening, something to be survived, managed or limited. Yet the concept of power that we wish to explore here is quite the opposite, what colleague John McLean describes as an expanding pie model: if I empower you, the whole group has greater capacity. Leadership is not the largest slice of the pie, but the ingredient that can grow the pie, multiplying and harvesting capacity.

Of course, there are times when power-over is important: in child rearing, occupational health and safety or within a crisis. Yet too often power-over is used unhelpfully in a limiting or controlling way, easily ending up as abuse or bullying.

Figure 6.1 Two views of leadership

Developing a leadership lens

WE NEED TO develop a *leadership lens*, a way of seeing and naming leadership contributions or interventions around us. Spotting them is a first step to harnessing them.

For those responsible for teams, this approach can help reinforce or reshape team culture and help everyone refine their own practice and behaviour. It is also important for those not in positions of authority to see what is going on, and recognise the right time and moment for critical interventions or encouragement.

Find a good vantage point to monitor what is happening around you. In our experience, almost every organisation has people with abilities, ideas or energy they aren't bringing to the table. Your extra vigilance might reveal game-changing ideas or contributions that might otherwise have been lost.

Creating the right team

JUST AS OUR bodies need a variety of food groups to remain healthy, so our healthy teams need a variety of leadership contributions.[8] Who do we need around the table to best achieve outcomes?

Over the years the New River team has regularly explored together the various leadership contributions identified in the previous chapter that we each bring. A poster on the office wall highlights our individual strengths to guide us. When looking for additional staff we look specifically for people with the particular leadership strengths needed.

Does your team or organisation do anything similar? To what extent do you know what you have to offer? We turn to that in Part 4.

Bringing together a team with the range of leadership capacities needed is important to effectiveness. A childcare co-ordinator with strengths in listening and engaging with others could easily spend too much time with individual children while chaos reigns around him/her. They might value someone else who can stand back to provide an overview. Or someone in positional authority with strong, analytical skills may suggest so many diagnostic processes and reviews that it leads to analysis paralysis unless they are balanced by people with other strengths.

Different leadership contributions may be important in different seasons as illustrated in Figure 6.2. Innovation strengths and new ideas might be distracting once initiatives are underway. A desire to move to action might be unhelpful in a phase of learning and listening. Everyone needs to better discern when to contribute and when to step back and encourage others.

Ask yourselves: what leadership contributions are needed now in our situation, and who is best placed to contribute them?

There is a time and season

Margaret Thatcher, British Prime Minister in the 1980s, was strong and self-assured and became known as the Iron Lady. It was something the country was looking for at a difficult time. She was confident and could stand up to opposition.

At the same time, there was a less palatable shadow side: she was merciless with people who did not fulfil her expectations, capable of publicly humiliating them, of not listening to advice, and being unwilling to compromise, seeing it as a form of cowardice.

Her iron will served her well in her early years, making her attractive to a public looking for strength and confidence. Eventually though, it came to be less effective and less appropriate and, ultimately, she was ousted by her own cabinet.

The leadership strengths needed in different seasons

- **Creating a new group:** Initial stages will require engaging strengths - *connecting with others and listening deeply* to what is going on - before going ahead with a new initiative. As a group develops, *empowering* strengths will help people feel they belong.

- **Early in a group's life:** Groups will need to develop shared direction. Helping the group *envision together* a positive future and *inspiring heart commitment* to that vision will be critical, as will *exploring options creatively* together.

- **Taking stock of progress:** Envisioning, inspiring and exploring together are also important when pausing to take stock and look ahead, when renewing shared directions.

- **In the middle of a major project:** This may not be the time for new ideas. *Clear positive structures, a culture of optimism and empowering people to contribute* will be critical.

- **In a time of growth:** Growing from a single-celled to a multi-celled organisation will need others to join leadership teams as senior people move into roles more removed from direct engagement. Creating *clear positive structures* and systems for the new situation will be vital. *Reliable communication* will become harder and more complex but no less important.

- **When faced with complex issues:** We need to invite lateral thinkers who can *explore options creatively* and suggest new ideas for ways ahead.

- **As an organisation matures:** Over time organisations can become rigid, in danger of losing touch with their initial purposes. To remain fresh and connected, they will need to continually redefine their purposes and directions. Strengths linked with *developing shared directions* will again become important, as will a willingness to *grow from experiences*.

Figure 6.2 The leadership contributions needed in different seasons

Mapping the leadership strengths in your team

DESIGN ROLES WELL matched to people's strengths. The entire team will benefit from it.

Do those in your team know the leadership capacities they each bring? Mapping team strengths can help us make the most of what we have, and help us discover untapped potential.

We need to ask:

- Are those in our teams working to their strengths?
- Do our teams have the necessary strengths?
- Do we need people with other strengths to complement those already in our teams?

Mapping leadership strengths with your team is important; we may not be aware of all the strengths a person may bring because we are only experiencing them in the roles they perform.

There may be leadership capacities missing from your team. Recognising this might suggest adding people with those strengths: as temporary outside support or a permanent team member.

Diversity can be a great strength, whether of age, experience, skills or energy. Effective teams will seek to expand their collective perspectives by valuing diversity. It might take time and energy to build up a diverse team but it can reap dividends.

Apart from creating well-balanced teams with the required strengths, you also need to consider other questions in building collaborative leadership teams:

- Do team members represent your organisation's breadth and scope? Can those in the team help build stronger commitment across your organisation for what is proposed?
- Are people with different perspectives included, as well as newcomers or people from the fringes of your group?
- Does the team feel cumbersome or is it small enough to be effective, keeping everyone involved?
- Do team members have enough stakeholder credibility to take outcomes forward?[9]

Growing a quality team

JUST CALLING A group of people a team doesn't make it one. Not all teams are effective. The whole is not always better than the sum of its parts. Introducing a team approach to a group used to take-charge leadership won't be straightforward.

The following traits of quality teams are commonly identified by researchers:[10]

- *Trust:* The team needs to be a safe space underpinned by clear, reliable communication, good systems and members listening deeply to each other. People need safety to learn and make their contributions without fearing their vulnerabilities will be used against them.[11] Trust takes time to build, and is easily destroyed.
- *Clarity of focus:* The team needs clear focus and purpose that is fully owned by all involved. Teams become dysfunctional when members put personal needs, status or agendas ahead of group purpose. Is everyone pulling together? How focused are they on team goals?
- *Resources:* The team needs to set realistic, sustainable goals and expectations, supported by adequate resources and expertise.

- *Inclusion:* In a strong team, everybody matters, has something to contribute and is taken seriously, including those on the fringes. Commitment to the growth of everybody in a team distinguishes high performing teams from others.[12]
- *An atmosphere of openness:* Members are made to feel comfortable and encouraged to contribute. They feel they are part of something worthwhile.
- *The ability to handle difference:* The team is comfortable with disagreement and welcomes constructive exploration of difference. Difficult issues are addressed; important conversations take place in meetings rather than outside them. Conflict is managed as a creative process potentially producing better outcomes.

Creating a healthy environment

The responsibility of leadership is not to come up with all the great ideas but to create an environment in which great ideas can happen.

– Simon Sinek[13]

FROM RESEARCH INTO organisations performing well above what might be expected of them, Kim Cameron suggests four strategies for building positive organisations.[14] First, develop a positive climate where positive emotions dominate, enhancing both individual satisfaction and organisational performance. Second, nurture positive relationships that enrich people rather than leaving them feeling dispensable. Third, encourage positive communication that invites inquisitiveness. Finally, develop positive meaning. When people pursue purposes that matter to them, they become more engaged and that improves wellbeing.

Together these create reinforcing positive spirals, enhancing wellbeing, job satisfaction and performance and reshaping organisational culture.[15] This can help organisations innovate and respond creatively to challenges.[16] While not naively ignoring challenges we can intentionally seek to build a positive climate.

The challenge of shared leadership

IN AN APPARENT paradox, those in positions of responsibility need to believe they can make a difference but have the humility to know they can't do it alone. While their own contribution matters, more important is growing leadership capacity and contribution across the group. The question we need to ask is *not*: how can I be *the* person who is going to rescue this group? Better is to ask: how can I weave together well the range of leadership contributions available in my team so it becomes more than the sum of its parts? Those with positional authority need to create an environment in which leadership can multiply and flourish.

This approach may feel challenging or uncomfortable as it requires different skills, taking a risk in trusting others and a loss of control. Some people may not want additional responsibility, preferring to leave it to those who already do all the leading. Yet this is limiting and unlikely to succeed because no one person brings all the capacity or perspective needed to engage complex challenges. Shared leadership is not an abdication of responsibility by those in assigned roles.

Modelling the practice of distributed leadership

Our colleague Jim had a significant experience about 20 years ago, working in an executive position for a large, state-of-the-art hospital. The CEO was a quiet, reserved man with an innate understanding about leading an organisation. Watching him over the 18 months until his retirement Jim learnt more about exercising positional authority than from any book or his MBA. What did this CEO do?

- He had a light touch. He did not get rattled. Problems would arise, things would go wrong, but he calmly dealt with them, seeking out a solution while others around him were getting upset.

- He surrounded himself with others with particular expertise. Hospitals are multifaceted organisations needing many specialist skills. Rather than pretending he knew everything, he accepted his own limitations and built a specialist, executive team.

- He selected people who would get on with each other and gave them room to do so. Executives were chosen carefully. Candidates would meet the existing team to see if they would fit in. Once employed they were made to feel part of things through team-building activities. He was consciously building a team where everybody could come to know and trust each other.

- He recognised that a person's expertise was only part of their story, that everyone brings a different mix of personality, experience, expertise and emotion. He sought to understand what each person might bring beyond their specific training and expertise, quietly blending together a high performing team. In Jim's words:

With different personalities we would see problems in different ways, and would approach issues differently. Some of us were dreamers who could think ahead and see possible ways forward. Others were focused on the day-to-day who could get things done efficiently. Some could intuitively see a way through a problem, while others could brilliantly collect and interpret hard data. Some could work the room while others listened quietly to understand things more deeply.

This CEO's approach to leadership was where possible to allow the team to do what they each did best. Jim discovered later that years before in another organisation the CEO had tried to be more controlling, making every decision, trying to know everything about the business. His way of shared leadership was the result of hard-won wisdom!

Collaborating across groups or organisations

COMPLEX CHALLENGES OFTEN require groups within organisations to work together collaboratively, and sometimes to partner with other organisations.[17]

To be effective, collaborating groups need a set of common goals to guide their joint activity. They will agree on shared resources, people or assets because their goals can't be achieved alone or are better achieved together. They will have their own strategic objectives from the partnership and can withdraw if the partnership is not delivering.[18]

Collaborators need to understand where other groups are coming from, their needs and hopes. They will need to learn how to explore possibilities together, hear different points of view and experiment together to find ways forward.

Key roles will be holding together the collaboration and linking with key people in each partnering organisation. Critical in this will be high levels of trust and commitment underpinned by clear structures and roles. Communication will be critical. When crucial individuals move on, collaborations can founder.

Collaboration is important but seldom straightforward, given that people from diverse backgrounds or interests are around the table. It is about learning to lead across difference.[19]

Geoff Aigner and Liz Skelton identify three major traps in collaboration.[20] First, there is *competition*: diverse motives and agendas might compete. Second, partners need to let go of full *control* of what is going to happen and how. Finally, there may be differing levels of *commitment* to what is happening.

Collaboration or espionage?

A community welfare interagency group met for years to share information and build partnerships. There was a lot about achieving social outcomes in the region together. A few members asked whether it might be possible to work more collectively on some projects beyond information sharing.

Beyond superficial encouragement such suggestions were not welcomed. Under the surface the biggest, best-funded organisations wanted to maintain control, to achieve their own organisational outcomes rather than broader shared objectives. Collaboration was in fact a code for interagency surveillance!

A new paradigm

MANY PEOPLE INVOLVED in leadership development are recognising that there has been too much emphasis on growing individual capacity rather than developing overall leadership capacity in teams. Current thinking is moving from ideas about the great *leader* to a great *group* view of leadership.[21] In Hillary Armstrong's words, we need to ask not about the capacities of individuals with positional authority but rather the extent to which a team or group is *leaderful*.[22]

The implication for leadership development is that we need to think of broader leadership-capacity building, as opposed to turning selected high performers into higher performers. Everyone needs to explore what they have to offer, building a quality team together.

A culture of shared leadership can strengthen the ability of organisations to navigate complexity and change. Figure 6.3 highlights what the shift might entail. The contrast is stark between the two models. How we see, exercise and build leadership can make a huge difference. American leadership writer Bill Drath puts it well: "What people are looking for is a new source of leadership…and I believe it is right under our noses. Leadership can come from the activity of people making sense and meaning of their work together."[23]

Old World leadership paradigm	New World leadership paradigm
A noun: a leader or a position.	A verb: an action, something we do.
The Man out the Front, the Head, the Captain, the Chief, the Voice, the CEO, the inspirational speaker, the one to follow.	Different people contributing their unique combination of strengths to make a difference and move something forward.
A sense that certain people are born leaders and this is discovered as they grow up	We all have different leadership strengths that we can offer and discover in ourselves.
A position of authority.	Positional authority is only part of the bigger leadership story.
A position people compete for.	People contribute leadership from wherever they are.
A superhero-type character to save the day. A strong person who makes all the decisions.	The right to contribute or ask the right question at any time.
Coming from the top down.	Coming from the ground up.
Groups move forward if they let the leader have his or her way.	Groups thrive and move forward when people trust each other.
Research into leadership explores the characteristics of a great leader.	Research into leadership explores the kinds of contributions a group needs.

Figure 6.3 Old World/New World paradigm shift

Summary:

How can our collective efforts create impact?

Cultivate effective collaboration in balanced teams

LEADERSHIP IS A team thing. It is fundamentally cooperative: sometimes one person will contribute leadership, at other times they will benefit from the leadership of others. No one has all the necessary gifts, yet everyone can contribute. In a quality team, the whole is more than the sum of its parts.

People in positions of authority need to encourage and harness capacities in a group, choreographing the right balance of leadership contributions for the group to be effective. To lead is not to make others depend on you but to encourage and equip them to make their own contributions.

Mapping a team's various strengths can help us discover untapped potential as well as additional capacities that may be needed.

Beyond leveraging capacity, there are two other key reasons why collaborative leadership is critical. First, it will multiply not just capacity but also motivation, trust and commitment. The net result will be more agile and effective teams and organisations. Second, a collaborative approach will increase our chances of more fully grasping a situation. In anything but the simplest situations we need the perspectives of many. No one person can see the whole picture.

Reshaping practice 6

Actions for you

Identify and ask: We all need different things to feel able to contribute and be able to contribute well. What do you need from your team to contribute your best? How can you ask this from them?

Teams are made of individuals, just like you. What teams or groups have you had a positive experience in, that you have learnt from? Can you think of a team that was a negative experience that also provided learning? How can you apply this learning in the way you participate in your current team?

This chapter invited you to think about the different seasons in which leadership is necessary. In what stages do you have the most to offer? When are your contributions most effective?

Actions for your team

In your team who brings which leadership strengths? To what extent does your team make full use of members' capacities?

What leadership contributions does the current challenge or season you are in most require? Are there people in the team or organisation who can (and are invited to!) offer these?

How empowered do people in your team feel? How can you build this?

Reshape: On a scale of one-to-ten, currently in your team how important is nurturing and empowering people to contribute from their strengths? What might move it one or two steps up that scale?

What are the first steps you can take to cultivate the strengths of individuals in your team?

What question can you ask in your next meeting that will help people recognise that leadership comes from everyone, not just from the head of the table?

Consider the Old World and New World paradigms. What paradigm operates most often in your work place? Pick an element of the New World paradigm. What conversations or actions could you take to help this grow?

How might your meeting or communication practices need to change to reflect a distributed model of leadership?

Part 2

Epilogue

Surviving shipwrecks: Leadership in complexity

Part 2

How can we build effective leadership for complex times?

4 Look widely for leadership.

5 Uncover the various *People*, *Purpose*, *Safety* and *Strategic* leadership contributions needed.

6 Cultivate collaborative leadership in balanced teams.

Figure E2.1 Rethinking Leadership – How can we build effective leadership for complex times?

HOW CAN WE build effective leadership for complex times? Let's take stock. At the beginning of Part 2, we outlined the sad fate of the crew of the *Invercauld*, wrecked on the Auckland Islands in 1854. Few survived starvation on the island, despite reaching dry land and finding a safe harbour, fresh water, food and shelter. What kinds of leadership might have made a positive difference? Through a quirk of fate, we have some clues. The *Invercauld* crew were not the only reluctant visitors to the islands in 1854.

About 27 km south Captain Thomas Musgrave, Frenchman Francois Raynal and a crew of three from a schooner, the *Grafton*, had already been shipwrecked, struggling to survive for five months.[1] Having travelled from Sydney, Captain Thomas Musgrave had been prospecting for seals and was sheltering in a channel near the island when the *Grafton*'s anchor broke in a storm, washing them onto the rocks.

Planning their evacuation carefully, they waited till morning to leave the ship, salvaging a dinghy, tools, provisions and tobacco. Raynal had been very ill before the shipwreck and could easily have been seen as dispensable, but Captain Musgrave was committed to his entire crew and put considerable effort into rescuing Raynal from the stricken vessel.

With a damp box of matches they managed to light a fire and took turns to ensure the precious flame didn't go out. Over the next few days, sleeping in wet, exposed conditions, their well-being declined. The men searched for a cave without success. Maggots invaded their clothes and Musgrave feared that without shelter they would die.

They decided to try to build a cabin and for three days scoured the area for the best position, and cleared the site of dense undergrowth. Raynal was too sick to work, so contributed by tending the fire, cooking, mending clothes and conceiving a cabin design. From previous experience, he suggested an internal fireplace and thatched grasses for insulation. Roasted seashells produced lime and by adding gravel they mortared a safe hearth and chimney, lining it with copper sheets off the *Grafton*.

The men worked hard and provisions were shared equally. During breaks in construction they hunted seals and birds, salting or smoking any excess meat. They observed seal behaviour, becoming more efficient hunters. Musgrave and Raynal wrote journals using seals' blood when their ink ran out. They planted a flagpole and large canvas flag that might be easily seen out at sea.

Over 18 months the crew fought to survive, and escape. From the outset (and throughout), Musgrave prioritised the wellbeing of his team. Early on, for instance, he shared the tobacco equally among them, setting the tone and culture for their time on the island. After just a few weeks he noticed unrest and fragmentation in the group, noting in his log: "Up to the present time the men have worked well and conducted themselves in a very obedient and respectful manner towards me, but I find there is somewhat of a spirit of obstinacy and independence creeping in… We stood so much in need of each other!"[2]

Concerned at the consequences of growing bitterness Musgrave's response was intriguing. He invited the group to select a person to be Chief of family on the island, to take on positional authority in the new situation. The group chose Musgrave and they all developed a simple charter to guide behaviour:
1. Be firm but fair in keeping order.
2. Work to avoid disharmony and controversy.
3. Adjudicate quarrels and hand out punishment that initially should be a reprimand, followed potentially by ostracism for those failing to change their behaviour.
4. Assign daily chores fairly to everybody, including himself.
5. For major decisions, take a vote.
6. That the community reserves a right to depose a chief of family and elect another if at any time he abuses his authority or employs it for selfish purposes.

The cabin took two months to build but significantly improved their living conditions as they could escape the rain. It was built so well that one night an earthquake shook the island, and the cabin remained intact. They made furniture from items scavenged from the wreck and worked hard to avoid despair that might come from purposelessness. Raynal notes in his journal: "if we had not been continually focused on work we might have succumbed to madness."[3]

Experimentation and innovation was a part of life together. Over the months, through trial and error, they learnt how to cure seal skins to make them strong but soft and pliable enough to use for clothing and blankets. Raynal, an innovator by nature, wanted to create replacement shoes as theirs were deteriorating. After a week of hard work the first pair proved useless, so he adapted and redesigned until something worked: shoes constructed from tannin extracted from native trees, tanned seal leather and pitch made by mixing tar from the wreck with seal oil. Sea lion hair and sailcloth threads held them together. When the signal flag blew down, a sturdier white signal board was designed.

Figure E2.2 Wreck of the Grafton[4]

Winter forced the men indoors so they passed time teaching each other languages, mathematics and reading, also fussing over some parrots they had tamed. They carved a chess set and made a solitaire board. Musgrave also made a pack of cards but, valuing team harmony, put them in the fire when card games caused friction between them.

With spring Musgrave considered sailing for New Zealand in the dinghy salvaged from the wreck, but the others dissuaded him. A few months later, and now a year since being shipwrecked, Raynal suggested constructing a small ocean-going boat from the remnants of The *Grafton*. He commenced work, improvising with wreckage and sealskin. Initially sceptical, his work infected Musgrave with a spark of hope and eventually everyone became involved, splitting time between work on the boat, hunting and domestic chores.

Three months in, they hit major obstacles. Wood from the wreck was too old and inflexible and the island's trees too twisted to provide workable timber. They also lacked key tools. Disappointed, they started to build another boat around the core of the dinghy. With winter approaching, they worked 17-hour days for two months. Eventually hard work and ingenuity created a five-metre boat/kayak with a mast and sail. And, on 19 July 1865, Musgrave, Raynal and one of the other men set sail for New Zealand.

The little boat leaked, but thankfully Raynal had installed a small pump. In deteriorating weather and storms, they worked the pump constantly for days, soaked and lacking sleep. On the fifth day they sighted land, but failing wind left them drifting back out to sea, possibly dying within sight of land. Finally, however, a breeze drew them toward the coast. Around a headland, civilisation awaited them: houses, gardens, children playing and a man walking his dog. They had reached Stewart Island.

Despite exhaustion, Musgrave was anxious to rescue the rest of the crew and both he and Raynal were keen to be part of the mission, heading out in a large fishing vessel. A faulty compass and appalling weather meant it took 25 days to reach the islands and collect the remaining crew. Before heading home, they combed the coast for other possible shipwreck survivors and discovered the old settlement where the *Invercauld* survivors had stayed, finding and burying the body of an *Invercauld* crew member, before heading back to New Zealand.

The combined contributions of the crew of the *Grafton*, wisely choreographed by Captain Musgrave, saved the lives of all five men. It was collaborative leadership at its best.

Building effective leadership for complex times

ONE CAN'T SIMPLISTICALLY compare the fate of the two expeditions. The *Invercauld* sunk in mid-winter in an inhospitable cove and very little was retrieved. The *Grafton* wrecked in better weather and location, so on occasions they could retrieve materials from the wreck. Yet there is much to learn from their experiences.

Both crews shared similar purposes: to survive and be rescued. But that is where the similarities ended.

The two experiences highlight the importance of looking carefully at the challenges to be faced, as was explored in Part 1. Earlier we noted how little those in authority on the *Invercauld* looked at the situation they were in, appearing helpless and in shock from the moment the dangerous cliffs of the island came into view. Onshore they responded in haphazard ways to their circumstances, quickly factionalised and resorted to lying to avoid challenging work. It was far from an effective collective response to their plight.

By contrast, the *Grafton* crew examined their situation carefully, and sought to develop an adaptive response, using the time they had to plan step-by-step their evacuation from their wreck, collecting tools, provisions and a dinghy to help them survive.

The two experiences also highlight how our approach to leadership in complex times can make a huge difference.

In stark contrast to Captain Dalgarno's approach on the *Invercauld*, Captain Musgrave sought from the start to encourage leadership practices that harnessed the capacities of their team, letting go of heroic models of leadership to find better ways forward.

As their challenges multiplied on land - food, shelter, clothing, rescue - they used their capacities together to maximise their chances. Each person contributed as they could, recognising they needed to deal collaboratively with what might lie ahead. They faced impulses to avoid the work they needed to do and helped each other to face the challenges. In this way was multiplied both capacity and resolve.

How we understand and live out leadership can make a real difference. Here are some key elements explored in previous chapters.

4. Look widely for leadership: People with roles or responsibilities need to bring out the best in others, helping ordinary people do extraordinary things together.

Crew responses to the moment the vessels floundered set the culture for their ordeals. The *Invercauld* crew were overwhelmed, some abandoning their posts; it became a broken culture of every-man-for-himself. By contrast, Captain Musgrave, the person with positional authority on the *Grafton*, worked for the wellbeing of the whole group, seeking to empower them all to work for their survival. He valued his human assets enough to work hard in the initial crisis to get a sick team member onto shore, an action that later would repay them greatly: Raynal's innovation and exploration of possibilities showed leadership that greatly enhanced the team's overall capacity.

The *Grafton* crew focused on the overall group purposes of survival and escape, and recognised the importance of each other for achieving this. Take Musgrave's invitation to the team to decide the best person to take positional authority on the island. By voluntarily offering to surrender authority, the Captain empowered the crew and was empowered himself. Knowing the value of common purposes and a well-functioning team, he demonstrated commitment to act as servant to the team. In turn, the crew were motivated to make their contributions for the good of the group.

Positional authority is important. People with such roles can help multiply leadership capacity, open-up space for ideas and contributions and positively shape organisational culture. They can provide direction, protection and order. This was not provided by the *Invercauld* officers. Consequently, most of the crew acted in short-term individual self-interest, costing most of them their lives.

5. Uncover the various People, Purpose, Safety and Strategic leadership contributions needed: Leadership is everyone's business and concern. Many contributions are needed in a healthy group if we are to respond constructively to whatever we are faced with.

This was the case with the *Grafton* survivors. Each contributed differently. Musgrave made important people and purpose-focused decisions, listening to others, understanding their situations, building community and maintaining morale. He actively promoted collaboration in a desperate situation and built shared purposes.

He also made important safety contributions, surfacing the positional authority question. Once elected, he worked to create safe structures, communication and an optimistic culture.

Raynal explored options in ways that built and refined shared purpose. He brought practical ingenuity, lateral thinking and experimentation, exploring strategic possibilities using learning and persistence thereby giving hope to the others. Even when ill, he contributed design and housekeeping work that kept the group safe during construction of the cabin.

Others were empowered to contribute in various ways, such as in strategic decisions to dissuade Musgrave from setting sail for New Zealand in a boat before it was seaworthy. The crew took turns to keep the fire going, then each contributed to building a shelter.

The *Invercauld* survivors were given little encouragement to contribute leadership, perhaps because of Dalgarno's rigid view of positional authority leadership and status. As we shall see in a later part, some brought significant capacities that were undervalued and underutilised.

There was leadership capacity within the *Invercauld* crew, capacity underutilised and undermined by the approach taken to leadership by those in positions of authority and by a lack of a quality team and trust before things turned nasty.

6. Cultivate collaborative leadership in balanced teams: Building teams of people with the right blend of leadership capacities is important, as is helping them contribute their capacities to the fullest. A priority for Captain Musgrave was to maximise the capacities at his disposal. Most obviously, he encouraged the ingenious Raynal to contribute to his best, rather than being threatened by him. This probably made the difference between survival and death.

A culture was created that multiplied the capacities of the crew. Everyone worked on the design and construction of shelter and the escape vessel, even though they wouldn't all be able to sail to safety together. Cohesive groups like the *Grafton* have the best chance of navigating complex or challenging situations through their organisation, collective skills and strength.[5]

At the other end of the island, Captain Dalgarno seemed to have little understanding of the importance of growing collaborative leadership capacity and collective endeavour. With an old-school view of leadership as being about prestige and authority, he did not try to reshape their culture towards the shared purpose of group survival. Throughout their ordeal there were falling outs and internal strife, reducing overall capacity.[6]

In his account of their ordeal Seaman Holding, a young sailor picked up in Melbourne, was critical of the lack of teamwork and collective action. At one point when others had refused to help cut a track to a possible safe-haven, he noted: "if we had been better acquainted with each other things might have been different"[7]. In his report on the tragedy senior officer Smith acknowledged he didn't know the names of some of the dead. With many crew members only joining a few days before, they hardly knew each other. This lack of bonding had devastating consequences.[8]

In anything but the simplest situations we need the perspectives of many to assess situations well and find ways forward. The *Invercauld* crew were quick to provide disinformation to reduce short-term effort, generating learned helplessness, diminishing their capacity to survive and sowing seeds of distrust. Group malaise undermined everything.

By contrast, Captain Musgrave and the *Grafton* crew made decisions based on shared perspectives, as when dissuading Captain Musgrave from prematurely sailing for New Zealand. Collaborative leadership builds ownership of directions, motivation and trust.

Rethinking leadership for complex times

As we negotiate the shifting landscape of our lives, we encounter opportunities to exercise leadership and help others do likewise. We need to constantly assess our situation, the nature of the challenges to be faced, and the leadership needed to move forward effectively.

To engage complicated or complex challenges we need to grow leadership across our whole team or organisation, as outlined in Figure E2.3. Choosing to contribute is an important step and sometimes an individual choice. From then on, however, leadership is fundamentally co-operative and collaborative; the interplay of a wide range of people making different contributions is essential.

Seeing leadership as a collaborative strengths-based contribution is one thing, but just asking people to contribute doesn't guarantee they will. There are barriers or reasons why people do or don't contribute. Surfacing those issues and reshaping a group's culture will start to normalise a different way of being, freeing up people to act differently. It is to growing agile cultures and responses to complex change that we turn now.

Rethinking leadership Parts 1-2

Part 1

What are the challenges we face?

1 Distinguish between simple, complicated and complex challenges, and be clear on your purposes.
2 Move through work avoidance to face the deeper challenge.
3 Positive change requires leadership from many.

Part 2

How can we build effective leadership for complex times?

4 Look for leadership capacity right across your organisation.
5 Uncover the various *People*, *Purpose*, *Safety* and *Strategic* leadership contributions needed.
6 Cultivate effective collaboration in balanced teams.

Figure E2.3 Rethinking Leadership Parts 1 and 2

Part 3

Developing Agility With Ongoing Change

Introduction

How can we develop agility with ongoing change?

Change is inevitable - except from a vending machine.
– Robert C Gallagher[1]

IN PART 2 we invited you to rethink your paradigms and mindsets about leadership, and the different contributions needed in a healthy group engaging *complicated* problems. Quality teams will leverage the leadership contributions of as many people as possible, also getting wide perspective on situations and encouraging ownership and commitment to common directions.

We move now to focus on what else might be important in effectively engaging *complex* challenges. If change is constant, how can we develop agility and responsiveness in our teams? What leadership practices might foster such agility?

Finding your way around Part 3

IN THE CHAPTERS that follow we move from *how we lead to the culture in which we operate.* Chapter 7 identifies a range of factors that can hinder or enhance organisational agility, and identifies the limits of top down change 'management'.

Adaptive responses require moving through personal uncertainty and anxiety in others and ourselves, as well as navigating unknown territory and unpredictable systems. Chapters 8 to 10 explore in turn the implications for leadership of each of these. In Chapter 11 the focus is on effective leadership practices that can help create and shape agile cultures and organisations.

Chapter seven

Rethinking change
How can we prepare for ongoing change?

CHANGE MANAGEMENT HAS traditionally been conceived as a linear, top down process[1], following steps like those shown in figure 7.1. Delegate someone to *diagnose the situation*, then *develop desired objectives*, *decide a plan* and, finally, *do it*, unfreezing what needs changing, resetting things, then refreezing it in the new format.[2] Sounds simple?

Traditional change manangement

- Diagnose the situation and the challenge

- Develop desired purposes and objectives

- Decide a plan

- Do it together

Figure 7.1 Traditional change management

Yet we already know from Part 2 that leadership involves a wide range of people in quality balanced teams. At the very least there needs to be another important step, as shown in Figure 7.2.

Because leadership needs to be collaborative, we need to add a step:

- Assess together the nature of the challenge

- Develop desired purposes and objectives

- Decide a plan

- **Build collaboration and quality teams**

- Do it together

Figure 7.2 The importance of collaborative leadership

And, the more one looks at change, the more it is evident that the reality is different to this model. Change follows curious paths. In the 1850s, the market for motorcycles in the US was spread between British companies and Harley-Davidson. Until the 1970s, though a market leader in Japan, Honda sold few motorcycles there. Yet, half a dozen years later, they enjoyed more than 60% share of the US small motorcycle market. Was this clever planning?

Actually, no. Honda's plans were to build a powerful motorcycle to compete head-on with Harley-Davidson. Fearing it might hurt their image, Honda explicitly instructed US dealers NOT to sell their smaller motorcycles. Sadly, their large bike encountered technical problems that forced its withdrawal from the marketplace.

Using smaller bikes to run errands in the US, Honda staff were regularly asked where to buy the smaller bikes. After repeated pestering, the company finally allowed a few representatives to sell some. The massive take up shocked senior Honda executives. Honda's sales reps' on the ground experiment succeeded where the grand plan from headquarters failed.[3]

Change can be so rapid and unpredictable that it is hard to effectively manage from one central position. Yet, on the ground, people and organisations still regularly use such top down, refreezing approaches.

The limitations of 'top down management' of change

TRADITIONAL CHANGE THINKING assumes that complex change can be *'managed'* and controlled, that organisations function like machines. To best solve problems break them down into components, tune or improve each part in isolation and then reassemble them. Not true. In factories where separate teams design specific components, valuable information about how parts work together gets lost. Dividing medicine into specialties dealing with specific body parts, can be limiting when a more complete view of a patient is needed.

Mechanistic planning makes use of limited sets of eyes and misses information about linkages between components.[4] Conventional change thinking - that assumes people in key roles can specify desired futures, then direct the change - can lead to disappointment and damage.[5] Throughout this book we have provided examples of how this doesn't work: school principals eliminating middle management (Chapter 1), managers trying to achieve change without staff consultation (Chapter 2), Rick and his novice team in the flooded river (Chapter 3), the community sector agency facing a sudden financial crisis and shedding program staff (Chapter 3), the CEO exercising control by dangling staff over the balcony (Chapter 3).

Yet in schools, social welfare agencies and businesses today we cling to top down management approaches to change. The more challenging the problem, the more we try to control it, or seek the quick fix of handing control to an 'expert'.

So how can we best create change in complex systems that will last and not spring back to how it was? Humans are not machines, nor are organisations. Change will be neither linear nor mechanical. To make a lasting difference deeper change is needed. More than implementing a new strategy, this is about **reshaping culture.**

Reshaping culture

FLOCKS OF STARLINGS fly in amazing formations called murmurations. They twist and turn and move as one. Thousands of birds in tight configurations fly perilously close to obstructions in spectacular displays of teamwork. Together the birds form a unique and amazing system that is complex and resilient.[6]

There are many examples of this in the natural world. On the Great Barrier Reef hundreds of Big Eye Trevally swim closely together in schools, seamlessly navigating currents, rocks and hungry threats.[7]

How do these creatures have the discipline to stay in formation during uncertain weather, contours and environments? Is there a commander bird calling the shots at the helm instructing each bird what to do as they hurtle towards unexpected objects? Obviously not.

Starlings stay in flock formation by following three simple rules or organising principles:
1. Keep the minimum distance from other birds.
2. Match velocity with the others.
3. Seek to move towards the centre of the flock.

These three organising principles regulate the behaviour of thousands of birds through rapidly changing environments, threats and weather. It is a useful illustration of the power of culture and how it operates. The starlings have evolved a culture that embodies **a readiness for and capacity to deal with change**, enabling them to respond to continuous or surprising change in agile ways.

What do we mean by the culture of an organisation? On one hand, culture is a simple concept including the feel of an organisation, its values and how it operates, often displayed in aspirational posters on the wall. On the other hand, culture is complex. Like icebergs, much lies under the surface: deeper ways of being, shared values, beliefs and assumptions, and shared experiences, many of which go unspoken.

There is much in traditional organisational culture that can hold us back in facing complex challenges or in making the most of any presenting possibilities.

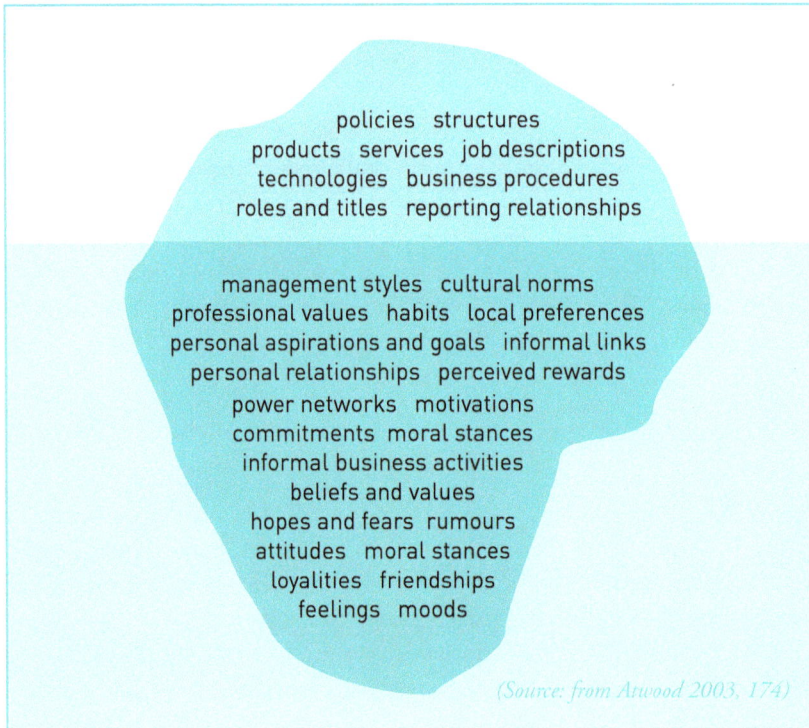

The iceberg diagram text (above surface):

policies   structures
products   services   job descriptions
technologies   business procedures
roles and titles   reporting relationships

(below surface):

management styles   cultural norms
professional values   habits   local preferences
personal aspirations and goals   informal links
personal relationships   perceived rewards
power networks   motivations
commitments   moral stances
informal business activities
beliefs and values
hopes and fears   rumours
attitudes   moral stances
loyalities   friendships
feelings   moods

(Source: from Atwood 2003, 174)

Figure 7.3 The organisational iceberg: above and below the surface

Unhelpful elements of organisational culture

Why do we create controlling bureaucracies when we attempt to form visionary enterprises? Why do we persist in piecemeal analysis as the world becomes more and more interconnected?

– Fred Kofman and Peter Senge[8]

IN THE 1960S Douglas McGregor warned of the dangers of segregating people into occupational groups that institutionalise particular views about things.[9] Silo members can become so preoccupied with their focus area that they lose the bigger picture. In 1991, Peter Senge wrote *'The Fifth Discipline'* about the need to create quality *'learning organisations'* that encourage new ways of thinking, where individuals are invited to look at the bigger picture together.[10]

Senge identified various organisational barriers to learning and agility:

- *Highly fragmented organisations*, with teams in silos trying to deliver in their own area, without a clear view of the whole. There can be significant learning losses when teams do not work or fit together.
- *Splits between people delivering services and those in management*, resulting in diminished knowledge, trust, understanding, and quality of service.

- *Competition that generates fear.* While competition can enhance performance and promote invention and daring, it can also reduce people's willingness to take risks through increased fear of failure. We feel in competition with the very people with whom we need to collaborate. It can also create the fear about asking questions.
- *Professional self-confidence.* People depending for their identity on feeling competent and expert in their field can be brittle or resistant when it comes to learning.[11]
- *Organisations seeking 'quick fixes' for complex problems* generating confusion or disillusionment when things don't change as expected.
- *High turnover of personnel* leading to loss of knowledge, limiting cumulative learning.
- *A consequent lack of trust and fear of change* hindering learning that might improve how things are done. Swapping a known present for an uncertain future can be challenging.
- *Lack of time for reflection* due to tight timelines and urgent demands. No margin for learning can prove costly when solving problems arising from ill-considered decisions.[12]

Each of these barriers reduce the capacity of organisations to navigate complex change. In steady-state situations, hierarchical organisations can be highly efficient. However, in times of change and uncertainty, the importance of flexibility, communication across silos, learning, experimentation and innovation come to the fore. Achieving change is not just about retraining, changing structures, or vision statements. It is about the deeper work of reshaping culture, rethinking our ways of working together. There is a common saying in change literature: *Culture eats strategy for breakfast.* It is one thing to say we want to change, quite another to achieve it.

Peter has played football almost his entire adult life. One particular year he played in a talented team with a very unhelpful culture: when things weren't going well people would vent frustration criticising each other, channelling energy away from rethinking their performance together, reducing self-belief and team capacity. Despite commitments to change, under pressure people returned to old habits.

Attempts at change often fail because they focus on strategies rather than a deeper shifting of organisational culture. Opening up office spaces won't necessarily increase collaboration and communication if the culture is one of working separately. We need deeper change.

If we have no experience of anything different, how can we know how to act differently? Habitual ways of working become so ingrained that we see no other way of operating, and become threatened by alternatives.

Ways of operating are under the surface and hard to see. They meet deep down needs for some or all, and become embedded in an organisation's culture. To change it everybody needs to think more deeply about it and together reshape it. It is about modelling alternatives. If senior management doesn't model the values on the workplace posters, then the lived culture of the entire organisation won't enact them either.

Back to that football team. Over time the small, consistent actions of individuals tilted its culture. Conversations and group emails invited everyone to develop a new story focussed on building each other up, putting the team first. One person chronicled each game to shape a positive approach. Step by step a more positive culture was developed through leadership contributions from a range of people, and work done by everybody.

A different approach to change

The world is not calling for faster change processes; it's calling for organisations that can change faster.

– Christopher Worley[13]

ABOUT A CENTURY ago a young retailer J. C. Penny sought to describe the kind of company he wished to create. The manager listening understood what was being proposed: "What you are wanting is an organisation that will always be renewing itself from within", an organisation with a more agile culture embedded into it.[14]

Agility is the capability to make timely, effective and sustained changes in response to what is happening around us.[15] It involves creating a climate and culture that makes the most of people's capacities. Complexity leadership theorists see those in positions of authority as having an opportunity to not simply focus on the management of change, but to at the same time be consciously developing an organisation's ability to be agile in the midst of complexity.[16]

Organisational agility frees an organisation to respond creatively and effectively to changing circumstances, by nurturing a culture that encourages such behaviour. Rather than a culture of blame, we need a culture of active learning from both setbacks and successes.[17]

Leadership does not need to speed up change in organisations, but to reshape organisations so they can change more adeptly. By working on developing an agile culture we can become better prepared to face complexity naturally and effectively.

It is about relearning how we flock and fly. What might an agile organisational culture look like? Let's look at two very different examples: one corporate, the other a school.

Agility in innovation: W.L. Gore

IN THE EARLY 2000s, Fast Company magazine set out to find the most innovative company in America, one with a long history of innovation that didn't rely on one idiosyncratic individual. They finally chose W.L. Gore founded in 1958 by Wilbert Gore, a chemical engineer with DuPont who was exploring the properties and possibilities of a chemical polymer connected with Teflon. DuPont were not interested in the polymer and granted Gore the rights to do his own development work. He and his wife invested their savings in the company, which eventually developed Goretex, a ground breaking breathable rain protection fabric used extensively in outdoor gear.

Fast Company's writer observed: "I've had the opportunity to peer inside a lot of organisations. Most big companies are pretty much the same. The rituals of goal setting, planning, budgeting and performance appraisal differ only slightly from firm to firm. Hierarchical authority structures, top down leadership appointments and order-following employees…One amazing exception is WL Gore and Associates."[18] His first impressions were that the company's culture seemed weird but, after initial surprise, he was taken by its humanity, a company where innovation was the main show rather than a sideshow.[19]

What do rain jackets have to do with guitar strings?

ANYONE INVOLVED IN mountaineering or outdoor sports will be familiar with Goretex, a remarkable breathable waterproof rainwear product that has dominated the market for decades. W.L. Gore has also achieved significant innovation in guitar strings, space suits and dental floss.

What does it take to be a company able to lead markets in each of these seemingly diverse areas? What does it take to maintain sequential experimentation over a sustained period, developing insulated wire and electric cabling applications (1950s and 1960s), rainwear (1970s), space suits (1980s), dental floss and Elixir guitar strings (1990s), as well as innovative medical technology and implants, electronics, sealants and membrane technology for filtration and incineration?

One of Wilbert Gore's ambitions was to use the polymer in creative ways. Another was to create a company that would genuinely support experimentation, collaborative innovation, communication and learning. At DuPont he witnessed how real communication tended to occur in the car park after meetings. He set out to be innovative not only with the polymer, but also in how the company was run. Experiencing the power of collaboration he wanted to explore its possibilities.

The Gore story is an impressive story of serial innovation over decades where innovation has not come from large-scale research budgets but from a culture where people are given the space and incentive to innovate and encouraged to work and explore together with people from different backgrounds. Collaborative innovation is structured into their culture, to how they fly together.

The guidelines for flight

IN 2010 CEO Terri Kelly summarised three core values in Gore's organisational culture:
- *Encourage innovation through cross collaboration*, where project teams form across departments to co-develop any product. A culture of celebration is also fostered, recognising achievements, or good attempts that didn't work. This encourages a willingness to take risks as mistakes are seen as part of the creative process.
- *Avoid over structuring and unhelpful bureaucracy*, by creating flat organisational structures where decisions don't have to make their way up to the top and back down again all the time.
- *Generate motivation and commitment among staff.* Senior associates are selected as much for their ability to motivate and innovate, as for technical competencies. Part of their remuneration is in profit-sharing with the company, increasing commitment and ownership and connection through aligning personal goals with those of the company.[20]

There is also an emphasis on elevating people from within the company to positions of responsibility, with the promotional decisions made by a group of peers who look for the right person within the team to take them forward. This makes it easier to maintain core aspects of the Gore culture through staff transitions.

We will return to look in more detail at the W.L. Gore culture in Chapter 11.

Rethinking education: one school's journey

WHY IS IT that schools can feel like inflexible, top down organisations operating from old information-transaction models of learning? In complex times, there is an oppurtunity to focus on growing student capacity to problem-solve, explore possibility, do original thinking and develop action and reflection patterns of living. Just where we are growing the learning capacities of the next generation, too often rigidity is deeply embedded.[21]

Though their role is to grow learning practices, teachers can sometimes be resistant to change. Having gone through school, then studying to be a teacher before moving back into the system they have spent a lifetime in a particular culture and have only known one way of operating.

But there are also teachers and schools daring to reimagine education, exploring new approaches to learning.

Whitebank, an inner urban school, is one of an increasing number of schools trying to rethink education from the ground up, to equip students for the world which they will move into, a world of increasing change and complexity, where exploration and agility are vital. The senior staff at Whitebank wished to transform their educational approach to one that builds learning capacity for the twenty-first century.

The Principal was challenged to consider what might best equip students for an unknown future. Perhaps not fully aware of it, he took on a challenge that required adaptive responses.

The idea that attracted him was co-teaching – two teachers combining their student groups in larger classrooms, providing greater opportunity for flexibility and modelling of teamwork. Merging classes and enabling co-teaching could create diverse learning experiences, promote student initiative and model collaboration by teachers. Children would have role models of living and learning together, and it could open up possibilities for more diverse activities that encouraged initiative and curiosity. A class could access a wider range of teacher gifts and students could develop more exploratory and self-motivated ways of learning. Rather than just receiving information, students would be learning how to learn.

It became evident that co-teaching would require major changes to both the classroom, and the culture in which they worked. It would involve engaging with complexity, navigating unknown territory, facing and working with personal uncertainty among staff and families, and the various unpredictable responses of stakeholders in the wider school community. It was a journey requiring significant transitions for everyone.

Five years on a very different school and culture is bedding down. The rebuilding of classrooms was just one technical aspect of the broader changes needed. Far more complex were changes in culture, understanding and commitment needed across the 40 staff. All of which would be very challenging, when added to the various personal, health, relational and family issues people face in life. This was a truly complex challenge, but proved well worth the journey.

Reshaping culture: A new way of flying

BEYOND REBUILDING CLASSROOMS, Whitebank's journey was fundamentally about changing their culture and ways of operating: changing their *guidelines for flight*. In the past, conversations had often centred around what systems could work best for staff in their work. Guidelines for flight could have been bluntly summarised as:

- Run an efficient school under the supervision of the Principal and Deputy Principal.
- Deliver an engaging curriculum.
- Help each other in that delivery as is possible.

This has significantly shifted. Today staff discussions are much more likely to be around the school's core purpose: what drives student learning? Now the guidelines for flight are described as follows:

- Maximise the school's capacity to create spaces and experiences that promote active teacher and student learning.
- Model collaborative learning and capacity-building at all levels of school operation
- Work as much as possible in accountable teams.

The school has developed different rules for 'murmurating'. We will look at aspects of this change more closely in Chapter 11. It involved the entire staff team and school community in a journey of change, facing fears, refining purpose, exploring effective ways of both team teaching and growing collaborative leadership, moving forward in a carefully paced way.

Summary

How can we prepare for ongoing change?

Agility begins with culture,
so discover new ways of working together

TOP-DOWN CHANGE MODELS may quickly prove inadequate in complex situations. A more effective approach within organisations is to *create a readiness for and capacity to deal with change*, enabling them to respond to continuous or surprising change more readily.[22] More than implementing a new strategy, it is about *reshaping organisational culture.*

Getting beyond rhetoric is vital, yet often elusive. The first step is to look deeply at the team or organisation's values and culture. Next it is a question of developing leadership that tilts or reshapes this culture in positive ways to better navigate complex challenges.

Reshaping practice 7

Actions for you

What are the norms within the teams and organisations where you work or live? How might you develop a deeper understanding of the values and culture?

To what extent do they feel impervious to change? How might this impact on your contributions?

Actions for your team

Look beneath the surface: Take a look at the iceberg diagram (Figure 7.2). Engage some people in your team in some 'submarine' conversations: What is the shape of things beneath the surface? What are unspoken rules or norms? What are the 'flocking rules' that bring people together, the norms by which they interact?

What is one step or action you could take that might tilt your team's culture towards agility?

Agile organisations have clear purposes and 'guidelines for flight'. How might clarifying purpose and generating owned 'guidelines for flight' make a difference? What's the first step in this? What rules for flight serve your team well, and what might you want to change?

Chapter eight

Moving through personal uncertainty

How can we move through the destabilising effects of uncertainty?

COMPLEX CHANGE GENERATES personal uncertainty. And, like fire and smoke, where there is personal uncertainty, anxiety and fear will follow. Change asks us to exchange a known present for an unknown future. To move forward, it also asks us to acknowledge and address personal concerns and fears.

We need to engage with people not just for their wisdom, but also to understand their concerns. In leadership, we need to recognise anxiety and uncertainty and help people cope and adapt through it.

The three phases of transition

WHEN FACING PERSONAL loss,[1] people will often experience significant grief. Similarly, significant change has its implications. Transition management writer William Bridges describes three phases of transition for people in organisations changing visibly.[2]

First is the *ending, losing and letting go*, as people grieve for the old that they have lost. Such grief may come in waves. Just as we think we have got over it, something triggers it again. We may deny this at first ("this cannot be happening") followed by anger, blame or helplessness. People get upset, confused or withdraw.[3] As with personal grief, people need to define what is lost and mark its passing in some way.

People then move into what Bridges describes as the *neutral zone:* a "nowhere between two somewheres". People feel suspended between what was and what will be.[4] They recognise the past is finished, but can't yet see what the future might hold. It is a time of readjustment.

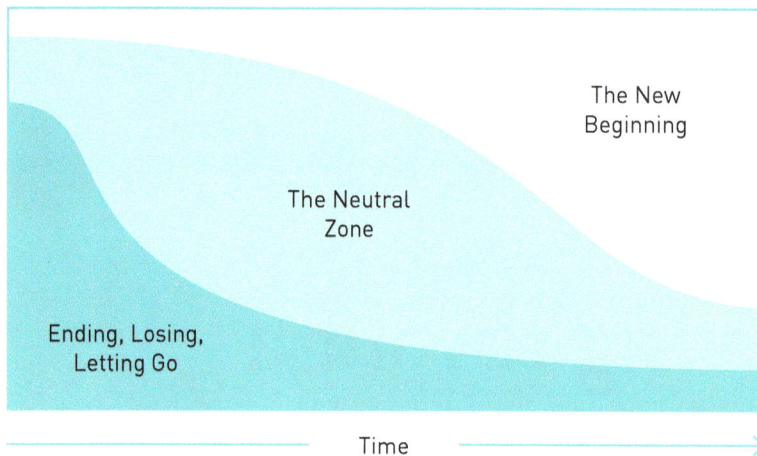

Figure 8.1 Three Phases of Transition

Those in positions of authority may want to push people through this transition but it cannot be rushed, sugar coated or pushed below the surface without causing damage. If people feel safe in their relationships with others, quality time in the neutral zone allows them to explore possibilities, taking advantage of short-term systems and structures which can create a safe space for conversation.

If supported well people can then begin to discover possible ways forward – the *new beginning* – and then regain a sense of purpose and a common direction. Take time to understand the emotional landscape for people around you. Flying blind to this is highly dangerous.

Look carefully: what are people feeling? What are their deepest hopes and concerns? Put yourself in their shoes: what challenges might each person be facing? If we understand what they are dealing with, we can better address their concerns, inviting them to discover what they could contribute in the new era. Otherwise, there is a danger of flying blind, leading to resistance from people.

Trying something new

IN 2005, THE principal of a prestigious Sydney private school returned from an educational conference in South Africa with a nascent idea. Some education initiatives in Johannesburg among black South Africans fired his imagination and fuelled his passion. Could something similar make sense among Indigenous students in Australia?

Back home he assembled an experienced task group, including a respected local Indigenous person, to explore possibilities and develop a plan. They proposed a school for around 30 children to be based in an inner-city area with a high Indigenous population. They spoke with residents, community groups and applied to council to use a local community centre for the new school.

The school task group talked widely in the community about this potential venture. It generated heated debate, with support from some Indigenous parents and community members yet anger and hostility from others. There were concerns about a well-funded private school using a community facility and also about the potential segregation of

Indigenous students from their Anglo counterparts. As the private school had religious affiliations some were also resistant because of the negative past involvement of religious organisations with Indigenous people. There was significant distrust of institutions generally.

Despite much listening, visiting and consulting with various stakeholders, the uncertainty, hostility and anxiety was overwhelming and the school withdrew its application. The way forward wasn't clear. Indeed, the project appeared doomed.

Finding the gems

HAVING FAILED TO appease many in the local community, the task group became despondent. Yet their investment in wide engagement paid unexpected dividends. One Indigenous mother raised an idea that would turn the direction of the project on its head. "This idea is too important to let go. Why don't we try doing it on the main school's own property instead?'"

This most challenging and critical leadership contribution came from someone in the wider community, not from a person in a position of authority. It shifted the whole project. New ways forward may come from anywhere and only the most careful listening will catch this kind of insight from the edges. Had the woman's voice been lost or her leadership contribution neglected, the entire initiative might have faltered.

Identifying anxiety

CHANGING THE SITE of the Indigenous school to the main school campus dealt with one set of anxieties, but generated others. Now it was the private school community's turn to raise their objections, fears and anxieties. What might be the impact of this site change on the existing school community?

Some parents were highly anxious, even antagonistic. They supported the idea of a satellite school for struggling Indigenous students but having them mix with their children challenged their comfort levels. Would standards drop? Paying sizeable school fees to give their children a privileged education, they were concerned their educational dollars might be diluted or siphoned off to support other children. Concealed, but still there, were concerns that the tone of the main school might be compromised. They were being asked to swap the comfort of a known present for an uncertain future: some seemed to hold racist attitudes, others fear of the unknown.

Indigenous parents were also anxious, with fears and hostilities of their own. With lifetimes of feeling marginalised by white Australia, they were not sure they wanted their children mixing with *them*, the children of well-off white families. Will they be victimised or taunted? Or misunderstood? Or judged by a different set of standards?

Anxiety isn't always unhelpful; it can provide insight into what is really happening and help signal to a group that it needs to carefully manage its pace of change, maintain ongoing communication, and encourage people to share their perspectives.

Balancing risk and safety

FOR THE PRINCIPAL and task group it was again a matter of listening carefully and reassuring the various groups that it was alright to move beyond their fears.

The principal finally took a well-crafted proposal to the school board: that the initiative proceed on the school campus on the proviso that no general school funds be used in its development. The design of the Indigenous classroom would involve Indigenous contributions whenever possible. The principal trod a fine line between risk and safety, keeping the pressure on to proceed while also providing enough safety to get the proposal through. It "shrank the change"[5] alleviating some anxiety by reducing risk for the school community. People could move beyond their fears in smaller, more manageable and less risky steps.

The project was approved. The process of seeking leadership and contribution widely engendered ownership, shared responsibility, and slowly built trust.

The principal's approach also placed responsibility and work back on to the relevant people. Anxious members of the school community had to face their fears about the Indigenous school's impact on the main school. Project supporters had to find financial support and wide Indigenous involvement was needed in its implementation. It was an invitation to everyone to step up and do what they had to do.

Teachers, Indigenous families and designers set up a classroom, and the school opened with 8 students and the potential to involve 30, with staff supported by Indigenous volunteers. It was underpinned by several core values: cross-age education with extensive parental involvement, a valuing of kinship links and Indigenous identity, small class sizes, constructive celebrative engagement with the wider school, and benchmarking results against national education standards. The initiative eventually provided a space for growth for parents and families of both the school and Indigenous communities to work on their attitudes and fears. It provided meeting points and a driver for some important personal transitions on all sides. It also provided a model from which others could learn.

Although waves of anxiety and hostility had nearly sunk the ship, it also led to the listening and engagement that highlighted deeper fears, attitudes and necessary individual transitions. These led to a reshaped proposal that balanced risk and safety, enabling the project to get approval but also for stakeholders to move forward themselves.

Supporting internal transition

PEOPLE WILL MOVE through change at different rates and levels of enthusiasm.[6] Those in positions of responsibility need to know where people are on this journey, supporting their personal transitions. They must create a quality holding environment that, like a slow cooker, allows an issue to cook in a carefully paced way.[7] Everyone's small steps will build the growth of the whole organisation, tilting and reshaping its culture. Transitioning people is the fuel for broader change.

Assisting people to face their fears can be pivotal. When people feel threatened they quickly look for who to blame. There is a danger of getting trapped in personal criticism or abuse; the challenge is to stick with the issues.

Seeing the invisible

ANXIETY IS NOT always immediately obvious. A natural reaction in times of anxiety is to try to become invisible to avoid embarrassment, humiliation or stress.

In one of New River's activities for exploring fear and anxiety, teams regularly find their more anxious members drifting across the room seeking invisibility. Understandably, many teams fail to notice this happening.

If our eyes are only focused on the centre, we miss critical things happening undisclosed at the edges. While we think everything is fine, under the surface people feel too pressured, anxious or unsafe to say anything, yet for all we know, they are applying for jobs elsewhere.

It is when we feel most vulnerable that we are least likely to share our real feelings. To avoid facing our fears we might act in ways we may later regret, such as being absent from work, aggressively opposing colleagues or the manager, forming cliques or engaging in work avoidance.

People's flight or fight reactions kick-in to hide their vulnerabilities. There is that moment in a crisis where we consider *not* calling that ambulance, opening that parachute or talking with someone who might help, because we want to pretend nothing is wrong.

When leadership does not deal with what is happening below-the-surface, the consequences can be catastrophic.

Being a non-anxious presence

BEYOND FEAR LIES panic. People's personal uncertainty and anxiety can turn into fear and panic, generating strong unhelpful responses.

"Panic gathers volume like a snowball", writes WW II historian S.L.A. Marshall.[8] Hysteria and pandemonium are typical first responses to disasters. At the very moment when teamwork and clear-headed responses are needed, our instinctive behaviour is to do the exact opposite.[9] We start to behave irrationally. A September 2011 World Trade Centre disaster survivor noted afterwards: "Your brain – at least mine – just shut down ... one thing you don't ever want to do is have to think in a disaster".[10] A chain of physiological reactions in our brains releases powerful hormones and critical thinking skills seize up.[11]

To get beyond this neurological script we need to be aware that our responses can affect everyone around us.

A multi-storey Japanese building shook from a small tremor, interrupting adult education classes. In one classroom the teacher suddenly stopped, gasped and started to panic. In turn the students also panicked and pandemonium set in as everyone rushed to escape. Next door another teacher simply noted the shake and kept teaching. Everyone remained seated, calmly completing the class.[12]

We need a strategy to hold and calm fear. Someone with a non-anxious presence can make a huge difference, providing strength to others and generating the stability for discovery of creative solutions. Such a presence can help people behave more responsibly, with the group's needs first and foremost.

Calm in the storm

In 1982, British Airways Flight 009 encountered volcanic ash over Indonesia causing all four engines to shut down, filling the cabin with fumes. The plane dropped 7,300 metres before being restarted.

Yet there was relatively little panic. The chief steward calmed things down over the PA. The captain then followed, acknowledging the problem, but stating that "we are doing our damnedest to get it under control. I trust you are not in too much distress."[13] Everything was comparatively calm.

As a baby, Naomi's family were passengers in a light plane piloted by her father when both engines failed and they started rapidly losing altitude. In the minutes that followed her father had to remain calm and focused so no-one would panic, while carefully following the procedures to identify the problem and call for help. Unruffled, his presence was crucial and potentially life-saving.

Dealing with discord and anxiety

IT MIGHT TAKE more time to manage uncertainty and anxiety than to push on regardless but, in the long run, initial groundwork will reap dividends. Simply saying "anyone who doesn't get it, doesn't matter" can rebound badly.

Early in a particular change project Naomi remembers there were many doubters. The more those responsible exhorted or explained, the louder the questioning became. Then, in a change of tack, they invited people to share their questions, fears and concerns. Questions previously skipped over, such as why particular changes were proposed or evidence for likely positive outcomes were now asked. These conversations built wider ownership, and improved the project itself. Some writers suggest people not fully aligned with a group's vision should 'get off the bus'. Getting bogged down can be dangerous.

But removing (or threatening) questioners to silence them or force them forward can be equally dangerous. Groups can lose the wisdom, energy and capacities of members because leadership is listening only to early adopters and supporters. Ask for the perspective of someone who has left an organisation or project and consider the value these insights might have brought. If people can positively communicate their fears, they will develop their own capacities and resilience to face challenging situations in the future. Here are some questions to guide decision-making:

- Have doubters been heard, carefully and more than once? Do they feel heard?
- Have their anxieties, fears or perspectives been addressed?
- Is their position a reflection of broader issues affecting people's engagement?
- Have we stated their value, and the place we see for them in the change with space to decide for themselves whether or not they fit?
- What might be broader consequences for the group if they leave disgruntled?

Summary

How can we move through the destabilising effects of uncertainty?

Create safe spaces for people to process their emotional responses to change

NOT EVERYBODY ENGAGES change as easily as others or with equal enthusiasm. We will all need to face our personal or group work avoidance tactics and be assisted to move beyond them. Responding to the challenges of change will involve assisting people to make necessary personal transitions. People will need to understand why new directions or priorities are necessary, eventually choosing to own them.

Dealing carefully with personal uncertainty can take more time initially than relentlessly pushing on but will reap better, long-term dividends.

High levels of personal uncertainty can quickly unravel grand plans. Personal anxiety can generate very unexpected or unhelpful responses. We need fully to understand people's experiences of uncertainty.

To be aware of people's feelings we need to involve people well in all stages of engaging a complex challenge, hence the important change in language in Figure 8.2 to collective involvement. Collective engagement is also critical to gaining people's perspectives and wisdom, to building ownership of shared directions, and discovering ways forward.

**To move through personal uncertainty,
we need to involve people widely in the process:**

+ **Assess together the nature of the challenge**

+ **Focus on shared purposes and objectives**

• Experiment carefully to discern effective ways forward

• Build collaboration and quality teams

+ **Implement strategically a well-paced journey**

Figure 8.2 The importance of wide involvement

Reshaping practice 8

Actions for you

What is your relationship to change? When have you been a part of changes (intentional or circumstantial) that have been life-giving, positive or meaningful and when has the outcome been damaging or negative? For both, think about what contributed to the outcome, and what, had it been done differently, may have enhanced it.

We all have anxieties and stressors that will diminish our ability to offer our best. Do you have a clear sense of what these are for you? What might you need to do or to ask for when these issues arise?

Actions for your team

How involved is your whole team in reflection, direction setting, experimentation and implementation? How could you increase this kind of involvement?

When faced with change, how could you invite more communication within your group?

Create calm: If faced with a sudden disaster, what might be your strategies to create a calm culture within your group? What does each person need to cope well with change? Discuss this with your team.

Chapter nine

Navigating in unknown territory

How do we navigate unknown territory?

Cross the river by feeling for stones.

– Deng Xaioping[1]

CHALLENGES THAT REQUIRE adaptive responses generally involve travelling in unknown territory. How can we effectively engage with new situations we have not experienced, with no maps to guide us? What might be key leadership priorities?

Walking in high country in wild, misty weather is very much a case of travelling blind in unknown territory. It is easy to lose one's bearings. How does one travel in conditions where snow poles, route markers or natural features are hidden?

Standard practice is for one person to test the way ahead, looking for the next marker, while another remains in earshot at the previous marker. If the search for the next marker fails, the tester can safely return to the previous marker and try in a slightly different direction. Only when the next marker is found does the whole group move forward.

This is 'safe' experimentation and is critical when journeying into the unknown. Staying immobilized where you are can lead to disaster. So can jumping ahead and losing contact with that last known position.

Experimentation and innovation are vital in times of change. Unquestioningly saying, 'That's the way it's always been done around here' can lead to ossification. Healthy organisations or groups need to continuously ask, 'How can we do things better?' Team members need encouragement to continually explore new ideas or opportunities, while maintaining their 'safe' base. Quoting Amazon founder Jeff Bezos: "every once in a while, you go down an alley and it opens up into this huge, broad avenue."[2]

We need to conduct thoughtful experiments to explore possibilities and find quality ways forward.[3]

Innovation and learning

LEADERSHIP THINKING HAS long recognised innovation and experimentation as key to solving complex challenges.[4] Kouzes and Posner suggest exemplary leadership will always be on the lookout for new initiatives that might make a difference.[5] Ron Heifetz sees experimentation as more useful than developing overly detailed plans for the future, particularly if they have been devised by people far removed from the situation.[6] Contemporary educationalists take a smiliar view: the more detailed the plan on paper, the less flexible and achievable it might be.'[7]

This requires openness to learning, growth and possible failure. Carol Dweck identifies two approaches to learning. Some see their knowledge as set in stone, validated via grades, titles or recognition, and failures as setbacks threatening self-worth. Others take a personal growth mindset, seeing learning, exploration and failures as opportunities for growth.[8]

Engaging unknown territory requires "lateral thinking", looking at problems in new ways, not just "vertical thinking" based on logical steps to a final solution. Vertical thinking is about digging the same hole deeper, lateral thinking about digging the hole in a different place.[9] Gifted innovators able to think laterally, even under pressure, can see possibilities that others miss, pointing to ways forward.[10]

Research suggests that business managers typically use sequential approaches to problems, following plans and instructions, while entrepreneurs approach challenges interactively, improvising as they go.[11] No surprise that small entrepreneurial groups can often find success faster with fewer resources than larger mainstream organisations. Jennifer Garvey Berger describes this as moving from "managing the probable" to "leading the possible", requiring quite different patterns of leadership.[12]

A friend of ours with a passion for designing computer and phone games was excited to join a prestigious game development company. Yet the experience proved discouraging. After international success with one game, the company developed a rigid structure, with only certain people able to work on new projects or offer ideas. The culture felt controlling and risk-averse. He couldn't work at his best and left to work more independently.

Within 18 months he and two others had developed an internationally successful game, rated as one of the most innovative of 2016, surpassing any releases from the development company in the same period.[13]

Encourage experimentation

Imagination is more important than knowledge.

– Albert Einstein[14]

GIFTED INNOVATORS CAN see possibilities that others miss, pointing to ways forward. Consider the potential value of fire-fighter Wagner Dodge, who we met in Chapter 5, who could think laterally even in a firestorm. When organisational learning is taken seriously, a more agile culture is likely to emerge.

Yet innovators can be uncomfortable to have around. Wired to identify opportunities, they may not bring other key leadership strengths, or they may get discouraged by scepticism from others wary of change.

Allow a margin

MANAGEMENT LITERATURE OFTEN encourages efficient teams utilising the least resources. However if an organisation is stripped too bare it will be unable to experiment. Having some redundancy in the system - space and time for experimentation - is critical in unknown territory or times of adaptive change. Many innovative organisations allow a margin for experimentation. Google, for instance, allows staff to spend 20% of their time on creative exploratory projects. Many fail, but some point to Google's path forward.[15] So too with W.L. Gore, as will be seen in Chapter 11.

It is critical to develop patterns of experimentation before they are needed. In the midst of disaster, it is far too late to start developing a culture of innovation!

Look widely for new ideas

SOME SITUATIONS ARE best approached with a fresh pair of eyes. Physicist Max Planck noted how many ground-breaking ideas in science come from relative newcomers to a field. Those heavily invested in a given discipline have developed particular ways of thinking that can blinker them to alternative points of view. Newcomers are more likely to question assumptions and ruts we may be in. Quality innovation may come from surprising people and places. Those on the edges, dissident voices, and those at the 'coalface' with hands on experience of what does and doesn't work can also make creative contributions.

Going where you want to go

Since his twenties, Peter has spent extended time exploring the craggy mountains and wild rivers of Tasmania. Carrying 20-25kg of camping gear and two weeks food on one's back is a heavy load, but adding an inflatable boat and paddles (another 9kg) was too much. Groups he was part of experimented over time with airbeds, various craft and strategies, sometimes walking 20-30 kilometres to a river with some gear, then returning for a second load. They slowly developed better options but also had some disastrous failures: over-burdened on one trip they had to give up and spend three days walking out.

After this disaster one of the team met a foreign hitch-hiker with an extremely lightweight (2.5 kg) inflatable he got in Alaska! Peter ordered one and trialled it, then bought three more and paddled down the Jane, one of the remotest rivers in western Tasmania. They felt almost amphibious! After decades of experimentation there was finally a way forward from an unexpected source.

And that way forward was itself the product of experimentation. This game-changing innovation was not developed by a major company but by a mother whose son wished to travel remote Alaskan rivers. With a background in outdoor sports she founded an outdoor clothing company, before raising a family. With some experience with outdoor materials, she designed the inflatables from scratch, then with others refined and developed them. The inflatable itself is the product of years of experiments, re-design, and feedback, and a shared purpose: "Our vision is not focused on the boat. It's about going where you want to go"[16]

In generating adaptive responses we need to look widely for ways forward.

Innovation: it's a team thing

RESEARCHING A BOOK tentatively titled *The Leap*, psychologist Vera John-Steiner interviewed many exceptional creators, expecting to hear about sudden flashes of insight causing creative geniuses to leap naked out of bathtubs and run to their labs in excitement.

What she found was quite different. Whatever the endeavour, ideas were put out in the world, engaged with by others and later, via a zig-zagging path a quality creation emerged.[17]

While some personalities are more adept at looking creatively at challenges, the individual creative genius model is a myth on two counts. First, *creativity usually comes from many years of hard work and exploration.* Creative people tend to be both highly curious and possess great drive. Fascinated by their subject, they do the hard work because it drives them and, when engaging the puzzle, get into a state of flow. There will likely be many false starts and dead ends. Persistence with experimentation may turn a series of failures into progress.[18]

Albert Einstein wrote more than 240 scientific papers, mostly uncited by other scientists. Picasso produced thousands of pieces of art not displayed in major galleries. Bach composed a massive collection of uncelebrated works. Thomas Edison filed thousands of patents, saying: "When you have exhausted all possibilities, remember this. You haven't."[19] These were all small steps in creative experimentation. Breakthroughs usually involve a lot of effort and experimentation.

Second, *innovators need others to bounce off.* In a vacuum their creativity is unlikely to flourish. Creativity flows out of interaction, what Keith Sawyer calls *'group genius'.*[20] While some are more able to create because of the nature of their personalities, we can all make creative contributions given the right circumstances and support.

C.S. Lewis and J.R.R. Tolkien were both remarkable and creative authors. They met at Oxford University as young adults and shared a common passion for writing fantasy and poetry. With some others they formed a group they named 'The Inklings'. It met regularly to explore ideas and creativity, discussing myths and epics, reading aloud from their own work, honing each other's capacities. While writing seems like a solo pursuit, here is a good example of a group refining and enhancing individual creativity.

Likewise scriptwriters spark off each other in writing television programmes, bringing ideas to the table to be scrutinised by others to hopefully generate a truly remarkable script. Comedians and musicians try out their ideas on informal audiences, refining them after each engagement. In quality meetings people bounce ideas off one another, generating better ideas and possibilities. The ideas may come from one or many but everyone is engaged, contributing, growing from the experience.

In 1968 a research scientist developing glues for adhesive tape created something with weak bonding properties. Not useful for tape he often talked to people about it. A friend, and member of a choir, was frustrated at how regularly bookmarks fell out of song-sheets. A weak adhesive that might temporarily hold a bookmark but wouldn't mark the book would be helpful. The result was 'post-it' notes.

Create a culture where innovation thrives

AN ORGANISATION MAY recognise the importance of innovation and as a result set up an 'innovation department'. While possibly useful, the danger is its value will be limited because possibilities are only being explored in one corner by a few people.

Far more leverage would be gained by deciding that creativity is going to be a core value within the whole organisation, and space made for it. Creativity needs to be part of the culture, language and practices rather than in one department or job description. A playful, encouraging atmosphere may surface unexpected things that become seeds of possibility.

Some organisations create temporary innovation collectives, where people come together from different parts of the organisation for a time to think about particular issues, before returning to their normal roles. The benefits are twofold: creativity and thinking about ways forward is enhanced, while trust and new linkages are built across the organisation.

What might an innovative culture look like? Consider a group of jazz musicians. They start altogether then improvise into amazing places. They play off one another, each contributing an idea for the next stage. Together such improvisational teams can create something really amazing. Yet such creativity is not completely spontaneous. It is built on foundations from a lot of hard preparatory work developing and mastering individual and collective skills and getting to know each other, developing ways of working and creating together.

Likewise in creative teams. Bound by common purposes they start with the known and then together explore possibilities, each bringing their own capacities and perspectives, creating an effective culture of innovation.

When the process is working, people experience what Mihaly Csikszentmihalyi calls a state of *flow*.[21] They are totally engrossed with what they are involved with, losing track of time. Have you ever experienced that?

The many leadership contributions needed

THOSE WITH A flair for lateral thinking need to be complemented by people bringing other strengths. Innovators might find it difficult to communicate with the wider organisation, or complete the detailed work needed to bed down an idea. They might be so passionate they don't tolerate useful modifications or get so excited that they lose sight of the bigger picture. Innovators in control of decision-making can sometimes generate brief displays of fireworks or unhelpful gimmickry: when your remote has 50 buttons, you can't change the channel anymore.[22]

Wise leadership builds innovation teams with a good spread of perspectives and capacities. The innovative capacities of Wagner Dodge in the firestorm may have benefitted more of his team had that been the case. Innovators need to be given a voice within a committed community, alongside others with complementary strengths. They need to be supported with good systems and relationships if ideas are to mature into reality.

Ensure experimentation is 'survivable'

EXPERIMENTATION HAS TO be safe enough that, if it fails, the consequences are not too catastrophic. Innovators need to be given freedom to explore but not to the point when it might seriously damage the organisation. 'Safe' innovation is ensured by subjecting innovations to appropriate scrutiny, evaluating both their value and the risks involved. The development of bungee-jumping in Chapter 5 is an example of safe experimentation in a very risky field. Balancing risk and safety is a critical and finely balanced tension to hold.

Jennifer Garvey Berger talks about the value of small *safe-to-fail* (or *safe-to-learn*) experiments in looking for ways forward.[23] Creative groups will pick several good but different solutions, and experiment with them in small safe ways.

Experiments worth pursuing are those from which we can learn and create forward progress. They need to start small but be developed in ways that enable them to be ramped up. Sometimes innovation can be fostered by initially keeping it at the periphery of an organisation allowing for exploration and maturing of ideas without pressure. As ideas develop into solid proposals for the future they can be brought closer to the centre.[24]

Establish clear criteria for outcomes

PART OF AN effective culture of experimentation will be clearly enunciated criteria around what success might look like. Focussed experimentation requires a series of compass points to provide direction, and some guard rails to prevent experimentation going offtrack.[25] What criteria will need to be met if experiments are going to progress to wider implementation?

Without this, experimentation will lack focus, and people may not push edges in the right strategic direction. They might also be less willing to take risks with new ideas in case they are inappropriate.

With explicit criteria people involved will have an acceptable finish line on which to focus and will know what bar their idea needs to reach. It will also take eventual decision-making away from personal preference or loud voices.

The zig-zagging path of serial experimentation

WHETHER WALKING IN wild country, working in business, science or any change, finding a way through unknown territory involves serial experimentation. As two time Nobel Laureate Linus Pauling says, "The best way to get a good idea is to have a lot of ideas." While many innovations will fail, some may provide important new information.[26] Many criticise the expense of high-energy physics particle accelerator research such as by CERN in Switzerland. Yet one consequence of their work was the basis for the internet!

Consider the following experience. Two development workers in Zambia recognised a need: the greatest killer of children was dehydration from diarrhoea, due to a lack of simple medications in remote areas.[27] They defined their goal: to get medication to children.

They saw that in remote areas soft drinks were still easily accessible. Could they get diarrhoea medications to the villages using the same channels? They came up with a cleverly designed package for the medication that fitted between bottles of soft drink and could be transported with the same delivery. Incredibly clever, it won a British design award.

Yet there was a twist in the story. When talking with soft drink distributors about their delivery system, the development workers discovered the importance of the *value chain*. Soft drinks reached remote destinations because there was a small profit for each person in the distribution chain. The development workers defined their next goal: they had to add value to each stage of the distribution chain. Funding and an incentive plan for each stage was established and the medication reached its destination. But it arrived in ordinary boxes; the clever packaging had become irrelevant.

Or had it? While irrelevant in terms of the final solution, it was an important step on the road, leading them to engage with soft drink distributors.

This story is an illustration of the zig-zagging path that experimenting provides through unknown territory. Determined to get medication to children in Zambia, the development workers did not rely only on their own wisdom and ingenuity, but sought wide perspectives to find a way forward. Holding firm to their core purposes they achieved their goal by looking beyond their own creativity to find solutions that worked.

The evolution of the smart phone

The arrival of the iPhone in 2007 was a dramatic step forward, not because it was the first, but because it was the result of various creative experiments. Over time phone developers included ever more features while retaining a keyboard, resulting in smarter but harder to use devices. Seeking to solve this, Apple realised the answer was in using existing touch screen technology. But how to touch it? A mouse wouldn't help, a stylus could be lost. What about finger control? That would need bigger screens, so lose the keyboard. Step by step a new concept emerged, sparking a revolution in mobile phone design.[28]

Summary

How do we navigate unknown territory?

Actively encourage careful experimentation

THE TOP-DOWN LINEAR change management model described in Chapter 7 is inadequate in navigating unknown territory, where grand plans can quickly become the stuff of nightmares.

We need to add a step in our culture as shown on below in Figure 9.1: to experiment carefully to discern effective ways forward. Serial experimentation needs to be an on-going part of an organisation's life.

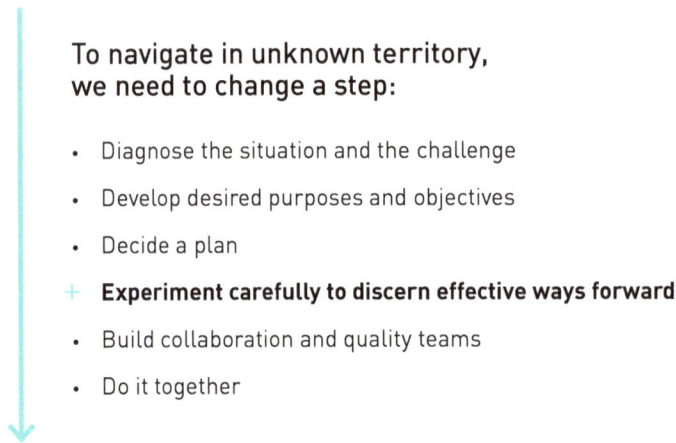

To navigate in unknown territory, we need to change a step:

- Diagnose the situation and the challenge
- Develop desired purposes and objectives
- Decide a plan
- **Experiment carefully to discern effective ways forward**
- Build collaboration and quality teams
- Do it together

Figure 9.1 The importance of experimentation

As people explore and interact together new possibilities emerge, generating energy and 'flow' among those involved. Many small sparks of possibility will start to add up, creating a zig-zagging path forward. It takes a team to take an idea through the experimentation phase to implementation, with people offering many different leadership contributions.

Actions for you

How do you tend to approach change and venturing into unknown territory? What do you need to feel safe, to be able to take risks?

Think about unknown territory you want to traverse. What's the smallest distance you can travel without losing earshot of the last known point?

Experiment: Whether you see yourself as a natural 'innovator' or not, you can ask questions, try new things, experiment and learn: in short, practicing the skills of innovation. Where might innovation be of use to you in your life? What people and resources could you draw upon?

Actions for your team

Who in your team brings innovative capacities? How supported are they?

How could space be given for 'way out' ideas to be heard in your team?

What steps could your team take to allow and encourage safe exploration of ideas and possibilities?

How well do people in your teamwork together around experimentation and innovation? How can this be improved or built on?

Organisational agility requires different attitudes to failure than do command and control models. If it is unsafe to risk, innovation won't happen. What stories does your team tell about 'failure'? How can people be empowered to understand what 'safe risks' are – for both themselves and for the organisation?

What might be ways to highlight and encourage innovation in your team or organisation? How could you share stories or encourage initiative in this area, even in small ways. Try and come up with a few concrete ideas that are a fun and inclusive way to start.

Chapter ten

Engaging unpredictable situations

How can we safely
engage unpredictable situations?

CHANGE IN COMPLEX systems can be highly unpredictable. Armies have an expression: No battle plan survives contact with the enemy. When dealing with people and the complex systems to which they belong, predictability cannot be guaranteed. This chapter explores some of the effects of unpredictability on groups or organisations, and constructive ways of engaging it.

In his 20s, Peter was part of an inner-city public housing community centre working with children and teenagers. The small team wanted to provide school holiday activities that encouraged self-directed creativity. Looking around to see what was available they found a team which was developing adventure playground programs where a vacant space was filled with creative objects, art and craft materials. This was designed to encourage play, self-confidence, self-direction and autonomy. The developers planned to organise and video it for both the kids and for wider use. It was a grand plan and, with much excitement and anticipation, a block of vacant land was found.

What actually happened was quite different to their expectations. Children and young teenagers were certainly drawn to the place but instead of using the tools to create, they turned them into instruments of destruction. Hammers were used to demolish things and materials were thrown around threatening the safety of smaller children. Some materials were even used as barricades behind which to hide from flying objects and from which to hurl their own. A creative play space had become a battleground.

Those running the initiative became increasingly anxious wardens of a fenced prison. Then someone started a fire with some of the craft materials, and the prison began to burn. That was the end. A five-day program lasted only two days. The shiny new plan was up in smoke - literally

This high-profile, accredited program seemed like a great learning and play option. But the outside experts did not understand its context, nor the pressures and frustrations that had built up inside the kids. As a result, despite the best of intentions and reputation, the initiative had unexpected and almost catastrophic outcomes.

In the years that followed, the centre staff developed less ambitious but more effective programs, concentrating on smaller groups of children and catering separately for subgroups. Less secure children valued being part of what they regarded as a club. Others needed wide open spaces to let off steam, still others safe spaces to explore creativity. These activities were less dazzling than the adventure playground, but more effective.

Where do we find unpredictability?

UNPREDICTABILITY CAN BE found in every aspect of our lives. No-one knows for certain what tomorrow holds: maybe a new government policy, sudden illness in a work team, something happening to our children at school. While habits and routines can reduce the likelihood of unpredictability, when something unexpected happens in our lives, as it no doubt will, we can be caught off guard.

Complex systems are made up of many sub-systems which interact in various nonlinear ways. Sometimes minor changes can cascade dramatically with serious consequences. Interaction with a complex system needs to be handled carefully. If we don't want things spiralling out of control as with the adventure playground, an iterative approach is essential. To use the words of influential environmentalist Donnella Meadows, it is about "learning to dance" within the living, changing system.[1]

Jumping too far too quickly

A tourism commentator observed that many ideas for grand tourist ventures are acted on far too hastily. In their excitement, developers make grandiose investments while failing to adequately consider the disruptive potential of changes in global tourism, exchange rates or travel costs. The result is over-capitalisation and white-elephant tourist developments, now empty and deserted. More iterative and careful multi-stage development would have better tested the market.

Unanticipated disruption from the actions of others

THERE ARE VARIOUS possible sources of unpredictability. One is the surprising actions of others, generating unexpected consequences for us.

Consider the Indigenous school initiative examined in the previous chapter. The project was developing well with one of the parents, Tricia, stepping up to manage fundraising. Initial support was encouraging.

Then, quite unexpectedly, the principal who initiated the vision announced his resignation. Tricia was shocked and anxious. He had been her inspiration, providing her with strength and courage. Much of the promised sponsorship was based on confidence in him, and his resignation might undermine that confidence.

Tricia and others had to move from supporting a vision to living and breathing it, embodying it and holding it. Previously acting in the principal's strength, they now had to find their own resources and provide strength to others. The resignation presented a serious choice: step up and contribute leadership, or risk the collapse of something they believed in. Staff, families and supporters each had to transition, recommit, face the challenges and eventually see the future as potentially positive.

Key staff did rise to the challenge, managing to maintain everyone's confidence. Responsibility passed from the pioneer to a broader leadership group. At times, Tricia and others had to step beyond normal role boundaries to offer stability. Throughout, they maintained the confidence of supporters and sponsors, without losing financial support.

What would happen if any of the people in this story were taken out of the equation? The initiative may well have folded. The art of leadership in unpredictable situations is for those in positions of responsibility to listen carefully amid the confusion and uncertainty, and to develop a leadership lens to spot, and grow, leadership capacity and commitment.

Many contributions were needed to develop and nurture the Indigenous education initiative as summarised over the page in the leadership 'map' in Figure 10.1.

Steps	Leadership contributors	Leadership contribution
Principal visits South Africa	**Conference speakers** share stories	Build mutual connections Learn from experience
Principal returns home	**Principal** shares ideas with team.	Envision together
Task group is put in place	**Task group** explores possibilities.	Listen deeply Build mutual connections
Task group engages widely with local community	**Community** shares concerns, providing insights into a complex situation.	Listen deeply Explore options creatively
Why not on the main campus?	**Indigenous mother** suggests an alternative, reshaping the initiative.	Explore options creatively Maintain resolve
Discussion in school community about this option	**Various school staff** listen to people's anxieties, exploring ways of dealing with them.	Listen deeply Build mutual connections Explore options creatively
A plan is put to the school board: It must fund itself	**Principal and Task Group** develop a proposal with enough safety for existing parents.	Move to action Create clear positive structures Build a culture os optimism
Board gives go ahead	**Board** takes risk to move forward.	Move to action
Classrom is set up	**Staff and Indigenous community** create a space that celebrates their cultural identity.	Inspire heart commitment Empower people to contribute
Initiative commences	**Staff and Indigenous community** implement plans, building links and support across school community.	Build mutual connections Create clear positive structures Develop reliable communication
Fundraising commences	**Parents and businesses** generate hope through support.	Build a culture os optimism
Principal resigns	Contributions from **senior staff** and **key supporters** maintain community confidence and funding.	Listen deeply Build a culture of optimism Maintain resolve
Transition to new principal	Contributions from **people across school** enables initiative to develop and maintain funding.	Maintain resolve Envision widely
More broadly	**Former Principal** looks to develop a similar initiative, as do other schools.	Envision together Explore options creatively

Figure 10.1 Leadership Map of the Indigenous Initiative continued

Unpredictable interactions of multiple sub-systems

ANOTHER SOURCE OF unpredictability is the interaction of multiple systems.

Consider child rearing: doing it well once won't guarantee a good outcome with the next child. Families are complex systems that interact with a range of social systems, educational systems and communities of interest. One child's experience of school might affect how the next child fares. Children relate to wider communities that, in turn, affect them. Cultural diversity can further complicate this. Much as we might try to shape things, we can't guarantee outcomes. A family is part of an interconnected system.

We might understand or feel we can cope with each system separately, but their interactions may surprise or overwhelm. Underestimating unpredictability and complexity can be catastrophic, as in the experiences below.

The 1953 Mt Everest expedition that first reached the summit faced a very complex challenge. They were climbing into unknown territory on a mountain that had never been climbed and faced the personal uncertainties generated by a team of mountaineers from various countries and cultures each with their own motivations. There was also the unpredictability of wildly fluctuating weather, the potentially catastrophic effects of high altitude and relatively untried oxygen apparatus. Yet, they succeeded by taking small steps and evaluating the outcomes: carefully experimenting with equipment, developing the team meticulously and building on decades of accumulated experience from previous parties.

By 1996 the unpredictability could have been less, with known routes, better equipment and accumulated experience. Yet there were new complexities connected with potential overcrowding by multiple parties climbing at the same time.[2] Run by unregulated climbing businesses, climbing parties often included wealthy, less capable, paying customers needing help to climb and survive. Mountains over 6,000 metres high are still unpredictable and surprise disruptions can snowball chaotically as systems unravel.

Below the summit on 10 May 1996, cold and oxygen-depleted climbers from different teams overlapped, with slower climbers struggling lower down in a veritable traffic jam. Then a fast-approaching storm changed everything.

Journalist climber John Krakauer recalls: "Later, after six bodies had been located, after surgeons had amputated the gangrenous right hand of my team mate…people would ask why, if the weather had begun to deteriorate…did veteran Himalayan guides keep moving upwards, ushering a gaggle of relatively inexperienced amateurs…into an apparent death trap? But nobody can speak for the leaders of the two groups involved, because both men are dead.'[3]

Twelve people died that day. Everest remained a highly complex proposition with new forms of unpredictability. Key people were overconfident, a key ingredient in things going wildly wrong.

The surprise storm triggered chaos but the seeds of disaster were planted well before.

Multiple agendas: Commercial companies with multiple agendas lacked the focus and precision of the 1953 team. These teams were competitors, needing to build business reputations and maintain success rates. They needed publicity, hence including a less experienced journalist and celebrity in their teams. Including relatively inexperienced amateurs required safer practices, greater teamwork, and careful leadership, yet disagreements, poor teamwork and distrust marred all teams.

The turnaround moment: Critical to safety on Everest is an agreed time when summit climbers must turn around to descend safely, whether or not they have reached the summit. Team leaders agreed on 1 pm, stressing to their teams the importance of this. But with so many parties trying to summit at once, the route became so overcrowded this would not be possible, particularly for slower climbers. One team leader summited with a slow customer around 4 pm. The other also climbed way past their agreed turnaround time.

Perhaps getting customers to the summit overrode safety priorities. Foggy thinking at altitude, competition, or a need to succeed, led them to ignore their own stipulations. By the time people in positions of authority on Everest recognised their plight, it was far too late. They, other guides and customers paid with their lives.

Systems falling apart: Because of less skilled teams, more responsibility was thrust on expedition leaders. Their drive for success with amateur climbers meant pushing themselves too hard, with no one in place to support them or take over if their own well-being deteriorated, which indeed happened to one or both of the expedition leaders. Over-extended at high altitude, they suffered oxygen depletion, making irrational decisions.

Critical teamwork and systems quickly fell apart in the storm. Confusion reigned, plans were in tatters. Climbers were left to their own devices, some staggering alone off the ridge.

In appalling conditions without radios, guides lost track of customers. Poor communication meant that full, potentially life-saving oxygen bottles left on the mountain were mistakenly assumed to be empty.

Agreements were broken: Prior agreements between teams to summit on different days, and to fix ropes on the icefall and upper mountain, were broken in the desire to summit during the narrow window of reasonable weather. Without fixed ropes in the blinding storm, climbers couldn't find their tents in the dark, costing several lives.

Conflicting purposes, multiple agendas, inadequate systems, poor teamwork and decision-making, and competition on an unpredictable mountain created a disastrous cocktail. Those responsible overestimated their ability to control things, treating the mountain as a complicated rather than complex system. The culture within the teams (and others around them) was not agile enough, preordaining a disaster long before the surprise storm hit.

An iterative approach to unpredictability

AN ITERATIVE APPROACH is essential in both unknown territory and unpredictable situations if we don't want things spiralling out of control. Progress will usually come from the accumulation of creative micro-steps rather than one big dangerous one. The adventure playground catastrophe recounted earlier could have been averted with an iterative development process.

By taking small steps we minimise risk, allowing learning to affect next steps. If one small step works, it is forward progress. If it doesn't, it provides valuable learning.

1. Experiment with a small step.
2. Evaluate it from the balcony.
3. Apply what has been learnt.
4. Experiment again.
5. Again evaluate it from the balcony.
6. And repeat.

The Marshmallow Challenge

A leadership development exercise used the world over is the Marshmallow Challenge. Teams are given set amounts of spaghetti, tape, string, scissors and a marshmallow. They must construct a tower to enable the marshmallow to be as high off the table as possible in a limited time. The task is about teamwork and creative experimentation.

People from some backgrounds tend to do better than others. Indeed, kindergarten children tend to perform better than business college graduates.[4] Researchers argue that children experiment more and learn from the experience, bringing a more creative and playful spirit, and are more likely to discover fresh approaches. More concerned to prove themselves, and more averse to failure, business school graduates tend to develop grand plans and not engage in so many experimental iterations. If the plan is wrong, the result is a disaster.

Learn, learn, learn

CONSIDER THE STEP-BY-STEP approach of the team at Fukushima Daini power plant (Chapter 5). When in potentially unpredictable situations, actions and priorities needed to be regularly assessed and revised.

This is not always easy; we are uncomfortable with chaos, and want to rush out of confusion as soon as possible. Yet, from her experiences working with the US army, Margaret Wheatley urges teams to stay with the complexity of things, resisting simplistic solutions or rushing to move out of confusion/chaos too quickly.[5]

Armies are highly interested in learning from experience. As one colonel said: "It's better to learn than be dead".

Key learning moments are After-Action-Reviews, where everyone involved responds to three questions:

- What happened?
- Why do you think it happened?
- What can we learn from it?

These three questions can help shape more agile responses to unpredictable situations.

Noticeably absent from this is a focus on establishing fault or blame. Wheatley is sharply critical of organisational practices where, after a crisis or failure, people try to bury it as fast as they can, and move on.[6]

Step by step

IN SO MANY examples in this book iteration has been critical. In establishing the Indigenous school, at least three serious iterations took place, each strengthening its strategies and identity, each growing capacity. Likewise with the Zambian workers trying to get medicine to children.

Dawn on May 29 1953, decades earlier than our disastrous Everest event, saw two climbers moving slowly up the final ridges of Everest towards the summit, successful after more than 40 years of failed attempts.

Yet this is not a story of one team's success, but of a climbing community adding bricks to the wall of knowledge and experience over decades. It is a story of both persistence and learning. Previous teams who reached 400 m below the summit, shared information about the route. One mountaineer observed that final ascents were attempted from too low down the mountain, making ascents long. He offered critical advice: "put your assault camp close under the southern summit...I shall never have any great hope of success unless a final camp is so placed."[7]

Previous parties reported they left oxygen high on the mountain. Knowing this, the 1953 team developed adaptors to use it. Everest 1953 was also one step in an iterative journey: development and learning would continue in the decades that followed, leading to new leaner alpine-style approaches. In his memoirs 1953 expedition chief John Hunt doubted people could climb Mt Everest without oxygen[8], yet two decades later climbers were doing just that.

Success in 1953 on Mt Everest wasn't just about one team, but an extended climbing community making iterative gains over decades. One step at a time, a way forward was found.

Traditional models of change management first size up a problem, then put together a plan and implement it. An iterative approach repeatedly engages and re-engages questions, experimenting and reshaping responses at every stage. Complexity researchers have found this approach tends to produce better outcomes.[9]

Rather than a linear model of engagement we need an on-going process of action and reflection as summarised in Figure 10.2.

To engage unpredictable situations, the process needs to be iterative:

- Assess together the nature of the challenge
- Focus on shared purposes and objectives
- Experiment carefully to discern effective ways forward
- Build collaboration and quality teams
- Implement strategically a well-paced journey
+ **Learn from the experience and repeat the cycle**

Figure 10.2 The importance of an iterative process

Developing agility routines

When the winds of change are blowing some build shelters, others build windmills.

– Old Chinese proverb[10]

FROM THE MOMENT we are born we are taught effective 'routines': ways of acting to navigate the complexities of life. There are *engagement* routines: how we relate to others, listen, learn and participate in shared activity. There are *perceiving* routines: we are taught not to touch a heater if it is red because it might be hot. There are *testing* routines through which we are taught iterative ways of exploring possibility: puzzles, Lego or building blocks. There are *collaboration* routines, like using group play then team sports to teach us how to work together with others. Then there are *implementation* routines, about how to achieve outcomes while maintaining a good risk-safety balance: we learn how to cross a road safely to venture into new territory. Such routines provide the foundations for effective living in a complex world.

Organisational agility routines

CURRENT RESEARCH SUGGESTS that creating organisations able to effectively engage on-going change requires embodying similar routines within organisational culture.

Christopher Worley and his research team studied organisational performance in over twenty industries between 1980 and 2012, to identify those demonstrating sustained agility in the face of change? What was different about them?[11]

They found consistently high performing organisations could better respond to change because their cultures had embedded in them key dynamic routines. They identified four key *agility routines,* to which others have added a fifth. These parallel our exploration of what is needed to engage personal uncertainty, unknown territory and system unpredictability as summarised in Figure 10.2.

1. Perceiving routines: assess together the nature of the challenge: Worley identifies the importance of effective perceiving mechanisms: agile organisations develop a wide range of processes for broadly, deeply and continuously monitoring their environment. Facing a complex challenge needs all hands on deck for two reasons. First, no individual will be able to understand the system from all perspectives, so collectively observing and assessing the situation is a pathway to a better understanding of things. Second, doing this together can also help us understand what is going on for people in the uncertainty.

Agile organisations will try to see with fresh eyes, understanding well the system and its underlying dynamics. They will invite, not suppress, conversation about key issues, deepening discussion that might bring quality ideas to the surface.

Indeed, conflict and difference can be constructive for progress, pushing people to think more deeply about their ideas. It is important for people having tough conversations to stay in relationship, even if they hold different viewpoints.[12]

2. Dynamic strategising routines: focus on shared purposes and objectives: Rather than relying on an expert to set direction, agile organisations will continually focus together on shared purposes and values and, as much as possible, seek to align personal and collective purposes. Worley describes this as a dynamic strategising routine, where new directions come to be widely owned. People will be eager to contribute, not because they have been instructed to, but because they want to help translate a shared vision into reality.

3. Testing routines: experiment carefully to discern effective ways forward: As was seen in Chapter 9, navigating unknown territory requires careful experimentation, in Worley's words: effective testing responses. Agile organisations respond to new situations via relatively simple experiments that encourage innovation and learning. They will tolerate honest failure, supporting experimentation with careful risk management.

4. Empowering routines: build collaboration and quality teams: Though not identified by Worley, other researchers have suggested key empowering routines relating to how people work together, build teams and empower others.[13] As explored in Part 2, this will be vital to living out shared group purposes.

5. Staged progress: implement strategically a well-paced journey: Agile organisations build capabilities in converting successful experimentation into applicable practices. Effective implementation depends on carefully pacing new directions, persevering when things get difficult, as well as being willing to learn from experiences.

Learn from the experience and repeat the cycle

JOHN F. KENNEDY argued that leadership and learning are indispensable to each other.[14] Agile teams and organisations will develop natural ways of learning and gaining perspective from what they do.

To be effective, such routines need to be a natural part of the life and culture of teams. To what extent are such agility routines embedded in the culture of your team or group? What steps might take you forward?

Such approaches to challenging situations or new possibilities are not just the preserve of organisations. They can also apply to each of us in daily life, enabling us to navigate life's many challenges.

Agile software development

In computer software design, agile software development describes an approach to programming that moves away from hierarchical, structured processes of design through to implementation.[15] Traditionally, software has been developed via a top-down process that begins with a customer brief and moves step-by-step through design to production, delivery, implementation and maintenance. Each stage usually involves a separate team operating in isolation. All requirements must be known right from the start. Sound familiar?

Agile software development approaches things quite differently, breaking composite tasks into smaller steps, engaging with the customer after each iteration. Collaborative work teams *(scrums)* work together with a high level of autonomy through all stages, back and forth with the client. Each step can be made up of a series of separate *sprints* to iteratively produce the various elements of a solution. Such a methodology is more flexible, bringing together appropriate people at the right times while maintaining high levels of communication.

Summary

How can we safely engage unpredictable situations?

Work iteratively with measured steps, observing and learning as you go

WHEN ENGAGING WITH unpredictable situations, grand plans can quickly look like foolish, naïve dreams. We need to approach complex change iteratively. To avoid surprising or dangerous outcomes, take one small step, evaluate its impact, then take another. We need a sense of where we are going without over-specifying it. It is a different way of being and acting.

Adaptive responses to complex challenges require more than managing it linearly. The hurdles described in the last three chapters suggest we need to be developing in our teams the agility routines described in this chapter. What kinds of leadership practices might foster that agility?

Reshaping practice 10

Actions for you

Gather complementary people: To what extent do you look at the big picture and possibilities therein? Or do you prefer to figure out the detail and steps required? Given that both are required to deal with unpredictable situations, what sorts of people do you need around you?

Actions for your team

Choose a positive move forward made by your organisation or team. Can you map the contributions of different people at different stages?

Building an agile culture is itself a complex challenge! Consider again the organisational agility routines outlined in this chapter. How might your leadership strengths, and the strengths of those in your team, contribute to developing routines like these?

Strengths matching: Identify a current complex challenge: use a map of your team's leadership strengths to identify ways these strengths could be directed towards each step of the journey.

Chapter eleven

Embedding agile practices

How might we grow agility with change?

Life isn't about waiting for the storm to pass... It's about learning to dance in the rain.

– Vivian Greene[1]

HOW CAN WE best foster the agility routines Chapter 10 describes? How can we practise and refine how we act together so that it becomes natural to our teams and organisations?

Take it step-by-step. A skateboarder uses muscles and balance to propel a board forward. Within a few days, a beginner can begin to build-up speed and distance travelled. Then good skateboarders test themselves, seeking less certain movements - steps, bowls, rail, and curbs. They fine-tune their balance not only to maintain momentum on uneven surfaces but to transform the way the board is used, moving sideways, rotating, flipping and kicking it. These movements are subtle, the adjustments fine, the skaters able to navigate unpredictable terrain developing their own agility routines.

As with skateboarding, an agile organisation becomes so adept at implementing routines that personal uncertainty, unknown territory and system unpredictability become the spaces in which it operates best.

Physicists exploring the nature of sub-atomic particles observe an effect called quantum entanglement, where groups of particles are so intertwined that the state of each particle cannot be described independently of the others, even when separated by large distances. They can only be described as a whole system. Sceptical about the idea, Albert Einstein referred to it as 'spooky action at a distance'.

Quality teams are a bit like that. They have developed an effective agile culture that can't be simply described by indentifying the gifts of each individual. Their patterns of being have become well entangled, the leadership contributions of all - formal top down, peer to peer and informal foot of the table contributions - have become so well entangled that the resultant agile culture enables them to effectively navigate what lies in front of them.[2]

So what might this look like in practice? And how can we develop such an approach?

Through the previous chapters we developed a model of agile behaviour when engaging complex change that is summarised again in the top half of Figure 11.1.

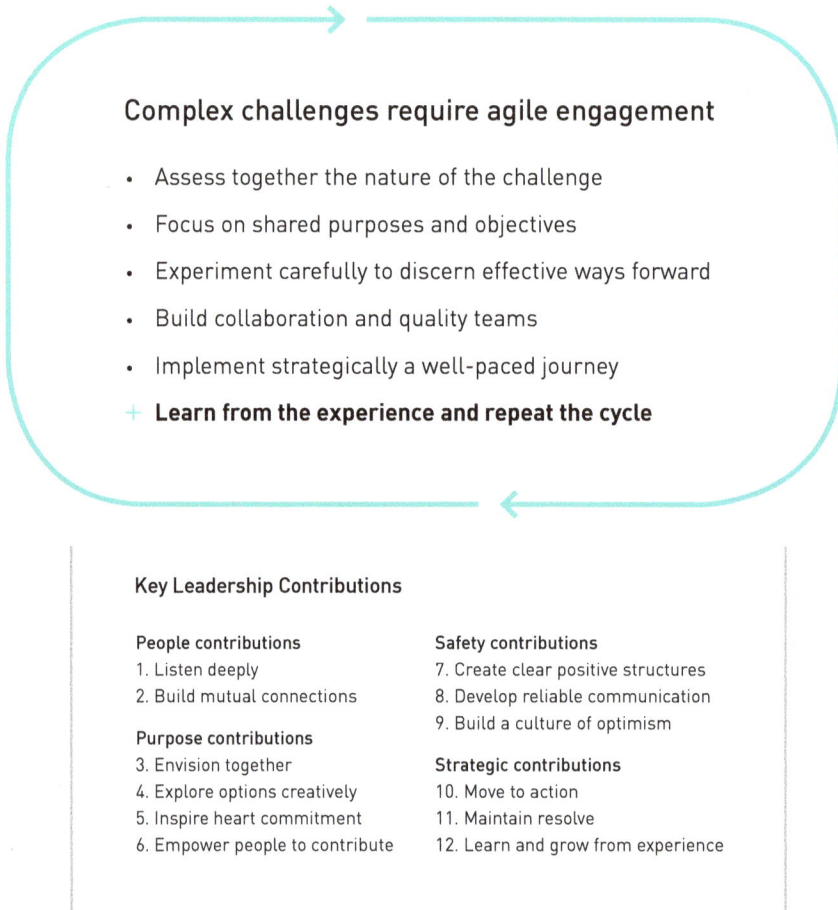

Figure 11.1 Engaging complex change and potential leadership contributions

Each routine in this approach will require a different blending of the various leadership contributions needed in healthy groups identified in Chapter 5 (also summarised in the bottom half of Figure 11.1). Simply knowing the range of leadership strengths in your team won't be enough. In entangling well top down, peer-to-peer and informal foot of the table leadership contributions, it is important to know what types of leadership contributions are vital (or unhelpful) in each aspect?

In this chapter we step through some practical ways to embed agility routines in our teams or organisations, and the leadership contributions critical in each.

Agility in action

IT IS HARD to use words to describe something as alive as 'agility'. It may be more useful to explore it in action. To do this, we reconnect with the two organisations introduced in Chapter 7: Whitebank School and W.L. Gore. You might find it useful to go back to Chapter 7 to re-familiarise yourself with these examples before proceeding.

Because we are exploring two case studies, this chapter is a little different in format. It looks at each agility routine in turn, exploring how they were embedded in each example.

Look carefully at each agility routine. What leadership contributions are most important in each? What might be practical ideas for implementation in your situation? Or road blocks you might encounter?

1. Assess together the nature of the challenge

AGILE ORGANISATIONS WILL assess together their situation, and the challenges and the possibilities it presents.

Whitebank: taking another look

CHAPTER 7 OUTLINED the desire of senior staff at Whitebank to reshape their educational practices. Achieving this was far from straightforward. It is a good example of a typical organisational challenge, where its adaptive nature required not only outward changes in practice, but also deeper cultural changes.

Initially the principal simply informed the staff about what was going to happen. This generated anxiety, fears and resistance. Most were concerned about the proposals, some openly opposing them. Lacking clear understanding of the rationale, they were unable to own them.

There appeared real losses for teachers, used to controlling their own classroom with minimal interaction or interference from others. In co-teaching they might face more scrutiny, with the additional complexity of communicating with someone else. There was an underlying fear: "What will this new world look like and how will I find it? Or will it find me out?" More experienced teachers were asking: "Am I too old for this?"

For a year negative feelings were rising, and the principal and deputy soon realised that, as a complex challenge, this needed a different approach. It was far more than a question of creating teaching teams and rebuilding classrooms. Forty or so staff needed to take the journey together, and tilt their culture in new directions.

Recognising the unrest, the principal and deputy put a priority on *listening* and *connecting* with staff, inviting them to look at the ideas and talk together about them. Staff were able to say 'we don't get it', to ask hard questions, and encouraged to bring their fears to the table. The fact that people might feel anxious was normalised. Staff felt heard.

While senior staff may not always have welcomed it, the surfacing of questions by dissident voices was a critical contribution, forcing deeper thinking and learning for all. The time taken helped bring people along but also improved the ideas and implementation. Real conversations ensured everybody thought carefully about what was proposed and why, addressing issues before things became too poisonous, building trust and mutual support.

Senior staff at Whitebank genuinely and openly listened, creating a quality environment for both learning and reshaping the way the staff worked together. Connecting, listening and learning paid significant dividends: anxiety and fear were understood and accepted, and better implementation strategies evolved.

Assessing together is valuable not only for generating ownership, but for making a space where surprising ideas can surface.

W.L. Gore: promoting wide perspective

WHILE WHITEBANK STAFF had to learn new skills, agility in assessing possibilities has been well enshrined at W.L. Gore. Getting wide perspective, *listening* and *connecting* across silos, and assessing possibilities are central to the Gore culture.

Rather than having a specific research department, W.L. Gore sought to provide incentive to all staff to innovate and *explore options creatively.* At any time innovative staff-led projects are being worked on across the company, encouraging learning and growth, with clear structures to maintain safety and communication.

Gore recognized the dangers of creating silos of people with particular skills or perspectives who become disconnected from others with different backgrounds. Associates are expected to spend 10% of their time experimenting with possible applications of the polymer with a team of collaborators from different departments.[3] The teams have to be small enough for people to know each other, yet large enough for cross-fertilisation of ideas and skills.

By requiring people to collaborate across specialities means that everybody can better understand the business and possibilities that might exist. Rigorous assessment of possibilities by peers enshrines collective *listening* and *learning* into company practice.

Significant leadership contributions needed in this routine

COLLECTIVELY CREATING ADAPTIVE responses can make all the difference to outcomes. In both examples **People contributions** are key to this phase, including the need to *build mutual connections* and to *listen deeply* to each other. An ability to *learn and grow from experience* will also be important.

Practical ways to assess complexity and develop adaptive responses together include:

- *Invite others onto the balcony:* Together we can gain better perspective, while understanding what is going on for people. Involve people from different backgrounds. Maximising group wisdom will build trust, a vital foundation for the future.
- *Develop shared language and understandings together:* This will enable more meaningful conversations.
- *Listen deeply:* Listen well to people's stories and aspirations to understand their perspectives. Allowing staff to air concerns was pivotal at Whitebank. Try to keep people talking together, even if they come from very different places.[4] Don't avoid difference just to keep the peace. Stick with the issues, and don't get trapped into personal criticism.
- *Identify the deepest levels of complexity:* Resist simplistic or cost-free solutions. Take a systems view.

- *Give oxygen to those asking important questions,* or *ask a provocative question yourself.* People in authority can add (or subtract) legitimacy to the contributions of others, giving them oxygen or snuffing them out. Create a safe space for courageous conversations about real issues. Often a desire to look confident means people don't ask questions, so ask a question that takes them deeper or unearths hidden logic, giving them permission to explore possible ways forward.
- *Allow yourself to be vulnerable:* An open, humble stance can open up deeper conversations. Those with a need to impress often build walls rather than bridges.

2. Focus on shared purposes and objectives

AGILE ORGANISATIONS WILL work hard developing clarity of purpose, refining those purposes with each step.

Whitebank: Building wider circles of ownership

REAL AND BRAVE conversations among staff ensured everybody thought carefully about what was proposed and why. Heart commitment to it also grew through time invested in this collective envisioning.

Sometimes this yielded startling results. Through long painful conversations some early critics worked through their fears and issues, and became key spokespeople for the changes, assisting others to embrace new concepts.

Initially not enough time was taken to develop ownership of ideas and directions among families, stakeholders and the school's umbrella organisation, again causing anxiety. Engaging stakeholders, taking time to both explain and listen, was a vital change in stance, allowing everyone to *explore options creatively.*

Early on there were fears that families might leave the school because of what was being proposed. Communicating the vision was challenging, given it was not fully formed but evolving and maturing as it was being explained. One presentation night the Principal managed to encapsulate succinctly why he was passionate about the changes, communicating it in a simple, attractive way. Staff often recall that occasion as pivotal to bringing on board the broader school community. That night they created an attractive postcard of the destination they sought to reach, around which the school community could align. *Communication* is vital.

W.L. Gore: holding fast to primary goals

W. L. GORE is so effective in part because they firmly focus on one of Wilbert Gore's goals: to create a company culture that genuinely enhanced communication and learning. Structures were put in place that maximised wide conversation and discovery, bringing people into *envisioning together, exploring options together,* building *heart commitment,* aligning as possible personal interests with company goals.

Significant leadership contributions needed in this routine

AGILE ORGANISATIONS WILL work hard developing clarity of purpose, refining those purposes at each step. Nurturing this will require **Purpose contributions:** *envisioning together* future possibilities, *exploring options creatively* and *inspiring heart commitment* in each other. **People contributions** will remain important since growing shared directions requires on-going *listening* and *connecting.* **Safety contributions** such as *reliable communication* are also key.

Steps you can take to create focus:

- *Take time together to regularly refine core purposes:* Create spaces for people to share their deepest hopes and aspirations for the group. In Peter Senge's words: 'As people talk, the vision grows clearer. As it gets clearer, enthusiasm for its benefits grow.'[5]
- *Encourage ownership of shared directions:* Seek to link group purposes with people's personal aspirations. If they see enough of their own hopes in the shared vision they are more likely to commit to the shared goals.
- *Engage both heads and hearts:* People need both passion and understanding before they commit to a difficult journey.
- *Frame shared directions clearly and attractively:* People need a clear, appealing and meaningful picture of their goal, an *attractive postcard of the destination*, to build energy for moving forward and translating a shared vision into reality.[6]

3. Experiment carefully to discern effective ways forward

AGILE ORGANISATIONS NEED to encourage creativity, learn from failures and celebrate steps forward. They need to foster and reward learning and experimentation that uncovers quality ideas, embedding it in their culture. Part of an effective culture of experimentation will also be clear *testing* routines. Setting clear criteria for outcomes is vital, providing focus for those experimenting as to what they need to achieve to be successful.

Whitebank: experimenting with co-teaching

SEEING A NEW idea in action is very powerful. Initially staff explored options and possibilities for Whitebank by visiting other schools. Then two teachers committed to the vision were given permission to experiment in a pilot co-teaching class established during the building works. Other staff could then reflect on what did and didn't work. This pilot enabled learning and growth. It provided tangible first hand experience of what might be involved, drawing many staff on board. Later new teams were also encouraged to experiment to find their own ways with co-teaching, learning from the experiences, and exploring multiple co-teaching models.

One outcome of these experiments was the development of teams of three people rather than two, including a specialist support person, who was encouraged to contribute leadership from their field of expertise. In the journey of experimentation to adoption, Whitebank had a clear criteria for the worth of an experiment, building an evaluation metric around student outcomes. Ideas needed to be evaluated against their impact on student outcomes.

W.L. Gore: promoting safe serial innovation

AT GORE, INNOVATORS are free to explore but, to move beyond dabbling in a project, developers need to convince the company that their product opportunity is real via a solid Real-Win-Worth assessment. Is the opportunity real? Will people buy it? Can we win in the marketplace? Is it unique and valuable?[7] In this way safe innovation is encouraged and managed through *clear positive structures.* The development of Elixir guitar strings is illustrative of Gore's innovation process. The application was actually developed through experimentation in their medical department in Arizona. In a side project an engineer was trying to make gears on his mountain bike shift more smoothly by using a layer of the polymer on the cables. It worked well so he tried coating strings to improve the cables used for puppets at places like Disneyland, before wondering how this might affect guitar strings. He connected with an interstate colleague who was a guitarist and together they developed strings that held their tone longer than conventional ones. Three years on they sought company support to take it to market. Elixir strings have become a popular choice for guitarists.

This is a good example of a lattice approach to collaborative innovation by people from different teams and backgrounds.[8] Associates with an idea found followers among other associates who were willing to put their own discretionary time into the project. *Connecting, listening* and wide ownership became a bi-product of the innovation pathway.

Significant leadership contributions needed in this routine

IN THIS ROUTINE key leadership contributions include *exploring options creatively,* and transforming insights from experiments into achievable plans. **People contributions** and **Safety contributions** (creating *clear positive structures* and developing *reliable communication*) will remain important in uncertain times.

Practical ways to undertake careful experimentation are summarised below from Chapter 9:
- *Encourage experimentation:* Include a margin in people's roles to allow them to experiment as a normal part of their lives, sowing seeds of potential new growth.
- *Look widely for possibilities:* A non-guitarist was critical to the development of Gore's Elixir guitar strings. Find and encourage innovators with capacities in lateral thinking, supporting them with others bringing other strengths.
- *Create a quality learning community where innovation can thrive:* Create a safe environment where curiosity reigns, where there is freedom to create and experiment. Model an open, ongoing learning stance that shapes organisational culture.
- *Ensure experimentation is survivable:* Evaluate risks and limits of time, cost and resources that can be spared.
- *Establish clear criteria for an experiment* to achieve if it is going to progress towards wider implementation. These criteria will be developed for your specific context and purposes.
- *Iterate experimentation carefully:* Take small steps, letting lessons learnt shape next steps in a carefully paced journey.

4. Build collaboration and quality teams

THE IMPORTANCE OF a quality team was explored in Part 2. Teams more than the sum of their parts are what Peter Senge calls 'communities of commitment', committed to core values, to working together and engaging possibility. If we cut corners in developing quality teams we will be less agile. Opportunity rarely waits. At both Whitebank and Gore, a rethinking of leadership as a collaborative endeavour has been central to developing agility.

Whitebank: enabling collaborative leadership

IT WAS SOON evident to the principal and deputy that the changes involved more than reshaping buildings and teaching teams. They also had to rethink the school's leadership culture, recognising the importance of collaborative leadership for the new era. No principal or deputy could bring all the leadership strengths needed, nor was that a good model for staff and students. It required growing capacity and distributing leadership broadly, *empowering people to contribute*. An entire staff team had to become more agile.

Staff explored together what collaborative leadership might look like, about how to make space for others, not taking up all the space themselves. Others had to find the confidence to contribute. Everyone needed to grow, and start to act differently.

Structures also had to change: an expanded executive and other leadership teams were set up, enabling more staff to gain experience, develop capacity and enhance communication across the school.

Constructive leadership contributions were also encouraged from people not in positions of responsibility. In addressing challenges the words: 'the answer is in the room' were regularly heard. Sometimes surprising people would step up and make significant leadership contributions. Relying on group genius was both powerful and empowering.

Slowly a new culture took shape, with the school shifting from a predominantly top-down management style to a more fluid collaborative model. Mutual encouragement, renewed structures and coaching support embedded the changes and quality teams emerged.

In the past parents had little influence on setting school directions. Now their voices were actively encouraged, and some were not afraid to question things. Because they had the school's interests at heart their contributions have been important.

W.L. Gore: constructing and encouraging collaborative practice

GORE'S INTER-DEPARTMENTAL EXPERIMENTATION teams build collaboration, trust and perspective. Honest failures are seen as part of the creative process. A culture is fostered of celebrating achievements and recognising good attempts that didn't work.

Criteria for success include whether such teams are forming and growing in capacity? And are new ideas rising to the surface?

Encouraging innovation teams has fostered not just innovation but also leadership capacity. Gore built an environment that was whenever possible a "bureaucracy free zone"[9], with a very flat company structure and simple decision-making processes. Leadership is conceived as a collaborative endeavour to which everyone is encouraged to contribute.

CEO Terri Kelly has observed that in most companies, those in senior roles are expected to be the most knowledgeable person on the team, all-wise and all-knowing. In her words: "At W.L Gore we take a different view. If you want to tap into the whole organisation you have to distribute the responsibility to the associates. The Gore model changes the traditional role of the leader."[10] She sees the main role of people with positional authority as ensuring the culture is healthy and maximising innovation: is the system working well? As a way of generating commitment and ownership, staff are invited to become partners in the company, increasing alignment between personal and company goals.

There is an emphasis on elevating people from within the company to take positions of responsibility. Peers select new CEOs from within the company, thereby consolidating core aspects of the Gore culture.

Gore provides a good example of structures that encourage and enhance teamwork rather than restrict it. Their guidelines for flight prioritise growing *human capital*, encouraging and celebrating excellence, creating a culture that maximises contribution across the organisation.

Significant leadership contributions needed in this routine

CRITICAL LEADERSHIP CONTRIBUTIONS here will include *empowering people to contribute*. An *optimistic culture* will also generate commitment and motivation to contribute. **People contributions** will continue to build trust while **Safety contributions** creating strong foundations remain significant.

Priorities in building quality teams include:
- *Develop leadership widely:* Look widely for leadership and multiply it. It might come from surprising places.
- *Help people discover and contribute what they have to offer:* People need to identify their capacities and find opportunities to contribute them.
- *Generate the team that is needed:* Ensure the team has the range of necessary leadership strengths. Include people who can help stakeholders move forward.
- *Put in place good structures, systems, communication and a culture of optimism:* Create structures that enhance collaboration and innovation. Build trust and confidence by modelling integrity, optimism and authenticity.

5. Implement strategically a well-paced journey

ALCOHOLICS ANONYMOUS CHALLENGES recovering alcoholics to get through one day at a time. To go a lifetime without a drink sounds impossible. Going one day at a time is more doable. Small victories add up to something worth defending, and eventually new behaviour becomes instinctive.

Whitebank: maintaining a delicate but critical balance

IMPLEMENTING CO-TEACHING REQUIRED carefully balancing risk and safety. Sometimes senior staff felt they were moving to action too hastily, that perhaps the pace of change could have been slower. However slower progress might have generated inertia, blocking progress.

Getting the right balance between long-term planning and allowing experiments to freely generate seeds of possibility was always a source of tension. Confidence in plans had to balance with a willingness to learn from experience and refine directions.

Five years on, there are new challenges but the school culture is more agile. Staff have less fear of change, having experienced the rewards gained by opening up to new possibilities. Their agility routines enabled progress with co-teaching and also set the school up for future change. Now there is a strong feeling that "What we are exploring is important if our children are to be well prepared for an increasingly complex future".

W.L. Gore: structures to ensure safety

THE GORE WAY of working together provides freedom and an incentive to explore yet requires people to work with others and to face rigorous assessment of a product's viability and worth. These structures encourage well-paced implementation, good balancing of risk and safety, and quality serial innovation over decades.

Significant leadership contributions needed in this routine

KEY LEADERSHIP CONTRIBUTIONS in this routine include **Strategic contributions** such as *moving to action, maintaining resolve* and *learning and growing from experiences.* **People** and **Safety contributions** remain important.

Practical ways to implement strategically:

- *Know when it is time to act:* In this phase we need good judgment about when to act or pause. Find the right balance between indecision and haste. Seek to be a non anxious presence.
- *Help people move beyond fears or work avoidance:* When anxiety generates resistance it can be tempting to push harder, resulting in passive aggression and loss of commitment. Be sensitive to people's fears, and help them get beyond them.
- *Shrink the change to achieve small wins:* One way to motivate people is to help them feel they are closer to the finish line than they thought.[11] Small wins can generate confidence to keep going, enhancing morale and willingness to take further steps. Celebrate successes that are aligned to intended directions, for encouragement re progress and to underscore valuable culture shifts.
- *Place your time and energy strategically:* Some favour change for its own sake, others always resist it. Concentrate on the potential of the majority in between. As they commit they increase group momentum for change.
- *Monitor progress carefully:* Raise the heat to move people beyond complacency and lower it if their anxiety begins to diminish performance. Balance perseverance with a willingness to learn. Every step of a journey holds new insights. Return to the balcony regularly.

Summary

How might we grow agility with change?

Nurture agile leadership practices in your teams

TO EFFECTIVELY NAVIGATE difficult or complex situations, teams and organisations need to develop leadership practices that nurture agility, entangling all the leadership capacities that are available to them. Learning to act and reflect together positively, while taking measured steps, is a pathway to more effective outcomes.

It will also be the pathway to creating a more agile organisation for the future, more adept at facing its next challenge adaptively. It is critical to develop the agility routines described in this chapter before they are needed; they can't be created suddenly midstream. Each routine requires a culture shift nurtured by various leadership contributions, different ones being important in each routine and season.

All of which is far removed from top-down command and control leadership or steady state management of efficiency.

Reshaping Practice 11

Actions for you

Select one of your leadership strengths from those described in Chapter 5. Pause to consider how utilising this strength more fully might contribute towards innovation and agility. In which agility routine is it most important?

Actions for your team

Map the leadership strengths in your team as described in Part 2. What strengths can you draw upon to build more agile processes in your organisation? Which team members have important contributions to make in each agility routine?

Tilt work habits: How could you promote safe and regular innovation? Start with simple aspects like flexibility in working hours, personal interest projects and professional development. Move towards more culturally ingrained practices, habits and mindsets that may help.

Part 3

Epilogue

Surviving shipwrecks:
Agile engagement with change

Part 3

How can we develop agility with ongoing change?

7 Agility begins with culture, so discover new ways of working together.
8 Create safe spaces for people to process their emotional responses to change.
9 Actively encourage careful experimentation.
10 Work iteratively with measured steps, observing and learning as you go.
11 Nurture agile leadership practices in your teams.

Figure E3.1 Rethinking leadership – How can we develop agility with ongoing change?

PLACE A COLLECTION of metronomes on a soft, flexible surface and set them going. At first, you'll notice they all tick chaotically at different times. Then something amazing happens. The metronomes gradually become more synchronised. Eventually they tick along to the same beat. This alignment won't happen on a rigid surface that creates reverberation. A flexible surface allows each metronome to both calibrate and affect the others. Leadership to enhance organisational agility is the equivalent of harmonising individual metronomes.

Managing what is requires one set of skills, exploring what might be possible in complex situations is quite another.

Time after time we underestimate the complexity of change. Positional authority in organisations often seeks to dictate rigidly the alignment among staff and priorities, expecting everyone to fall into line. Yet the reality of change is quite different. A group attempting to navigate change effectively needs a malleable environment that facilitates listening, absorption, and flow and allows everyone's contributions to affect each other. Eventually, because of these dynamic relationships, the flux settles and the organisation aligns itself.

We can't control complex situations but we can constructively influence them, helping them change in positive, significant ways.

So what have we learnt in this part about engaging challenge and change? Let's return to the Auckland Islands and our shipwreck survivors and step through how each Rethinking Leadership element was lived out.

The *Grafton* crew demonstrated that, though challenging, engaging complex challenges is possible. They maximised their capacities and became agile in uncertain, unknown and unpredictable situations. Cutting corners, as with the *Invercauld* survivors, brings a cost. A detrimentally static culture, present from the outset, meant an 'every man for himself' dominated.

Was the leadership cupboard bare on the *Invercauld*?

THE IMMENSE LOSS of life among *Invercauld* survivors suggests a lack of leadership in the group. Yet the leadership cupboard was not bare. The group had the leadership capacity to face their challenges.

Seaman Holding took the initiative and sought to contribute at every stage. He was involved in early exploration beyond the wreck site to find a better, survival location. It was his plan not Dalgarno's to explore the two coves, which maybe contributed to the deceit of the exploration party only pretending they had explored theirs. How different things might have been had they actually done the reconnaissance and found the old settlement.

Holding contributed innovation from the start. He established a route up the cliffs from the wreck site and did extensive exploration with others and on his own, eventually discovering the old settlement. Though having no previous experience, he was the one who learnt to hunt birds and seals, collecting 37 of the 42 seals killed. Like those on the *Grafton*, he innovated with sealskins to create moccasins and fish traps. On several occasions, he moved camp to better access changing food sources or possible rescue sites, weaving a raft then building a boat to reach an outer island from which they were eventually rescued. At each step, he experiments, explores what might help, then takes another step forward.

Many of us might find ourselves in Holding's shoes, wishing to contribute something but lacking the formal authority to do so. Holding was seeking to tilt a static culture and he faced an uphill battle against rigid thinking, self-centred behaviour and low morale. Culture matters. For those of us in positions of authority the lesson is obvious: identify, encourage and harness all latent leadership capacity.

A failure of culture

THE PROBLEM ON the *Invercauld* was a failure of culture. Holding approached their predicament creatively, but he was not surrounded by a quality team or an agile leadership culture. His creativity and effort were in stark contrast to the effort and attitudes of others, who were happy to receive food and assistance in moving forward after the hard work was done but contributed little to the collective project of survival.

Critically, those with positional authority gave minimal leadership to growing the group's collective capacity. Preoccupied with notions of leadership as being about position and reward, they expected others to do the work. Often, they were unwilling to contribute to a team effort yet ordered seamen to do their bidding to increase their comfort. To the end, Dalgarno only accepted Holding's innovations when it suited him, giving his contributions scant recognition in his reports. What strengths might others in the crew have brought if encouraged?

This lack of support for Holding's initiatives gave everyone an easy way out, an excuse to sit motionless by the fire till death overtook them, or to plot treacherous alternatives.

Leading from the foot of the table, Holding was completely frustrated by the lack of oxygen provided for his initiatives. Their overall culture couldn't make the most of his agility.

Positional authority, class and title were the traits that carried weight throughout. Even upon rescue, Captain Dalgarno instructed the other two survivors that "he would do all the talking". On board he and the First Mate were promptly taken to the officers' mess leaving Holding with other sailors.

Yet, undaunted, Holding used his leadership strengths (described in Chapter 5) to move things forward. *Resolve, exploration of options, ability to learn from experiences, optimism* and sense of when to *move to action* helped keep him going, experimenting and learning, progressing and occasionally tilting the culture to get effective group responses.

And he did achieve some success. Sometimes he managed to convince others to act differently, even those with positional authority. It was a limited victory with all but three perishing. Yet it was a victory nevertheless: without Holding's efforts neither captain nor first mate would have survived.

The different experiences of the two shipwrecked crews highlights the importance of agile leadership practices in facing complex challenges. We illustrate this by stepping through elements 7 to 11 of Rethinking Leadership in light of each story.

7. Agility begins with culture, so discover new ways of working together: We need to look deeply at our stated and unstated ways of operating that govern our behaviour. How different were the lived cultures of the *Invercauld* and the *Grafton*?

A simple gesture of sharing the valued resource of tobacco equally among the *Grafton's* crew set the tone for the group to respect each other as equals and live together accordingly. Destroying the playing cards because they jeopardised team harmony is another example of the values enshrined in the crew's behaviour, as was the development of a constitution for how they would live.

8. Create safe spaces for people to process their emotional responses to change: Throughout the *Invercauld* tragedy no senior officer could provide a non-anxious presence or help people process and move through their emotions about the situation. Panic started the minute the Auckland island cliffs came into view. Chaos reigned as officers ran around issuing irrational orders that couldn't be obeyed.

The destructive effects of panic are all too evident! Onshore, anomie became the dominant mode of surviving, a mode with tragic consequences.

By contrast, for the *Grafton* survivors' purposeful activity became the dominant mode of being. Having spent time preparing to abandon ship, collecting useful resources and ensuring that everybody got off safely, Captain Musgrave took the time to try to understand what everyone was going through, aware of the ways fear might paralyse or disunite. He gave them space to own their own fears and choose to work for a positive way forward.

The *Grafton* survivors committed to the self-discipline of busyness and fighting fear by keeping focused and active together. In this way they grew their own capacities and resilience to face challenges.

9. Actively encourage careful experimentation: We can't see how things will unfold, but can still experiment with possibilities to find ways forward.

The *Grafton* survivors continually experimented and innovated: when building a hut, creating clothes and shoes, harvesting and preserving meat, constructing boats. Responding to their situation in this iterative way helped them survive – even thrive – in the hostile environment. Together they developed group genius, together discovering ways forward. And how much would that group genius have been diminished had Musgrave not rescued the sick Raynal from the sinking ship?

By contrast, attempts by seaman Holding to get the *Invercauld* crew to look for safe harbours was undermined by deceitful behaviour that led to learned helplessness, hopelessness, and in many cases, death. Other survivors were happy to reap the rewards of his experimentation in hunting, fishing, exploration and innovation when it suited them, but not to contribute or put effort in themselves. Possibilities were lost through poor culture and the lack of group genius in solving problems.

10. Work iteratively with measured steps, observing and learning as you go: Taking small measured steps was a mark of the *Grafton* crew's culture. They focused one step at a time: on making shelters, clothing, blankets, shoes and, ultimately, a vessel to get help. Each step was an example of careful trial and error, and evaluation that finally resulted in them being rescued.

From the *Invercauld*, Holding's attempts to approach their plight in a similar fashion were resisted or only grudgingly accepted by others, and far too late.

11. Nurture agile leadership practices in your teams: Effectively engaging a complex challenge will involve going through various phases over and over: assessing the situation together, focusing on shared purposes, experimenting, building a quality team and implementing strategically in a carefully, paced way.

Captain Musgrave prioritised building the wellbeing and energies of the *Grafton* survivors and melded an agile team, enhancing overall capacity rather than reducing it. They illustrate well cyclical learning and engagement, continually assessing their situation, setting priorities and looking at key next steps to serve their ultimate purposes. At every step they experimented to find ways forward, learning from each experience. They sought to maximise team assets, and to take next steps as safely as possible.

They demonstrated the value of an agile culture. The hallmark of such a culture is that each cycle produces quality responses that move the organisation forward while building both capacity and self-belief.

The *Invercauld* survivors, in their every-man-for-himself culture, were quickly overwhelmed by the challenges. Organisational agility needs to be developed well in advance before it is needed. Holding's innovative capacities could have been critical to saving more men, but their overall culture minimised that possibility.

Agile leadership in facing a challenge

In this book, we have sought to reconstruct leadership thinking to explore how to engage complex challenges in effective, adaptive ways. The figure here provides a map of our journey so far.

Is this the full picture or is there more? In the following part we look at one more critical aspect of engaging complex challenges, and it might surprise you.

It is all about facing the adaptive challenges within.

Rethinking leadership Parts 1-3

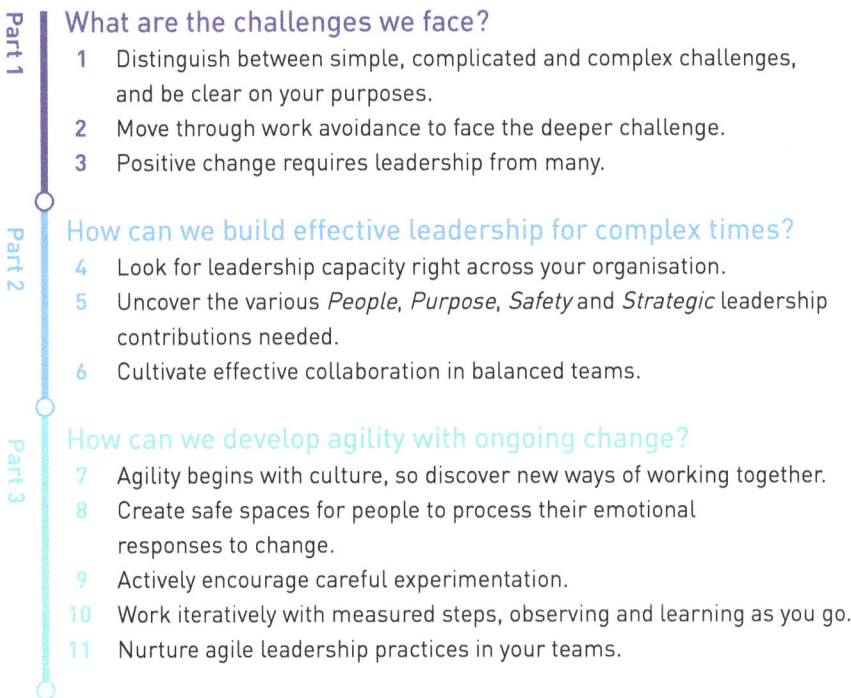

Part 1

What are the challenges we face?

1 Distinguish between simple, complicated and complex challenges, and be clear on your purposes.
2 Move through work avoidance to face the deeper challenge.
3 Positive change requires leadership from many.

Part 2

How can we build effective leadership for complex times?

4 Look for leadership capacity right across your organisation.
5 Uncover the various *People*, *Purpose*, *Safety* and *Strategic* leadership contributions needed.
6 Cultivate effective collaboration in balanced teams.

Part 3

How can we develop agility with ongoing change?

7 Agility begins with culture, so discover new ways of working together.
8 Create safe spaces for people to process their emotional responses to change.
9 Actively encourage careful experimentation.
10 Work iteratively with measured steps, observing and learning as you go.
11 Nurture agile leadership practices in your teams.

Figure E3.2 Rethinking Leadership Parts 1 to 3

Part 4

Contributing Leadership That Makes A Difference

Introduction

How can we each contribute authentically and sustainably?

IN PART 4 we invite you to look at the adaptive challenge within, to reflect on who you are, what you have to offer, what you value and why you are seeking to contribute leadership. We must do some personal work to prepare ourselves for complex situations.

Leadership is not just an external strategic contribution. Certainly it needs to be *effective,* with people contributing in ways that enable teams to become more than the sum of their parts. But our contributions also need to be *sustainable* amid turbulence. Too many people start with a flare of enthusiasm but burn out quickly. Yet, for real impact, we need to be there for the long haul.

Our contributions also need to be *authentic,* offered with integrity in ways that build our trustworthiness. If people do not have full trust in someone, as with the team of fire-fighter Wagner Dodge, they are less likely to follow them or their ideas.

Our own personal foundations will be critical, particularly in difficult or uncertain times. Both research and experience underline a critical ingredient of long-term, effective leadership:

What we do is important, but who we are is foundational.

Consider this analogy. A tree or plant blossoms and bears fruit that enables it to reproduce.[1] This is what we harvest or admire. But a tree is more than its fruit and flowers. Its trunk is just as fundamental to its growth and existence, providing strength, support, shape and stability. The more robust the trunk, the higher a tree can grow towards the sun, spreading its branches, leaves and fruit. A deep, strong root system is also important, nourishing and anchoring the tree firmly, stabilising it when strong winds blow.

Each part of a tree relies on the others and helps it mature and blossom. But the tree doesn't grow in isolation. It is part of a wider ecosystem, including animals, plants and soil. Trees will blossom in accordance with the health of the ecosystem.

So too with us. Contributing in effective, sustainable and authentic ways is about truly knowing ourselves and discovering both *what we have to contribute,* and *how to offer it with integrity.* It is also about developing *strong personal foundations* and *growing self-awareness.* What drives us? When are those drives healthy, and when not?

1. Discover and develop the leadership you have to offer

2. Act with integrity and authenticity

3. Anchor yourself with strong personal foundations

4. Consistently make time to grow self-awareness

Figure 14.1 Contributing leadership authentically and sustainably

Finding your way around Part 4

POSITIVE PSYCHOLOGY SUGGESTS it is important to identify and work with our strengths as much as is possible. Some contributions come more naturally than others, depending on our personalities, make-up and life experiences, as discussed in Chapter 12. *Understanding well what we have to contribute* is an important part of the self-awareness we need.

But *how we live and act* is also critical, and is the focus of Chapter 13. We must live and offer leadership with integrity. Like a tree, we need a sturdy trunk to effectively bear fruit through many seasons.

Chapter 14 explores the importance of *strong personal foundations*. Just as a healthy tree needs a strong root system to anchor it, provide nourishment and stability, we too must look below the surface at our personal foundations. Strong core values, clarity of purpose and our meaning systems - how we make sense of life and see ourselves in the grand scheme of things - are all vital to sustaining and directing us, keeping us on track.

This is rarely done in a vacuum. Just as trees mature in a broader ecosystem, we need quality, nurturing communities (family, friends, colleagues, life partners and trusted others) to nourish us, and help us grow and mature.

Discovering and developing our capacities, strengthening our personal foundations, and learning to live and contribute with integrity is about developing *self-awareness,* the focus of Chapter 15. Recognising what drives us will help us avoid being trapped by it. Self-awareness is an on-going journey of action and reflection.

Chapter twelve

Discovering our leadership strengths

Leadership: what do I have to offer?

Realising our strengths is the smallest thing we can do to make the greatest difference.

– Alex Linley[1]

CLASSICAL SINGING TRAINING seeks to perfect a student's ability to achieve a predetermined sound quality and tone. By contrast, contemporary training often sets out to help students find their own true voice. Success is determined not by achieving a predetermined sound, but by achieving strength in *your* sound.

People's perception that leadership must look or sound a certain way is often a major barrier to them contributing. They struggle to live up to that image or, because they don't match up, feel they have nothing to offer.

Encouraging everyone (including ourselves) to discover, develop and offer the leadership strengths they bring is critical. Organisational effectiveness depends on it.

That is the focus of this chapter.

1. Discover and develop the leadership you have to offer

Figure 12.1 The leadership we have to offer

What comes naturally?

WE ARE ALL unique. A novelist's personality probably differs from an economist's. People suited to developing purpose and direction will most likely differ from those who develop quality systems and safe structures.[2] In developing **Situational Leadership** in the 1970s Paul Hersey and Ken Blanchard made a significant contribution by recognising the links between personality and leadership. Some leadership contributions come easily to us, others we struggle with.

During the 20th century, personality theory emerged as an important branch of psychology. It provides a framework for exploring the reasons some people might be more effective than others in certain situations. While there is debate about the extent to which diet, mood swings and emotions affect personality, theorists see personality as relatively stable over time. Since the early work of theorists like Gordon Allport and Myers and Briggs, various personality models have been developed with associated testing tools routinely used in job selection and personal development.

Personality theories confirm that no one person will have all the required leadership capabilities in equal proportion. We are genetically different, with different traits, personalities and gifts. Some contributions will come naturally while others will be difficult because they run against the grain of our personalities. The strengths we bring, and the situations we are suited to, might depend on our personality types.

This has two critical implications. First, because no one person will bring all the leadership capacities needed in equal proportion, we need a team. Second, for each of us as individuals it is vital we identify our leadership strengths. Then we can develop them, contribute them and work alongside others with complementary strengths.

Consider these examples of people's particular strengths:

John has an amazing eye for detail. He picks up on seemingly small mistakes, which could have major consequences. While sometimes frustrating, his attention to detail means that, when he asks a question or makes a comment, it is important to listen and take it seriously. John needs big-picture people around him, and big-picture people who fail to get detail right need to work alongside people like John.

Sue lives spontaneously. For her, life is about relationships and community, about helping people to feel comfortable and that they belong to the group. Meaning and energy come from contributing to other people's lives. She gathers information intuitively, making decisions based on feelings. The result is sometimes wonderful, sometimes chaotic. People in her community feel valued and included when they are with her. She complements people like John, and needs others around her to contribute order and direction.

Rose and **Phil** are members of a leadership team with extensive experience and expertise. They both have a strong idea of the goals of the organisation and how their team needs to grow and develop. Yet both struggle with decision-making and closing options. They know they need others who can help make decisions.

We all bring a mix of strengths. Once we know what they are, we can then discover how to use them. A positive, strengths-based framework provides a whole new way of thinking about leadership, creating spaces to thrive in our work together. Knowing our strengths can be empowering and liberating, focusing us on what we bring, not what is missing. Be yourself, everyone else is taken![3]

Problems arise when our personality and the required leadership contributions do not match. Over time, working like this is frustrating, exhausting and reduces performance. We might eventually give up, our idealism turning to cynicism and defeat.

Contributing as only we can

Several years ago, Peter met Tom, a primary school teacher, on a desert journey. On top of sand dunes, Tom would sit and draw extraordinary images in the sand. While everyone else sat and talked, he physically connected with the dunes by shaping and reshaping it.

In a world where so much is about strategic planning and rational reporting, Tom often felt his creativity, appreciation of beauty and playful nature weren't useful. However, while running a camp for children at-risk, he was alone with a disturbed young boy seeking to self-harm, banging his head against a wall. Not knowing the boy well, Tom started to make shapes in the dirt where they were sitting. He wrote the boy's name in interesting shapes. Slowly, the boy became distracted by Tom's creativity and they started to talk. After an hour, the ground around them was covered with creative designs. Though conversation was minimal, the boy still felt heard and valued. Tom's unique blend of strengths had been put to great use in a difficult, dangerous context.

A different way of thinking

WHY WORK WITH our strengths? Surely we should be fixing our weaknesses? Consider this: A focus on problems can have very negative affects.

Think of a struggling community that is regularly described in negative terms and gains a label as a problem community. Welfare workers come in, focus on problems and use grant funding to fix them. The greater the deprivation, the better the chance of funding success. Over time the community and everyone in it becomes stigmatised, which compounds the challenge. What would it look like to start with the strengths of that community, and apply the available capacities to further building these up?

As individuals we are often conscious of our limitations, of what we don't bring. Focusing on this for too long will generate a downward spiral of helplessness, low self-esteem and reduced wellbeing in general. We start to lose perspective on what we have to offer, becoming stuck with a negative picture of ourselves and maybe even give up. What happens if we begin in a different place, discovering what we do bring - our strengths?

Positive psychology and leadership

The most important thing we learned was that psychology was half-baked, literally half-baked...we baked the part about mental illness, about the repair of damage. The other side's unbaked, the side of strength, the side of what we are good at.

– Martin Seligman[4]

ONE OF THE more dramatic developments in psychology has been the rise of positive psychology, built on work by Abraham Maslow, Carl Rogers and, more recently, people like Martin Seligman and Mihaly Csikszentmihalyi. Concerned that so much of psychology focused on mental illness, dysfunction and abnormal behaviour, positive psychologists explore the meaning of happiness, wellbeing and living purposeful, meaningful lives. Positive psychologists define it as the "scientific study of positive human flourishing that includes biological, personal, relational, institutional, cultural, and global dimensions of life".[5] It is being applied to a range of contexts, including education, clinical psychology and positive institutions. While there have been some critics[6] and get-rich-quick positivists, its significance is widely recognised. Positive psychology has value in rethinking leadership. First, it shows why strengths-based approaches work. Second, it suggests a pathway to increase the energy and wellbeing of those we work with. Both will improve our chances of achieving positive change.

Identifying or discovering strengths is important because:
- It encourages and affirms, enabling us to see what we have to offer.
- Identifying strengths is the first step to understanding how to best use them.
- We are more likely to be effective, we will feel better about ourselves, building self-esteem and self-confidence.
- It can release us from negative thoughts about who we are not.
- We can better assess how much we are working away from our strengths, in areas that do not give us energy.

Strengths, talents and hobbies

A CORE TENET of positive psychology is that fulfilment and meaning come from applying our strengths to wider purposes that matter to us.

What do we mean by a *strength?* A strength is something we both do well and get energy from. Peter enjoys contributing new ideas or ways of doing things. He believes he does this reasonably well, and it energises him, so he sees it as one of his strengths. Naomi gets energy from listening deeply and communicating. Building focused teams is one of her strengths. Connecting with the purpose of projects energises Sophie, and her strength of optimism is often valued in teams.

We also have *talents,* things we do well but that don't energise us. We use them when necessary but using them too often will tire us quicker than when using our strengths. Peter can manage and develop effective systems, but tires quickly with it. Several years ago he held twin roles as both director and senior researcher. Not able to manage an expanding workload he chose to remain as senior researcher rather than as director. Exploration gave him energy; management wore him down. Naomi prefers to work in a team with natural organisers. By contrast, Sophie sees organisational capacities as a strength she brings.

As well as strengths and talents, we can also have *hobbies:* things that energise us, but that we don't necessarily do well. Peter loves music, but has no natural talent for it. It is something he enjoys in private, using other pathways for making a positive contribution.

Working with our strengths

RESEARCH SUGGESTS THAT up to 85 per cent of people believe the best way to better performance is to find your weaknesses and get beyond them.[7] So we focus on them, berating ourselves about them, and try to be someone we are not.

Positive psychology suggests the opposite is true. Rather than trying to improve things we do badly, it argues growth is more achievable in our strengths, for the reasons outlined in Figure 12.2. We are more likely to fulfil our creative potential and be more effective working with our strengths, particularly as part of a team. Many people work in situations that have little to do with their passions or aspirations. So, another reason for thinking about our strengths is to make sure our lives are moving towards our natural capacities, and that we avoid, as much as possible, pressures that force us to operate in energy-sapping areas.

A proponent of strengths-based thinking, Marcus Buckingham, suggests a key lever for engaging and motivating people is getting them to play to their strengths: "pull this lever and an engaged and productive team will emerge. Fail to pull it and, no matter what else is done to motivate the team, it will never fully engage or become a highly productive team."[8]

What are your leadership strengths?

WHAT LEADERSHIP STRENGTHS do you bring? Reflect on this, and get feedback from trusted others. Figure 12.2 suggests some important steps you can take, based on the model in Chapter 5. Identify three or four of your leadership strengths from the list below by asking: What do I do well? What gives me energy?

Keeping strengths in perspective

DOES THIS MEAN that we should only contribute and work with our strengths? What about the times when we need to make other contributions? Few of us will have the luxury of being in teams covering all the bases, particularly if in small teams or more isolated contexts. Sometimes we have no option but to contribute from outside our strength areas.

Yet we can still use our strengths to make such situations easier.

1. Recognise the importance of working with strengths rather than dwelling on weaknesses.

2. Take time to identify the strengths you bring.

3. Get feedback from others.

4. Refine your understanding as you go.

5. Try intentionally working with your strengths and monitor the consequences.

6. Consider the leadership strengths needed from others to complement those you bring.

Figure 12.2 Identifying and developing your leadership strengths

Sophie is good at organising and developing structures but gets drained by tasks requiring detailed ongoing communication. So she uses her organisational skills to list what needs to be communicated and to whom, and sets deadlines for each so they get done efficiently. She ticks each one off to gain a sense of accomplishment, positively using her strengths to help her deal with, even enjoy, a task away from her strengths.

Sometimes those with responsibility for teams may not choose the most proficient person for a task, but rather encourage someone who may benefit from the chance to stretch and try themselves out. With an adequate safety net in place, this can be a good way to develop leadership capacity in a team. The question is who can best achieve the outcome **and** grow overall team capacity. This can be frustrating for people who might feel they could do the job more quickly with less effort. Yet sometimes that very confidence can shut others out.

Allowing others to grow

You probably know that highly capable person who people regularly seek out to get things done. While such people enjoy being competent, there is a downside: the rest of a team can avoid growing their capacities. Sometimes stepping back can give others a chance.

Naomi enjoys moving projects forward but has recognised this can close others out, while wearing her out.

Sophie brings natural energy and perseverance to what she does but has also found she can leave others behind, so must sometimes temper what she does to enable others to move at their pace.

Years ago, in Chicago, Peter met Bobby and Suzy, two educated young people seeking to support a local Hispanic community in a struggling urban area. While both had impressive teaching and communication skills, concerned to grow local capacity they did not always take on such roles, instead supporting others to do so.

A key leadership contribution is empowering others to act. Like sunshine and rain to wilting flowers, people thrive on appreciation and recognition. Encouragers look for the best in others, seeking out people who may make a difference. They believe in building on strengths and personally helping others reach their aspirations, so they take safe risks to give people opportunities, often supporting them via mentoring and coaching. It is important to stretch ourselves and others, to uncover new strengths and the breadth of our capacities.

Uncovering new strengths

Lyn, a 24-year-old whose mother left home when a teenager, is the oldest in a family of four. Throughout her life she has had to be the responsible one, and fills this same role in her work. Lyn has realised she is given managerial roles because she can do them and always has. It is a talent, but it doesn't energise her. On the other hand, innovation and exploring new possibilities energises, but she hasn't had the chance to see if they are strengths. She is keen to find out.

Naomi loves music and has played guitar since high school, seeing it as a hobby, playing only at home. In recent times, through the encouragement of others, she has ventured into song-writing and singing in public. It has opened up another way of living out her core purposes.

Summary

Leadership: What do I have to offer?

Discover and develop your leadership strengths, helping others do likewise

TO BE EFFECTIVE in leadership we need to find our own voice. We all have strengths to offer. It is tempting, and dangerous, to try to emulate someone we admire rather than look deeply at what we ourselves have to offer. We can't lead alone. We need to surround ourselves with people who bring complementary strengths, growing collaborative leadership capacity in our teams. We need to encourage everybody to identify and develop their own leadership strengths, enabling them to contribute constructively. While sometimes we must do things that do not come naturally, the challenge is to find others with complementary strengths to work alongside.

Reshaping practice 12

Actions for you

When has your contribution to a group made you feel fully alive? What comes effortlessly to you, and energises you in the doing? This will help point to your leadership strengths.

Pick one of your strengths. Try to use it intentionally over the next few weeks. Notice what happens, in yourself and in the people around you.

How can you reshape your roles to align more with your strengths? How could this sustain you, and make you more effective?

There are times when using our strengths may be unhelpful. When have your leadership contributions got in the way? How can you minimise this in the future?

Actions for your team

Do people in your team know their own and each other's leadership strengths? How might you encourage such reflection?

To what extent does your organisation's culture invite people's contributions as opposed to being limited by tightly defined roles? For three people in your team, consider a question to ask that would help them identify their strengths.

CHAPTER THIRTEEN

Chapter thirteen

Living out leadership

How do I best make my contribution?

One of the biggest failures of leaders at all levels today is the disconnect between what they say and what they do...Lead by example or you don't lead at all.

- James Kouzes and Barry Posner[1]

CONTRIBUTING OUR LEADERSHIP strengths means knowing ourselves well. It means acting consistently and living with integrity, being seen by others as behaving according to our beliefs and values. We are more likely to be respected and trusted if we act from a set of internally consistent frameworks and principles. People know what they are getting from us, which creates safety and trust.

Without trust and integrity things quickly break down. In 1822 Arthur Pierce was one of eight convicts who escaped from the notorious prison settlement on Sarah Island in Tasmania. The group set out across an unknown wilderness to find freedom, battling mountains, torrential rain and thick scrub. Food was running out. One evening, one of the convicts commented that he was so hungry he could "eat a piece of a man". A Pandora's box was opened, the unspeakable spoken, a private possibility made public.

From then on everyone was on guard, afraid to sleep. All trust was lost. They killed one person, cutting him up and eating him. Two others fled, ultimately dying of exhaustion. Three more were killed and butchered, finally leaving just Pierce and one other. They travelled for days, both desperately trying to stay awake, each afraid he would be slaughtered by the other if he fell asleep. Indeed, when his comrade succumbed to sleep, Pierce took an axe to his head.

Chapter thirteen – Living out leadership | **179**

The same occurred among the survivors from the *Invercauld*. Seaman Holding noted in his account that one day the boatswain suggested to a group they should draw lots for who should be killed when they ran out of food. After Holding indignantly rejected the idea there were many whispered conversations that he believed were about killing somebody to eat. Several men disappeared without trace.[2]

Later a survivor pushed a comrade showing signs of madness out of his tent, causing him to freeze to death. Later he was found eating his remains.[3] For Holding, this final manifestation of an 'every man for himself' culture fully destroyed any trust in others.

We too may find ourselves contributing leadership in less extreme but still deeply challenging situations where our integrity may be tested. We might experience organisational cultures that challenge our values, treat people as disposable or see the ends as justifying the means.

In Chapter 3 we met the CEO whose leadership style was to figuratively hang people over the balcony, suggest they were performing poorly and threaten to fire them. Did it indeed improve staff performance?

Absolutely the reverse. Employees lost trust and respect for him, only did what they had to, and spent much time seeking support from each other and outsiders. The survival culture that resulted reduced commitment, collaboration and organisational impact.

In another organisation where we were involved a major initiative was announced by the CEO with the assurance that no staff would lose their jobs. Another executive staffer pulled us aside to say: "don't believe a word of that". Sure enough, several staff were made redundant with consequent drops in morale and trust among those remaining. Albert Schweitzer was right, example is not the main thing in influencing others. It is the only thing.[4]

Double standards and poor modelling

On an outdoor adventure trip, those in charge asked their group of young adults to leave their mobile phones behind in order to fully engage in the experience. During the trip, those same supervisors made personal calls from the emergency satellite phone. This double standard encouraged participants to be dishonest, for example by not carrying out their rubbish as they had promised.

A school principal often left his door open and was regularly overheard discussing confidential issues raised by staff. As a result, the school's culture lost appropriate boundaries. Gossip was rife, drastically reducing confidentiality and trust.

Walking the talk

WHEN JAMES KOUZES and Barry Posner developed lists of the characteristics people admired in leadership, honesty was selected most: "whether into battle or into the board room, people will want to see leadership as worthy of their trust."[5]. How we act needs to be congruent with who we are, our actions aligning with our words.

Credibility is a foundation for good leadership without which strategies, skills and practices are empty. High credibility will motivate others to higher levels of commitment, performance and contribution. To believe in you they have to know who you are, and what you stand for.[6]

Leading and living with integrity also benefits our wellbeing. Psychologists and colleagues Maureen Miner, Martin Dowson and Sam Sterland carried out detailed research suggesting those with a strong internal sense of self are more likely to survive and thrive than those dependent on external sources for affirmation.[7] Peter's research also pointed to the importance of character, trust and respect for both effective leadership and healthy organisations.[8]

Trust: There is a problem out there

INTEGRITY BUILDS TRUST; it is critical glue for an effective team. Without it, teams disintegrate. Trust takes time to develop, but is easily broken.

Peter was involved in longitudinal research that charted major drops in confidence in a range of core social institutions and roles since the 1970s[9]: politicians, lawyers, corporations, churches and banks. In a 2007 national study in the US, 77 per cent of people felt there was a crisis of confidence in leadership in America[10]. In Australia in late 2013 only 27 per cent of people thought the federal government could mostly be trusted.[11] So what's going wrong?

Our social institutions seem to be losing integrity. This word stems from the Latin *integer* meaning whole or complete. In a work context, this can be about behaving according to expected professional standards and being transparent. At a deeper level it can be about being honest, with strong moral principles, being above reproach and not corruptible. We regularly make assessments of the trustworthiness of others, sometimes based on evidence and other times intuiting whether they walk the talk. Trust and respect will break down if leadership does not consistently uphold and model group values. This is particularly important for those in positions of authority, given the visibility of their behaviour.

Authentic leadership

WE OFTEN ASK the question in workshops: "Who are the people who have had the most impact on your life?" It is remarkable how often those identified are people whose lives and actions have demonstrated committed values and ways of being. Who they are, not what they do, inspires us. Their values, how they live them out, how they engage with others and shape their lives matter.[12] A willingness to care unconditionally, really listen or stand against injustice are the kinds of things that inspire and leave a lasting impression. Something is 'authentic' if it is genuine or real.[13] On a trip through Central Asia, Peter visited several magnificent mosques filled with devotees: seeing the place these sacred buildings held in their lives was deeply moving. He also visited splendid mosques in former Soviet republics now simply historic artefacts, largely empty of meaning except for tourists. Though beautiful, they felt false, lifeless and lacked authenticity.

People seen as 'authentic' seem genuine, know who they are, and accept themselves. Despite external pressures, they stay true to their spirit, core values, purposes and character, rather than being blown about by the expectations of others. In exploring authenticity, Bill George suggests that key to growing it is to take responsibility for our own development, seeking deeper self-understanding. The task of a lifetime, we will make higher quality contributions as a result.[14]

Research into authentic leadership suggests four key aspects: *transparency in relationships, balanced processing of ideas and possibilities*, firm *internal moral perspectives* and personal *self-awareness*. Below we look at the first two, as well as the importance good life balance and boundaries, turning to and the others in later chapters.

How to best make our contribution

JUST AS A tree needs a sturdy trunk to continue to bear healthy fruit through many seasons, we too need to base our lives on a sturdy way of living. Three key aspects are:
- Honest transparent relationships.
- Open, balanced and receptive consideration of ideas.
- Sustainable nourishing balances and boundaries in life.

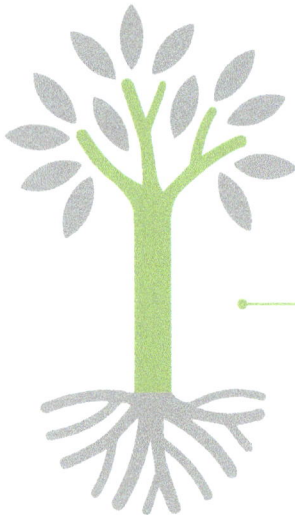

Act with integrity and authenticity
- Honest transparent relationships
- Open balanced consideration of ideas
- Sustainable life balances and boundaries

Figure 13.1 Act with integrity and authenticity

Honest transparent relationships

LEADERSHIP REQUIRES A commitment to openness in relationships, to appropriate self-disclosure and trust. It will make people feel they know a genuine person instead of interacting with someone hiding behind a mask.

Research has shown honest transparent relationships build more trusting, better performing teams.[15] NCLS Research found that those willing to come alongside others, share feelings, openly growing and developing, were less prone to emotional exhaustion. While there are obviously issues of confidentiality and self-protection, sharing some of our feelings can help people connect with our humanity.

There is a delicate dance to find appropriate levels of transparency. Those responsible for teams need sound, two-way relationships with trusted team members, making sure their sense of self worth does not depend on their positional authority or affirmation from others.

Transparency in relationships can be contagious, spreading and deepening to create a culture of authenticity. It sets a pattern that multiplies, promoting deeper personal trust.[16] Shared values and quality interactions enhance group alignment and commitment to each other.

Honesty in relationships cannot be faked. It is linked with self-awareness: we must know ourselves well in order to be authentic and transparent. If someone doesn't realise they are wearing a mask, attempts at transparency will fail.

Open, balanced, receptive consideration of ideas

AUTHENTIC LEADERSHIP ENSURES that discussions are not distorted towards vested interests, and that perspectives are sought from a wide range of people.

In nineteenth century England, canaries in cages were taken into mines, their greater sensitivity to carbon monoxide could warn miners of danger. Social canaries can help us gauge people's feelings about particular situations, helping us gain broader perspective.[17]

Open-minded processing including listening to dissenting voices, is important, though something difficult to do in pressured situations. Neuroscience shows that, under fear or threat, our brain struggles to process, and we become reactive.[18] We can short circuit this through open even-handed engagement with ideas.

Real issues need to be dealt with in an atmosphere of mutual respect and curiosity, recognising that learning is always possible and positions may change. Instead of ignoring uncomfortable feedback, we can learn from contradictory positions as well as more familiar, comfortable ones, listening deeply before reaching conclusions.[19]

We need to free others up to be able to challenge our ideas or opinions. Being willing to listen and possibly change our minds builds up rather than reduces people's trust in us,[20] encouraging them to do the same with others, generating a culture of mutual respect and openness.

Sustainable life balances and boundaries

Hurry is not of the devil; hurry is the devil.
– Carl Jung[21]

IT IS EASY to overstretch when it feels like important issues are at stake. Peter's past research highlighted again a critical issue for those in people-related or caring professions: the dangers of burnout and emotional exhaustion.[22] Making a significant difference in the lives of others is rewarding, but can lead us to forget our own needs, hoping to recharge our batteries later. While possible for short periods, 'compassion fatigue'[23] will catch up eventually, leaving us overcommitted, overextended and exhausted, seriously impairing our contribution to others.

Burnout is a state of physical, emotional and mental exhaustion marked by depletion and fatigue. It can cause feelings of helplessness and hopelessness, lowering self-esteem and generating negative attitudes to work, life and other people.[24] Our exhaustion, in turn, can affect family and friends, and cause us to lose perspective.

And, at different points, all three of the authors have experienced this personally. It can happen for many reasons. For Peter, a combination of perfectionism and a need to help others makes it hard to say no. Naomi and Sophie, unable or unwilling to delegate, just wear out. Many would-be rescuers create over-dependency that then breaks them. It can be caused by fatigue or frustration brought about by devotion to a cause that doesn't generate enough sustaining energy.[25]

Consider a rubber band. Apply some stress and it will stretch but return to normal when the stress is gone. Too much stress and the rubber band will snap, creating permanent damage. Positive stress can stretch us, help us reach for goals and give us energy to move forward, but too much stress for too long can break us.

Building balance in life

- Have a contingency plan to allow for blowouts, unforeseen circumstances, extra demands or increased complexity.

- Pace yourself. Life is a long distance race, not a sprint.

- Ask others to keep you accountable to your life priorities, and thus more likely to deliver on them.

- Celebrate the moment. To rewrite the words of Ecclesiastes: "For everything there is a season, a time for action and a time for reflection, a time to run and a time to rest, a time for work and a time for play. There is also a time to celebrate."

Figure 13.2 Building balance in life

So here is another leadership paradox: *effective and sustainable leadership for others also requires self-care*. We need to learn that we actually matter, and develop a leadership approach that upholds the value of people, including ourselves.

Addiction to rushing is one of the curses of this age. Caught up in a flurry of activity, rushing to achieve and accomplish, we have little time for reflection or self-care. On a treadmill of busyness, we overload ourselves with too much to do and too little time. Most organisations we know are significantly shaped by this.

Yet as individuals we must choose how to swim in whatever pressures, busyness, or chaos we find ourselves. We can mindfully act with purpose, build balance and set boundaries, something emergency teams practice and execute on a daily basis. Even small things like limiting when we open work emails, or a time of quiet before opening them can provide perspective.

Sustainability requires us to develop a balanced life with well-defined boundaries. We need to know our limits and balance our lives so that, if one aspect becomes difficult, other aspects can sustain us. Peter's research identified higher levels of emotional exhaustion among the overly busy, those having difficulty finding time for recreation, holidays or days off, who found it hard separating work from the rest of their lives.[26] While possible in emergencies, we must not get so involved in serving others that we neglect ourselves, our families, friends and other interests. However important our work, it is not all we are. Workaholism carries connotations of addiction. It can ruin relationships, wear us out and cause us to lose sight of who we really are.

It is important to erect and defend a perimeter around the private spaces in our lives.[27] Take time off, avoid unrealistic expectations, be clear about our roles and have a life away from them. This self-discipline is important for our wellbeing. It is not selfish, but essential to offering sustainable leadership long term.

Someone commencing a busy new role asked a friend for advice about starting out. After a long pause her friend replied: "You must ruthlessly eliminate hurry from your life." Not satisfied, she asked again. The reply came again: "Ruthlessly eliminate hurry."[28]

Summary

How do I best make my contribution?

Act with integrity and authenticity

DURING DIFFICULT, CONFUSING and pressured challenges we need to recognise the importance of learning to live and act with integrity in open, balanced ways.

It is critical to be transparent in our dealings with others and open to new ideas and possibilities. Aim to offer our best and, as a result, draw the best from those around us.

There needs to be a congruence between who we are and how we live. Express this by living a balanced life, characterised by good boundaries. Intentionally make space for this personal work. It is something we all need to do if we hope to contribute well and make a positive difference.

Reshaping practice 13

Actions for you

Ask yourself: When are you tempted to put on a mask rather than be yourself? Why? How is it helpful? How might this be a sign that something in the culture needs to change?

In what ways are you able to be transparent? When are you tempted to be less so? What allies or resources do you have to resist pressure to be inauthentic? How open are you to hearing ideas from others that might challenge your own thinking?

Consider the boundaries you have in place around work. Open your diary for the next week. Think of an action you can take that will add to balance in your life. Schedule it. Do it.

Actions for your team

Identify: Where are the less heard voices in your organisation? How can you give these voices more space? How might you develop a culture where people are more able to express openly their thoughts and feelings to the people impacted by them?

We often claim to value authenticity, but create organisational cultures that make it unrewarding or unsafe for people to be honest. In what ways can your organisation create processes and cultures in which people can be more authentic?

Chapter fourteen

Building our personal foundations

How can I stay on course
when strong winds blow?

WHEN LOST, WHETHER in a wilderness or big city, a compass or GPS can be a lifesaver. Similarly, when faced with pressure, difficult questions or decisions, strong personal foundations are critical to keeping us on course.

Robert is a late thirties Indigenous man. Born in a remote community in South Australia he spent time in Sydney's inner city and married a Pacific Islander. Several years ago, with children, they chose to go back to his remote community to contribute as community liaison officers, helping local people connect with wider social services and opportunities. They became significant bridge people.

This was an important decision, he said. *You can't underestimate the importance of story or place in life.* Robert made this decision based on his values and meaning systems, his sense of place in the universe. Given the many Indigenous people leaving remote communities for cities, here is someone whose sense of meaning and purpose moved him in the opposite direction.

Many people who have positively influenced our lives in the last hundred years - people like Nelson Mandela and Martin Luther King Jr. – built strong personal foundations on spiritual, philosophical or religious systems of one sort or another that nourished them, and provided compasses and anchors to keep on course.

Anchor yourself with strong personal foundations

- Solid core values
- Clarity of purpose
- Strong meaning foundations
- Quality relationships

Figure 14.1 Anchor yourself with strong personal foundations

This chapter explores the importance of developing strong personal foundations to effectively face challenging situations, when strong winds blow. It invites you to explore the following four questions:

- **Solid core values:** what are the values that guide you? Where have they come from?
- **Clarity of purpose:** what really matters to you in life? How should you live this out?
- **Strong meaning foundations:** how do you make sense of life, or see your place in the universe?
- **Quality relationships:** who are the key people who are your reference community? Who are your strongest personal supports?

Solid core values

If a man hasn't discovered something he will die for, he isn't fit to live.

– Martin Luther King[1]

OUR CORE VALUES provide frameworks for acting and decision-making, for how and when we contribute leadership at work and in our lives. Here are some examples of core values: 'equal rights for all', 'excellence deserves reward', 'people should be treated with respect'.

What are your core values?

Core values will vary across people and cultures. They are instilled in us from childhood through cultural, religious or social influences, but also through our own growing discernment as we mature. Peers, mentors, family and friends will all somehow influence them.

Our values should affect our actions, and be apparent in our behaviour and choices. For example, those who value altruistic behaviour should be more altruistic in their actions.

We may hold core values about outcomes (the importance of world peace, freedom, self-respect, happiness), or about how to live (cheerfulness, forgiveness, self-control, honesty, etc).[2] To be effective in leadership we need both: strong ultimate values that identify our destination and core principles to guide how we act to get there.[3] We need to know what we stand for, if we are to stay the course in the face of pressure.

Solid core values will reveal to us the gap between what is and what could be, perhaps indicating places in which to act and/or contribute leadership? What matters enough for us to act, or go against the grain of inertia, fear or self-interest? Where do we feel compelled to contribute?

It is easy to be swayed by strong voices.

Practised in using four-wheel drives in difficult situations, Naomi provided a support vehicle for a team on motorbikes travelling to Cape York. They brought their own approach to tricky situations: in a tricky situation hit the accelerator and see what happens.

Generally careful in her approach, Naomi felt pressure to act against her better judgement, negotiating river crossings or hill climbs without stopping to assess them. The pressure and jests slowly wore down her self-confidence and convictions. Near the end of the trip she buckled to pressure and, against her own judgement, in a water-covered muddy section, just went for it. The vehicle instantly sank in the mud with water up to the door handles. No amount of revving or reversing would budge it. For Naomi it was a harsh lesson in the importance of trusting her own values and holding her ground in the face of social pressure.

Clarity of purpose

WHEN ALICE IS in Wonderland in the Lewis Carroll novel, she comes to a fork in the road. There the Cheshire Cat skulks in a nearby tree.

"Which road should I take?" she asks.

"Do you know where you want to go?" says the Cheshire Cat.

"No," says Alice.

"Then any road will get you there."[4]

Many of us yearn to live lives that make a positive difference but struggle to discover direction, or to hold course in challenging times. We wrestle with questions about purpose: just what are *important life purposes for me?*

Nelson Mandela had a strong sense of purpose, stating in 1964:

I have dedicated my life to this struggle. I have fought against white domination, and black domination. I have cherished the ideal of a democratic and free society in which all persons live together in harmony. It is an ideal, which I hope to live for, and to achieve. But my Lord, if needs be, it is an ideal for which I am prepared to die.[5]

Is there anything you would die for?

Sometimes life events shape our sense of purpose. Tony Trimingham was a typical middle-class baby boomer with a family seeking to live the Australian dream. When his son died of a drug overdose, Tony committed his life to raising awareness about drug dependency and assisting those who had suffered similar losses. Through this he renewed his direction and meaning in life, which helped him deal with his pain and loss.

Other times it is less about a blinding purpose and clear summits to strive for, and more about general directions to travel.

Groups need clear shared purposes if they are to achieve them. A sense of our own life purposes is just as important. Indeed, to come alongside groups to develop shared purposes, we need to be clear on our own personal purposes in it. What really matters to us? If we are unclear on them we can easily be caught off guard, led astray, or left confused and disillusioned[6]. Clarity of purpose can sustain us when times are tough, energise us for action and keep us focussed.

A sense of purpose is an important internal compass and reference point as we seek new ways forward. Writing on authenticity, Bill George extends this image by inviting people to discover their 'true north': a fixed point in a changing world. This is about who we are at our deepest levels, our most cherished values, passions, motivations and the source of satisfaction in our lives.[7] Discovering purpose is a journey where at times there is intense clarity and times when the fog rolls in.

Purpose and wellbeing

CLARITY OF PURPOSE can be a pathway to greater wellbeing. How might this work?

We sometimes pursue pleasure, and presume it will lead to happiness. Society and marketing often suggest happiness comes from buying that new car or the latest fashion… but enduring happiness is unlikely to be found at the shopping centre.

Such 'mis-wanting' can seriously disappoint.[8] Research suggests those who most value wealth, excitement and success can be less likely to experience wellbeing in a range of ways. Beyond a certain level, happiness measures do not increase as countries become richer. Research suggests lottery winners are happier at first, but soon elation wears off and, with the pressures of instant wealth, they often become less happy.[9]

Positive psychologists like Martin Seligman suggest happiness is less about smiling faces and more about the extent our lives are spent on things that really engage us and have wider meaning. They identify three aspects to happiness: *pleasantness, engagement* and *meaning*.[10] If asked whether they are happy today, people may consider whether the day has been *pleasant* or fun. Asked about their happiness over months, people tend to consider deeper issues of *engagement* and *meaning*. Living an *engaged* life means being fully absorbed in doing things we have aptitude and enthusiasm for. Living a *meaningful* life involves contributing from our strengths to larger purposes beyond ourselves that matter to us.[11] They see wellbeing as flowing from living an engaged and meaningful life, from discovering our strengths, and finding opportunities to use them meaningfully towards our core purposes.

Peter's research in the wider Australian community supports this: people with clarity of purpose are more likely to help and trust others, volunteer or get involved in social issues.[12] Living out our purposes can improve our wellbeing because we feel we are making a meaningful contribution. It is associated with higher levels of self-esteem, optimism and life satisfaction.

Strong meaning foundations

WHERE DO OUR core values come from? What might guide our clarification of purpose? The answer to this may be many and varied: from the influence of family, peers, religion, political philosophy, the revolution (whichever revolution), or a mix of the above. However we have constructed them, our meaning foundations - how we see our place in the universe - can help us develop values, purpose, identity and place in the world, providing a solid foundation on which to live. Or not.

While in times past how we made sense of life was largely inherited via religion, ethnic identity or family background, in contemporary society individualism has made making sense of life much more of a personal project.[13] To understand the meaning threads of contemporary society we need to consider "not just the temples but also the market place".[14]

Many who have contributed inspirational leadership have drawn on a strong spiritual base: Wilberforce or Shaftsbury in the ending of slavery, or Mother Theresa and Helen Keller, Martin Luther King, Desmond Tutu in facing down apartheid, or Indigenous people with their strong spiritual connections with the land.

But think too of religious, philosophical or political meaning systems that have justified war, terror, hatred, violence, sects or division. They too have been self-evident in any age: consider violence in Ireland, Bosnia, the Middle East and Africa.

It is almost as if this is a potentially powerful thread in life that can magnify passion, purpose and resolve…for good or ill. This thread is more important than we sometimes recognise.

Today meaning foundations are often a hidden thread weaving through the fabric of society and our lives together.

What difference might it make?

PETER WAS INVOLVED in a research project with Edith Cowan University and NCLS Research using national samples of Australians to explore how people make sense of life.

This research found that people approach questions of meaning differently. Some accept a framework uncritically or dogmatically. Others approach it more openly and reflectively, embracing its complexity.

But how might how we make sense of life make a difference to our wellbeing, or to how we might offer leadership? Research suggests several avenues.[15]

First, our meaning foundations can help with *sense of purpose*. Those reflectively exploring questions of meaning were likely to have greater clarity of purpose, in turn helping with life decisions and keeping on course in difficult times. Presumably this would extend to identifying when to contribute leadership.

Second, if developed reflectively, they can encourage us to *personal growth*, which in turn can help us with self-understanding about how we operate and make our contributions.

Third, solid meaning foundations can help build *personal optimism* and self-worth. Seeing ourselves as part of intricate ecosystems, with an unbreakable connection with the land, or as being created in God's image can build self worth and sense of place.

Fourth, they can encourage us to place importance on more *other-centred core values* (helpfulness, social justice or environment concerns etc.), rather than more personally focussed values (enjoyment, success, excitement etc.). The research suggested such values generally translated into lived actions (concern for others, charitable giving, volunteering, trust in people from other races or religions etc.).

Reflectively developing our sense of our place in the universe can be a path to greater authenticity, purposefulness and wellbeing, compared to either inattention to this or an uncritical or dogmatic approach. As a compass to guide us and anchors to hold us, solid meaning foundations can help us cope, discern, and offer constructive leadership. And, beyond wellbeing, they can help us with a bigger picture, a framework, affirming the value of staying with complexity and working alongside others for shared goals rather than alone.

The rally

Peter was involved in the early 1980s in a major conservation battle against hydro-electric development on the Franklin River in Tasmania. In a few years, rallies had grown from handfuls of people till, by 1983, thousands were marching in capital cities.

A sense of meaning was critical to promoting engagement.

At rallies apologetic government politicians would try to look sympathetic though their government sat idly by. Opposition politicians and unionists would rail angrily from the other side. But when a young Bob Brown stood up it was quite different. The tone changed. Rather than angry rhetoric there was a message of hope - something like the following:

We live on a fragile planet. Together we are making a change, making a difference for good. For the sake of our fragile planet and the inter-connected eco-systems we are part of, we need to stand up with values different to those behind the decisions being made for us.

The crowd listened, hushed, inspired to keep going against the odds. Here was someone speaking with a different logic about the spirit of the thing, providing a meaning framework for why it mattered, and how we should therefore act.

Getting beyond the conspiracy of silence

IN A RESIDENTIAL leadership program a range of people spoke about contributing leadership in demanding situations, and the challenges and complexity involved. It was interesting how many of the presenters were working from strong meaning foundations: religious or spiritual, Buddhist, Eastern or ecological, or a strong spiritual connection to land.

Yet as a group no-one ever talked about these deeper aspects of contributing leadership. The group fled the question, as did the speakers. So, when asked how they sustained themselves, many gave superficial responses, leaving the very thing that motivated and sustained them unnamed and private.

We often shy away from questions like: *Why do I do what I do? Where does my sense of purpose come from? Where do I find meaning for my life?* In other areas talking about things can be helpful, even life-giving. So why not in this one?

It might feel too hard, divisive or scary. We may be faced with our own mortality, our worst fears and insecurities. We might lack a shared language to use. So we avoid this potentially vital area of who we are.

Helping a team develop a framework of *meaning* for their actions can be a vital, life-giving contribution. So why would it be different for us personally!

Like any challenge requiring adaptive responses, we don't need all the answers to engage the questions. What we need is a climate of respect and listening, and an openness to learning from others with different perspectives.

It is all too easy to let this go in the face of the seemingly urgent. But there may be dangers and losses in doing so. Certainly contemporary thinking is starting to take such concerns more seriously. Sometimes we need to cut out the clamour and noise of life to hear whispers from our depths.

Quality relationships

Being unwanted, unloved, uncared for, forgotten by everybody, I think that is a much greater hunger, a much greater poverty than being the person who has nothing to eat.

– Mother Theresa[16]

JUST AS TREES need fertile soil and a healthy ecosystem, we too need quality relationships and a nurturing context to flourish.

We generally learn and grow alongside others. Relationships are integral to our personal wellbeing and effective functioning, bringing out our individual gifts and helping us make sense of life. If isolated from our reference community it is harder to deal with struggles and get perspective.

We are strongly influenced by our upbringing, families, peers, schooling, contexts and communities we are part of. It is important to take time to build friendships and primary relationships, work at parenting, and find space for non-work activities.

All relationships matter as part of the stable mix in which we live and grow: acquaintances, colleagues, casual and closer friends, and our closest connections with whom we share our deepest hopes, thoughts, feelings and fears.

Similarly, quality relationships within teams are also vital. They need to be built on the basis of clear communication, mutual learning and integrity, balanced with appropriate boundaries. Those willing to positively interact and grow within the life of their group develop a more sustainable and life-giving role.[17]

Tough truth-tellers

IN RESEARCH WORK Peter was involved with, people were asked whether they had someone in their lives who encouraged and supported them, and with whom they could be completely honest. Such people can be tough truth-tellers. Those without such a person generally recorded lower levels of wellbeing, and higher levels of emotional exhaustion.[18]

The more responsibility we hold, the greater the need for strong relationships and tough truth-tellers around us. They can be incredibly supportive and honest, challenge us, help us curb toxic behaviours and provide important perspective. To help us grow and live authentically – and to contribute leadership effectively – such people are critical.

Yet times of challenge or difficulty can push those in leadership towards isolation and loneliness.[19] At the time when they most need support and perspective from others, they become more isolated.

It's worth taking time to build and nurture these relationships before they are needed, so they can sustain us when pressure hits. Too often we take such people for granted, cutting corners with them. That can be dangerous!

Finding shelter in a storm of change

After a promotion, Sylvie became the brunt of teasing and bullying by a tight group of colleagues, marginalised and ignored in meetings and in the staffroom. Surprised and wounded by this, she went to some friends outside of work for support and ways forward. They reaffirmed her purpose for accepting the promotion (to be able to make a greater difference to the operations of the organisation and have more opportunities to innovate). This gave her renewed perspective, energy and clarity to plan a new approach to working with her team.

Summary

How can I stay on course when strong winds blow?

Anchor yourself with strong personal foundations

It doesn't interest me what you do for a living. I want to know what you ache for and if you dare to dream…I want to know what sustains you from the inside when all else falls away. I want to know if you can be alone with yourself.

– Oriah (**Mountain Dreamer**)[20]

Growing our personal foundations can help us stay on course in the face of pressure, criticism or challenge. We need to continually refine our core values, life purposes and sense of our place in the scheme of things, working on them well before they are needed or tested.

Likewise it's important to develop quality relationships to hold us in our work and lives. We need supporters, but also tough truth-tellers who care about us enough to speak the truth in love.

Together these can provide a sound basis for effective living and leadership.

Reshaping practice 14

Actions for you

How clear are you on what you most value? Why do these values matter? Where do they come from?

How clear are you about your core life purposes? How much are they about end-goals or the direction of travel?

How have you sustained yourself in difficult situations? Who or what did you draw on in these times to anchor and guide you?

Can you express in a few words how your meaning foundations help give meaning to your life?

With whom can you be very honest? Who is it who understands you, and you feel encouraged and supported by? How can you build those relationships?

When did you last ask for, give or receive quality feedback?

Actions for your team

We spend much of our lives at work, yet often keep private our personal hopes, values and thoughts. How might it feel in your team to share more of your personal values, purposes and hopes? How appropriate do you feel it would be?

To what extent do you think members of your work team are fulfilling personal purposes by contributing to collective purposes at work? How might you talk about this together?

Personal foundations need to be nurtured. How might you help everyone in your team to do this?

Chapter fifteen

Self-awareness: the lifelong journey

How do I realise my true potential?

SELF-AWARENESS IS CORE to authenticity, and can help us develop our capacities, resilience and relationships. How can we grow such self-knowledge?

Joan Baez has been well known since the 1960s for her passionate social conscience and a rich beautiful voice. She is an example of someone who has lived a lifetime with a clear sense of personal purpose, and a willingness to go against the grain to live out her values. Her life has been one of both artist and activist.

Baez went through a period of not performing or recording for various reasons, one being that as she aged her voice changed, becoming more restricted. Visiting a specialist to see what could be done she was offered important advice: her vocal chords were exactly as they should be, healthy but changing over time. He suggested she accept her new sound, relax and find ways to settle into her current voice, continuing to use it to speak and sing about things that mattered.

Finding our authentic voice in leadership is a similar lifelong process of discovering who we are, then developing skills and practices to express this fully. Baez describes her voice now as having a tone that carries all of her many years of life, her struggles, disappointments and successes and the wisdom she's gained. So too does *our* leadership when it is authentic.

We can always profit from a better understanding of ourselves: what we have to offer, what drives us, who we are, and how to live. A costs/benefits analysis of developing self-awareness is clear. Drawing on his actuarial background, company director and executive coach Ian Pollard sees it as a precious opportunity where the gains massively outweigh any possible losses.

Often we feel too busy to devote time to personal development and growing self-awareness. Yet nothing is more important if we want to contribute effectively.

> **Consistently make time to grow self-awareness**

Figure 15.1 Realising our potential

Toxic leadership and toxic relationships

A LACK OF self-awareness can have devastating consequences, leading us to behave dangerously, particularly if we start to be driven by deep, personal needs. It can have consequences both for us and people or causes we aspire to serve. Knowing and managing our dark sides is critical.

What happens when these needs start driving our leadership practice? Consider these examples.

Craving significance

RICHARD WAS THE son of a pastor in a large church. Through his role in the church as a songwriter and music leader he influenced thousands.[2] One day he announced he had cancer and urged his followers to pray for him. Devastated, the entire community rallied around him, caring for him, raising money and praying. Richard battled on, sharing details of his medical progress and test results, and writing songs about his journey. The wide reach of his church meant he had global impact as he battled his illness.

The trouble was, none of it was true. Richard did not have cancer. He had invented the entire scenario to hold the hearts of a huge community and to avoid dealing with deeper personal issues. He deceived his family, making fake hospital trips and writing fake emails to doctors, even appearing on stage with oxygen and breathing equipment as he talked about his illness. Finally, two years after his cancer was supposedly diagnosed, he publically admitted to his deception, devastating everyone. He told a television reporter "I have told too many people how they should live their lives. And the last two years have been hell for me both physically and emotionally. I am plagued with guilt."

It had not been a premeditated hoax, but just fell into place step-by-step. Needing to feel significant and to avoid dealing with unresolved issues in his life Richard found himself slowly sinking deeper. Lacking self-awareness his needs drove him on, eventually leaving him at rock bottom. Only then could he finally face his demons and rebuild.

Success at any cost

GREAT SPORTS PEOPLE need to be talented, but also gifted with persistence and resolve, creating an overwhelming desire to succeed.

Consider Lance Armstrong, a cyclist with outstanding abilities and the drive to be the best in the world. His desire was so great that he went beyond the laws of his sport to maintain his position, creating a web of lies and deception to maintain his position… till it tumbled down.

His desire to succeed had taken over, with devastating consequences to him, cycling and to those who believed in him. A toxic mix of a 'win-at-all-costs' attitude and a weak moral compass cost him deeply.

Refusal to delegate

MANY FIND IT hard to delegate: they fear appearing lazy, have a need to control, or simply enjoy the affirmation from over-achieving. You probably know someone like Sandra, a super-efficient manager who prided herself on fully delivering on every task. A sign above her desk displayed the slogan: 'If you're looking to get a job done, ask a busy person'.

When her manager recruited an assistant for her, Sandra struggled to hand over even the simplest of tasks, fearing a drop in standards in what she delivered. An unhelpful, long term pattern of over-achieving to gain personal affirmation prevented her from being able to make space for her assistant, or get value from her.

Hunger for attention

SEAN WAS A member of a large family placing great importance on doing something significant in life. At his birth his mother had a dream about his future greatness. In adulthood he became involved in the theatre and became the centre of attention, meeting his needs for significance.

Sadly, he allowed these needs to spill into all his life, behaving at work as if still onstage, needing to be the centre of attention. Colleagues put up with it, complaining later that he never listened, and avoided involving him whenever possible. Though gifted, overblown childhood expectations diminished the value of his contributions and his wellbeing.

An unregulated need to serve

AMY GREW UP in a family where someone had mental illness they sought to conceal. The dominant message was that putting on a good show could be more important than truthfulness. Dishonesty became normalised.

This generated patterns of seeking self-worth by being overly helpful. Listening and caring was one of her strengths so she would seek out people with deep needs. She could not say "no" because saying "yes" met her own inner needs. Often her apparent helping actually created dependence, and others would avoid dealing with their real issues, a 'loss-loss' situation.

Toxic co-dependency, helping rather than being truly helpful, can become addictive.[3] Growing self-awareness led Amy to work hard on her issues and, as a result, disappointed some who sought dependency on her. She also had to face internal voices pushing her to be a helper to bolster her self-esteem.

A need to control

IN 2007 KEVIN Rudd was elected Australian Prime Minister. Initially very popular, over time things started to go wrong within the party. Rudd was criticised for controlling behaviour, poor interpersonal skills and an indifferent manner with those around him. History has shown the cost of this to Rudd, his party and advocates. He was replaced as Prime Minister, with many senior colleagues refusing to serve under him. He and others paid a heavy price.

Toxic co-dependency

IN 1978 OVER 900 members of the People's Temple in Jonestown committed suicide at the the instruction of Jim Jones, possibly the greatest loss of American civilian life in a non-natural disaster till September 11 2001.

Even in less dramatic circumstances highly damaging consequences can flow from unhealthy co-dependency. Strong, controlling leadership may be of short-term use in a crisis, but can open up a space for power-needy people to move in with their toxic practices. Because we seek to borrow someone's strength in a crisis, we hand them control. Once in place toxic leadership is difficult to remove.[4]

Toxic leadership situations result from collusion between power-needy people and those seeking rescue. Far from servant leadership, those offering leadership act out of their own needs, from their shadow sides, while those accepting it are often avoiding taking responsibility for their own situations.

Given powerful needs operating under the surface, it is easy to become enmeshed in toxic relationships. Without recognising how our needs drive us, our unmet unmanaged needs can bleed into our leadership practices, creating havoc. As human beings we have almost unlimited capacty of self-deception, to avoid facing deep issues about ourselves.[5]

What is the alternative? The antidote to toxicity and collusion is *self-awareness*. We need to know ourselves well if we are to make effective, authentic leadership contributions.

Developing self-awareness

Without reflection, we go blindly on our way, creating more unintended consequences and failing to achieve anything useful.

– Margaret Wheatley[6]

THE DIRECTOR OF an organisation believed they needed to be more open to new ideas. He realised his way of cutting people off, of not seeking their opinions was adversely affecting their culture.

Yet changing this was far from straightforward. Deep down he needed to have things done his way, to have all the answers, to bolster his identity and worth. Beyond learning to respond differently he would have to wrestle with his deeper self.[7]

We can only contribute effective leadership if our own house is in order. This involves identifying and working with our strengths, but also *acknowledging their shadow sides*.

Sophie's strength of perseverance, for example, can lead her to stick at a task long past the point of productivity, grinding herself and the project into staleness. With self-awareness she can choose to act differently.

What are some pathways to growing self-awareness? We can observe *how we act* in the world, *how we relate* to others and more deeply at *who we are*. We can try to identify deeper issues or defence mechanisms working against changes that might be needed. We can see this as our own internal adaptive challenge, involving both action and reflection.

We need to face the challenges within us to better face the challenges before us.

Here are some practical ways of making growing self-awareness a life priority.

1. Take a mindful approach: Contemporary leadership development thinking increasingly emphasises the importance of mindfulness as a foundation for effective relationships and contributions.[8] Mindfulness is about paying more attention to what is happening around us and within us.[9] Michael Bunting defines it as *maintaining an openhearted awareness of our thoughts, emotions, bodily sensations and the environment around us, paying attention to what is happening in the present moment.*[10] It is about being more attuned moment-by-moment to both the responses of others, but also to our own feelings, thoughts and motivations. We can observe how we make meaning out of life and our experiences,[11] getting better perspective on who we are at every step.

The starting point for this is to take some balcony time.

What might that look like? Here is one person's response after an extended desert retreat: *For me the challenge is to take the desert home with me: stopping and making space for that which really matters and living at a pace that allows for exploration. I need to be gritty in discovering more fully who I am and how to make a difference with my life. I must more fully trust my own heart.*[12]

Balcony time can be an extended retreat as in this case, or shorter regular times in meditation, prayer, writing a journal, gardening, painting, surfing or other activities. An intimate discussion can be a balcony moment if it generates introspection, slowing us to reflect on what matters.[13]

Many spiritual/meaning traditions include times alone, something also important in some leadership development programs. Outward Bound, for instance, develops resilience not just by pushing people to their limits on rock faces, but also by requiring them to spend several nights and days alone in the wild. Deeper reflection on life, hopes, struggles, pain, and purposes are typical outcomes from such times alone in self-reflection.[14]

At the end of a time of retreat a participant noted:

I walked, I fasted, but above all was quiet enough for long stretches to reconnect with my more radical, passionate and idealistic sides. My question was: 'What in me has to change so I can offer more effective leadership in my life, work and community?'[15]

We need to develop *ongoing cycles of action and reflection*, taking risks in moving forward then reflecting on what we have learnt. Slowly core priorities and ways to possibly live them out start to emerge.

2. Be willing to be vulnerable: To grow, we need to make room for honest reflection on difficult issues. We often flee painful issues; the more something scares us, the less likely we are to engage it.

Yet, as was explored in the previous chapter, it is vital to face such issues, to work them through with others who support us unconditionally but are willing to be tough truth-tellers. Our vulnerability and humanity doesn't disqualify us for leadership, it is a vital source for its authenticity.

One of Peter's mentors spent almost a lifetime in a mutual mentoring relationship. No matter how busy they were (and they were busy people) they would make the time to share deeply with each other, and keep each other on course.

Showing vulnerability – Helena's story

Helena is a refugee in her 70s. The combined challenges of her previous life and adjusting to a new culture and country left her an alcoholic. Eventually, desperate for help, she went to Alcoholics Anonymous (AA). The group included people from diverse backgrounds and was a place where everyone could be open, take risks and be vulnerable. The atmosphere of encouragement and challenge enabled people to move forward and, if they failed, to pick themselves up again.

For decades this group has been a critical part of Helena's growth. She says now she could not have survived without the ability to show her vulnerability and receive the support of the group. They became her anchor and compass.

3. Explore our edges and 'stretch zones': Early in World War II, Kurt Hahn was commissioned by the Royal Navy to understand an unusual phenomenon. When naval ships went down in the freezing North Sea, many sailors died. But surprisingly older sailors in their forties were more likely to survive than seemingly fitter younger ones.

Hahn concluded older sailors survived because they had been through more, knew better how to marshal their capacities, were more self-aware, and clearer about what they had to live for. Younger sailors hadn't yet developed the resilience that comes with experience.[16]

Resilience is about learning how far our rubber bands can stretch before they break. We all operate freely in our comfort zones. We also have a panic zone in which we become paralysed. Between these lies a *stretch zone*, in which we can work and grow. The challenge is to expand our comfort zones by taking calculated risks in our stretch zones, that will stretch us but not break us.

Sophie always saw a morning jog to the bus as a stretch. But by joining a local running club and building supportive friendships there, she set herself small enough goals in fun runs to be now training for a half-marathon. What seemed impossible is now quite plausible.

By taking on challenges, both individuals and the groups develop competence, confidence, capacity and character that can then be used in many other settings. It is about working out what is a safe risk, and having people around to support us to learn from the journey.

Building *resilience* is central to empowering people to flourish. Pacing change and balancing risk and safety well is critical to strengthening self-belief. Through incremental stretching we gain clearer perspective on our strengths and their boundaries.

We all have untapped capacity. The challenge and often the joy is to find it, tap it and help others do the same. Regularly going to our edges can consolidate our centre.

Seeing others in a new light

Over the years New River workshops have been richest when people from diverse backgrounds come together. One included members of an organisation which, the previous week, was involved in a public protest outside Parliament House. Passers-by heckled them, making it a very public altercation, providing colourful news footage.

At the workshop, protesters and one of the hecklers found themselves in the same room to learn together! The workshop started with frosty silence. Yet as the day went on small group conversations opened up communication. With careful listening and some levels of respect, people started to recognise depth in each other. A turning point came when a protester invited the heckler to have lunch with him.

By day two the heckler said publicly she had valued getting to know and better understand the protesters. The protesters also better understood her passion, its basis and the leadership contribution she was seeking to make.

Differences still existed but everyone had learnt how to engage constructively with difference, how to listen deeply and ask useful provocative questions to build understanding. A difficult situation had become a valuable learning experience.

4. Get perspective from others: Being completely immersed in something can make it difficult to get perspective. Because we are all capable of self-deception we need others to assist us in self-discovery.

If you want to know something about water, the last creature to ask is a fish!

As in the workshop story above, people from different backgrounds can help us question assumptions, even about ourselves. We all inherit ways of thinking or seeing ourselves. These go unquestioned till we meet people or organisations who think or act differently. This is the value of work exchanges, immersion visits to new contexts or communities of practice.

A psychological concept called the Johari window (Figure 15.2) highlights why this matters.[17] The window has four panes. Top left are the parts of us that we know and others know (our *public selves*). Bottom left are the parts of us we know that others don't know (our *private selves*). Top right are those aspects of us that others know about us yet we don't know about ourselves (our *unrecognised selves*). Finally bottom right are undiscovered parts of ourselves that neither we nor others know (our *undiscovered selves*).

Figure 15.2 The Johari Window

By revealing some more of ourselves to others we are likely to discover more about ourselves from them. Movement in any one pane changes every pane. As we reveal to others more about ourselves, they come to know more about us but, in their feedback, we are also likely to discover things about ourselves we didn't previously understand. It is a pathway to growth and self-awareness.

5. Work towards a more integrated self: Who we are might be quite different in our various roles in life. To what extent are we a different person at work, home, in the pub, with our parents or children?

While there will be aspects of who we are that will not surface equally in all contexts, authentic living (and leading) will be enhanced when our identities are congruent in each.[16]

Take the time to mindfully observe yourself in your different contexts. To what extent are you the same person, maintaining your sense of self in each? How much are you a different person, and why?

6. Reflect on our life stories: Our life stories shape us, and tell us a great deal about who we are and what matters to us. The stories we tell ourselves about ourselves will significantly shape our lives and actions.

Exploring them more deeply can be empowering, offering us new insights into who we are and why we act as we do. *Narrative therapy* is about exploring our personal stories and providing us the chance to choose to reshape our narrative and how we live.

We can describe our life stories in various ways.[18] One is by describing our natural progression through life, and key events or issues at different stages. Another is through identifying key themes such as overcoming the odds, finding a cause or learning from key experiences. However we describe it there is significant material for personal discovery and evaluation. Below are some useful starting questions:

- What key elements have shaped your life? Think about your parents and their contributions or disappearance from your life.
- Did you have early life crises? How did you resolve them?
- What pressures did you face from family or peers?
- What life events significantly shaped who you are? Consider relationships, travel, work experiences, roles or events.
- What experiences shaped how you understand leadership?

Often we have only developed *thin* stories about ourselves, *thin* because they have only one thread running through them. By way of example, a *thin* story could be someone describing themselves as always being late to things, and recounting many examples.

Sometimes it is important to try to *thicken* our stories.[19] Adding context and alternative perspectives to regular lateness, the person might recognise times they have not been late, or that they are often late because they stay at the previous commitment packing up, debriefing and planning. This can provide a broader more encouraging perspective and may point to deeper issues to work on.

In our work with New River we have found a number of techniques useful for exploring and refining our life stories in leadership, summarised in Figure 15.3.

- **Guided reflection.** Look at your life experiences, replay them in your mind and to others. This will help you re-examine them and draw lessons from them about your strengths, motives and values, getting you more in touch with your true self.

- **Draw a timeline.** Record major events and turning points on a time line, then reflect on what you see. The key is to notice what you recorded, and what you omitted.

- **Note the different spheres of your life.** Look at family, health, work, hobbies, goals, philosophies, the legacy you want to leave, and so on. Reflect on your aspirations in each area to see more clearly who you want to be. Often we put more effort into some spheres than others. Which ones are getting too much attention, which too little?

- **Your role models.** Who do you value and perceive as worth emulating? Understanding what makes them tick might help you better understand yourself.

- **Explore current issues or situations** to help you better understand your core values.

- **Legacy exercises.** Envision yourself at the end of your life, with all your family around you. One of your grandchildren asks, "How have you made a difference to the world?" How would you answer?

- **Examine your stories and experiences with leadership.** List key experiences then like a series of dots join them together to examine the story you tell yourself about you in leadership.

- **Other reflective exercises.** One useful exercise is to ask people who know you when they have seen you at your best. This will help you recognise your qualities and values. Or recall a time when you felt intensely alive and real. What was that like? What does that say to us about who you seek to be?

Figure 15.3 Possible ways of refining our life stories

Discovering ourselves in the context of others

Lily was a young woman brought up in a well-to-do neighbourhood, attended a private girls' school and quickly moved up the career ranks in education. She took every opportunity in life, travelling widely and experiencing the world.

As she matured, however, Lily began to question her place in the world, painfully realising she had little clarity about who she was, what drove her and her core values. Avoiding what she didn't like, rather than approaching what really mattered to her, had shaped her directions so far. With insecurity and vulnerability hidden under a tough exterior, she felt empty inside, defenceless when challenged or attacked.

A counsellor and key friends supported her to expand her sense of self and place in the world. With awareness came possibility: she could select people, activities and work to include in her life that strengthened her and connections with like-minded others, enabling her to open up to others her true self. She now feels like a 'fuller', better rounded version of herself, more centred and with clearer direction in life, and more able to make a positive contribution.

Summary

How do I realise my true potential?

Consistently make time to grow self-awareness

Think of your life as a house. Can you knock down the walls between each room and be the same person in each of them?

– **Bill George**[20]

BECAUSE LEADERSHIP AIMS to serve the deepest needs of a group, being well-grounded and self-aware is critical. A lack of a sense of self can lead us to behave in very toxic ways.

Self-awareness can make all the difference. It can provide a basis for flourishing and living constructively, for navigating uncertainty, unknown territory or unpredictable situations. They in turn can enable us to contribute more effectively to teams and organisations experiencing such complexity.

Indeed, effective leadership contributions will require an on-going commitment to personal development and growth. Realising our potential and growing the gifts we have is the work of a lifetime.

It takes hard work, time and committed energy, but can make a major difference to:

- the quality of our contributions;
- our wisdom in discerning how and when to make those contributions;
- the manner in which we contribute;
- the resources we have to sustain ourselves on the journey

It can be a critical gateway to better making a positive difference wherever we are. Exercising leadership is not just about our actions but also the transformations taking place within us as we take them.

Developing a more integrated self, and achieving greater congruity, may be a pathway to greater wellbeing and authenticity.

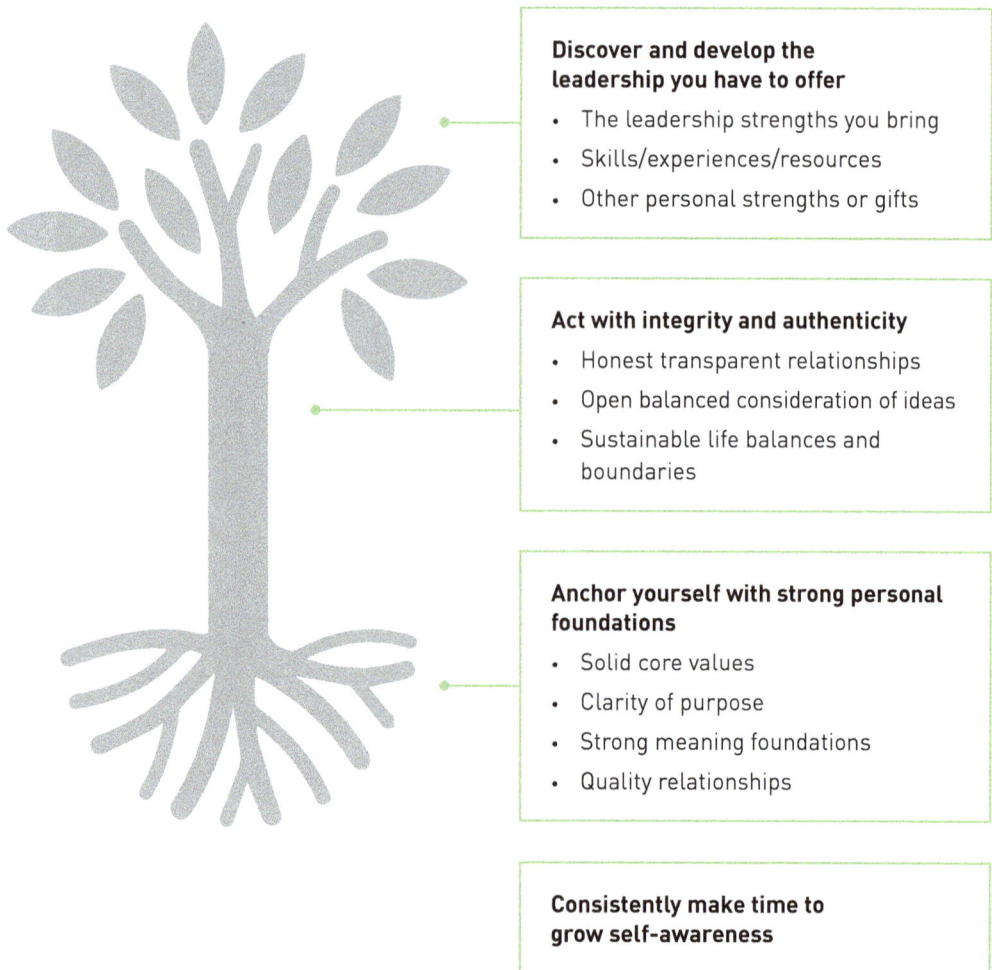

Discover and develop the leadership you have to offer

- The leadership strengths you bring
- Skills/experiences/resources
- Other personal strengths or gifts

Act with integrity and authenticity

- Honest transparent relationships
- Open balanced consideration of ideas
- Sustainable life balances and boundaries

Anchor yourself with strong personal foundations

- Solid core values
- Clarity of purpose
- Strong meaning foundations
- Quality relationships

Consistently make time to grow self-awareness

Figure 15.4 Contributing leadership effectively and sustainably

Reshaping practice 15

Actions for you

How could you expand the panes of your known and unknown self with trusted others in your life?

What are the shadow sides of your strengths? When are the times you could seek to satisfy your own needs by contributing ineffectively to a group?

What are some ways you take balcony time to observe and reflect on your life?

Who are the people with whom you can make yourself vulnerable? When was the last time you took a risk personally, trying yourself out in a new environment or with a new challenge? Did you take some time to reflect on the experience? What did you learn?

Has there been a time when you've stretched yourself beyond your comfort zone and surprised yourself with your capacity? What support do you need to bring more of those stretching opportunities into your life and the lives of others?

Actions for your team

How well does your organisation or team encourage members to develop their own self-awareness as part of their bigger life journey?

Look at the various practical ways of developing self-awareness discussed in this chapter. If people were prioritising these things in your team, what might be different? What is a first step in helping people in your team develop greater self-awareness?

Part 4

Epilogue
Surviving shipwrecks:
Who we are matters

Figure E4.1 Rethinking leadership – How can we each contribute authentically and sustainably?

HOW OFTEN WE start on a journey without realising how much we have to learn. That is typically the case with personal development. Much of growing our capacities in leadership is about cultivating our inner strength to stay true under fire: to ask important questions, stay balanced when things around us are turning upside down or when frustration and anger abound, to resist the temptation to slip into work avoidance.[2]

While in the final stages of completing this manuscript, two of us spent some time with Miriam-Rose Ungunmerr, a Northern Territory Indigenous Elder, as she shared some of the personal foundations on which she and her people build. For her, strength comes from surviving trials and challenges:

You are like a tree standing in the middle of the bushfire... The leaves are scorched and the tough bark is scarred and burnt; but inside the tree the sap is still flowing, and under the ground the roots are still strong. Like that tree, you have endured the flames, and you still have the power to be reborn.[1]

Each of us needs to develop strong personal foundations to sustain us through life's likely complexities. Who we are matters, and can dramatically affect how we act and what we can contribute. Careful, reflective internal reconstruction can provide us with resilience to survive the hard knocks, anchors to withstand storms and a compass to guide our actions. We each must face up to our own personal challenges and the work we ourselves have to do.

Ignoring the internal architecture of our lives is very dangerous. The strategy of dealing with the urgent and neglecting the important will quickly bring us unstuck. And, as we step through elements 12 to 15 of Rethinking Leadership we'll see how in challenging situations, such as those facing *Invercauld* survivors, it can have devastating outcomes.

For each of us: Turning leadership inside out

Following is a reflection on the final rethinking leadership steps, in the case of the *Invercauld*.

12. Discover and develop your leadership strengths, helping others do likewise: We must know well what we have to offer and how to best contribute our strengths constructively. We also need to help others on this journey. Dalgarno and senior *Invercauld* officers appear not to have recognised their own lack of basic survival capacities, or their need to leverage the leadership capacities of others around them.

Discovering and honing our capacities is an important step to making a meaningful contribution. No doubt each member of the *Grafton* team was stretched in discovering what he had to offer. A businessman and prospector, Raynal was tested in ways he could never have anticipated: yet by experimenting with new materials from wreckage and local resources in cabin, clothing or boat construction, he built and honed what he had to offer.

We each have the same opportunity.

13. Act with integrity and authenticity: While character flaws got in the way for many from the *Invercauld*, young Seaman Holding demonstrated strong personal character, sound core values and a desire to help the whole team survive. It appears to have been his unceasing purpose throughout the ordeal. He also demonstrated capacities in innovating and in strategising that helped the group survive.

Sadly, senior officers often seemed to resent his contributions, possibly due to their personal needs for status, respect or authority. When down to three in the final weeks of their ordeal, Dalgarno and the First Mate had serious falling-outs with Holding. For several weeks they had little to do with him, further reducing their overall capacity.[3] Character matters; it can and does make all the difference. The relational integrity of the *Grafton* team contrasts greatly with that of the *Invercauld* survivors. Comparing the two experiences it is evident how important matters of character are to effective leadership, and what a difference they can make. Perhaps it is no surprise that, while nobody was lost from the *Grafton* team, 22 of 25 of the *Invercauld* crew perished.

Effective leadership requires *seeking to* act with integrity, appropriately transparent in our dealings with others and open to new ideas and possibilities, offering ourselves at our best and drawing out the best from others.

14. Anchor yourself with strong personal foundations: As with the wrecks on the Auckland Islands, when a group is collapsing and conditions are steadily worsening, many individuals reach the point where selfishness overwhelms their commitment to the group.

While we do not know much about the motivations and foundations of those caught in the shipwrecks, two distinguishing features of these groups of castaways are the core values they carried as individuals and the shared culture they shaped as groups. The *Invercauld* core value seemed to be: *every man for himself*. Seaman Holding tried hard to reshape this culture towards the more collaborative, shared purpose of group survival, with little success.

By contrast, the core value of the *Grafton* survivors could be summarised as: *we all need to be at our best in this together*. Nowhere is this more obvious than in Captain Musgrave seeking to rescue the bedridden and feverish Raynal from the shipwreck rather than leaving him behind. Musgrave tied him on his back and carried him along a rope to shore.[4]

What might have happened had he not done so? How much innovative capacity would have been lost?

Yet was this a strategic decision, or a moral one? One indication of the moral character of a group is how it treats its weakest, most sick or injured members. On the *Grafton* Raynal had been so sick that at a previous port Musgrave dug a grave for him. Musgrave's decision was more than strategic.

Tom Page, a young sailor on the *Invercauld* was also unwell when it was wrecked. He was afforded no help, despite his pleas. With five others (including two teenagers) he was left to drown.[5] Too often leadership writing ignores this critical aspect of effective sustainable leadership.

We need to grow our personal foundations: our core values, life purposes and sources of meaning. These can hold us when loud voices yell or criticise, when winds of change blow or things get difficult.

15. Consistently make time to grow self-awareness: During the hardest times Captain Musgrave faced fears and guilt about abandoning his family back home and risking the lives of his crew. This may have spurred him on in trying to survive. Back home he experienced guilt and depression.[6]

From the *Invercauld* Holding framed it as an adventure and apparently suffered few ill-effects. Others were not so lucky: First Mate Smith went on to suffer pain and numbness in his legs. Captain Dalgarno aged greatly from the ordeal, was left in delicate health and could not talk about his experiences without bringing on a panic attack.[7]

We need to direct intentional effort into growing self-awareness. Long-term change is typically very demanding, requiring people who are ready and sustained for the journey. It will not just be an outward strategic contribution; we must always keep learning and growing ourselves, facing the internal work we need to do.

Strong foundations and resilience will emerge from a lifelong journey of mindful engagement, an oft-neglected aspect of leadership thinking.

Conclusion

Building capacity for positive change

Conclusion

Building capacity for positive change

Leadership is like the Abominable Snowman whose footprints are everywhere but is nowhere to be seen.

– Bennis and Nanus[1]

We can make a difference

THERE IS GREAT opportunity in these times to develop new ways of contributing leadership. We can choose to move away from cynicism, towards a more open and positive approach to change. Frustration with the status quo, complaints and grievances need to be transformed into energy for action and engagement. Disillusionment needs to be transformed into curiosity about new solutions. Feelings of powerlessness can also be transformed by discovering and valuing the power we do have. We can make the choice to contribute leadership.

Leadership matters

IN THIS BOOK we have looked at the turbulent world in which we find ourselves. We have explored the importance and nature of collaborative leadership and the range of leadership contributions a healthy group needs. We have also observed practices for building an agile culture that, once developed, can help us more effectively navigate the white water of change.

Finally, the need to understand better who we are, what we stand for and why has become evident, making growing self-awareness a daily priority for us all.

It's time to do leadership differently if we want outcomes more akin to those for the *Grafton* survivors than those from the *Invercauld*.

The following diagram maps out key aspects of effective and sustainable leadership.

Rethinking leadership: key steps

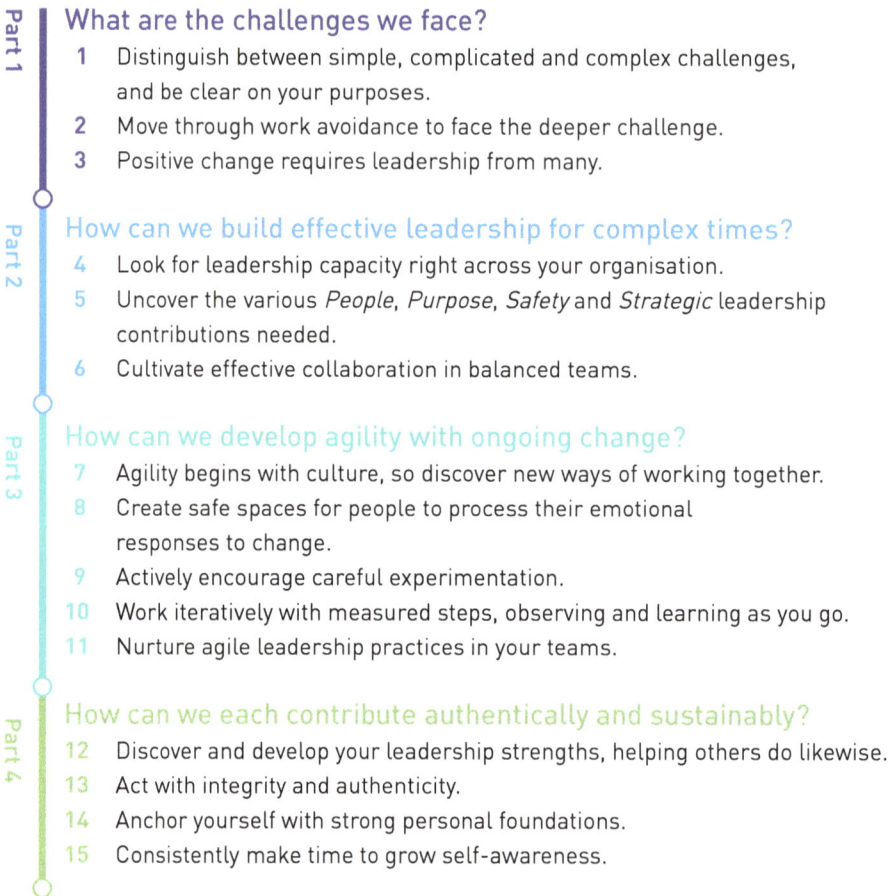

Part 1

What are the challenges we face?

1   Distinguish between simple, complicated and complex challenges, and be clear on your purposes.
2   Move through work avoidance to face the deeper challenge.
3   Positive change requires leadership from many.

Part 2

How can we build effective leadership for complex times?

4   Look for leadership capacity right across your organisation.
5   Uncover the various *People*, *Purpose*, *Safety* and *Strategic* leadership contributions needed.
6   Cultivate effective collaboration in balanced teams.

Part 3

How can we develop agility with ongoing change?

7   Agility begins with culture, so discover new ways of working together.
8   Create safe spaces for people to process their emotional responses to change.
9   Actively encourage careful experimentation.
10 Work iteratively with measured steps, observing and learning as you go.
11 Nurture agile leadership practices in your teams.

Part 4

How can we each contribute authentically and sustainably?

12 Discover and develop your leadership strengths, helping others do likewise.
13 Act with integrity and authenticity.
14 Anchor yourself with strong personal foundations.
15 Consistently make time to grow self-awareness.

Figure C.1 Rethinking leadership: key steps

Change is possible

A GROUP WITH which Peter was involved spent four days bushwalking through mist, rain and snow towards a mountain peak. On the way they saw nothing and navigation was tricky. Only minutes before they reached the summit they moved through the cloud cover and came out from the all-engulfing greyness to see a perfectly blue sky and a range of snow covered mountain peaks poking out to greet them. The half-hour on the summit will never be forgotten.

Helping groups move towards new possibilities in challenging situations is a bit like that. Achieving positive change in difficult situations is never going to be easy. It involves huge amounts of hard work, with limited visibility and tricky navigation. Moments of satisfaction seem few and far between, but when a group achieves an outcome there is little to surpass the sense of satisfaction at having made a positive difference. The joy of seeing the very issue, team or organisation you have laboured for move to a new place previously thought impossible is immense.

The good news is that change IS possible, new directions CAN be shaped, and core purposes can be lived out in new ways in a new era. Groups can reshape their cultures, families can change, grow and reconcile. Communities can be empowered and achieve goals and aspirations they hold dear. And, as individuals, we can generate adaptive responses to our own challenges, learning and growing from them and developing into the whole beings we are meant to be. Hard-won victories can provide energy, inspiration, self-esteem and hope to last a lifetime, and generate the hope we need to continue to make a difference.

Leadership is not a luxury item

SOMEWHERE ALONG THE line we decided as a society that leadership is a luxury item, attainable only by the special few. We developed an industry of high quality, proprietary training experiences and we put a high price tag on them to match. To walk through the door into the training room, you must be able to jump one of several hurdles: have enough money, and/or have a high enough position or social status.

What is behind these closed doors? Is it the world's best leadership thinking? Is it the most effective techniques for supporting change, managing resources, effectively navigating complexity, or developing authenticity in leadership and life? If it is then we need to ask the following question:

Why don't we want everyone to experience these ideas?

Why would we limit the number of people with this kind of knowledge, expertise and perspective? Surely, we want every member of our organisation or team to be operating with this kind of wisdom. This knowledge cannot be only for executives, directors, politicians and advisors at the top of their game. This knowledge is equally needed by teachers, small business operators, health professionals, social workers, community builders, volunteers, families, entrepreneurs, young people.

At a time where we are facing complex challenges on every front we need everybody to grow their leadership capacities.

An important starting question is: "where are we looking for leadership from?" Commonly the assumption is that it will come from the executive or CEO. That's where money is invested in leadership development and professional learning; all the leadership questions are asked at that level.

To unlock capacity, though, we must look more broadly: to front line people engaging clients, to those with fresh ideas or directions. Look for leadership across the whole organisation, as a responsibility and possibility for everyone.

That will change the conversation. If you send that message in a genuine way, it will create permission and mobilise contribution.

Who wouldn't want to live in a world where everyone knows what they can contribute and understands how to make that contribution effectively? Anybody with wisdom around leadership has a responsibility to the world to share it with anyone willing to learn.

If leadership is what a group needs to move forward on things that matter – then we cannot afford to limit it.

The questions we all must ask

THIS BOOK HAS been an invitation to explore four critical questions that we each need to face in order to make an effective contribution in leadership:

1. What are the challenges we face?
2. How can we build effective leadership for complex times?
3. How can we develop agility with ongoing change?
4. How can we each contribute authentically and sustainably?

The next step in *Rethinking Leadership* is to apply these ideas to your own context. On the following page is a practical tool for taking an intentionally deeper look at a complex challenge you face. There is space for you to respond to each of the above questions, noticing in particular the leadership capacity that could be built around you and ways in which your organisation or team can become more agile in their responses.

Completing this task is one way to begin integrating the key themes of this book into your own renewed leadership practice.

Rethinking challenges in your context

Rethinking _____

Describe your complex challenge

A. The complex challenge...

In a few sentences describe the situation or challenge to be faced. Look as deeply as you can at the elements requiring adaptive responses from you or others.

....

....

B. Growing and leveraging leadership capacity ...

In a few sentences describe what you see as key steps in growing and leveraging leadership capacity as widely as possible in your situation.

....

....

C. Developing agility...

In a few sentences describe what you see as key steps in growing each of the agility routines that might be needed for your teams to effectively engage these new or challenging situations.

Assess together: ....

....

Focus together: ....

....

Experiment carefully: ....

....

Build collaboration: ....

....

Implement strategically: ....

....

D. Contributing effectively, authentically, sustainably...

In a few sentences describe how you and those around you might need to grow to more effectively, authentically and sustainably engage the complex challenge you face.

....

....

....

Figure C.2 Rethinking challenges in your context

A final note

WE HOPE YOU have found the material in this book helpful, challenging and encouraging. Writing it has not been easy; it has been a long road from conception to completion.

But it has been immensely satisfying and we have stuck with it because we believe that it is important. Offering leadership is not easy, but it is extremely important, as the crew of the *Invercauld* wrecked on Auckland Island may well tell us with the wisdom of hindsight. It is critical for healthy individuals, healthy groups and healthy societies.

Our hope is that we have helped you look at leadership in a new light, to rethink what you have to contribute and where you feel compelled to contribute it. It is an invitation and a pathway to unlocking your leadership strengths and those of people in your teams and organisations.

In many ways, this book is simply a beginning, an invitation to shift your thinking. The real work lies in how you choose to live out these ideas, in your own leadership practice, sharing them with your team or using them as a framework for approaching a large change project or new initiative. As authors we look forward to continuing the conversation with you, hearing stories about the impact you are creating and how these ideas have helped you along the way.

Whatever complex challenges lie in your path, take courage and be confident in making your contribution. No matter what your role, it is vital to develop a leadership practice that is effective and sustainable across a lifetime. Exercise leadership where you believe it is important, and in ways that are life-giving.

Thank you...it has been a privilege to share the journey with you.

Appendix 1:
About NCLS Research

AT VARIOUS POINTS in this book we have drawn on research Peter was involved in between 1991 and 2007, primarily as director or senior researcher with NCLS Research.

Some of this research was based on NCLS/university partnerships designing large national sample surveys of Australians to investigate aspects of community life such as social capital, wellbeing, values and how people make sense of life. Large amounts of data were also collected from thousands of churches across Australia and overseas as part of the National Church Life Surveys, conducted every five years since 1991. Below is some background to this research.

Researching effective leadership in churches

CONTEMPORARY SOCIETY IS characterised by rapid and continuous change, increasing social diversity and lower confidence in social organisations. Many organisations need to rethink their place in a changing world, and churches are no exception. As can be imagined, such a process is far from straightforward, involving different perspectives, fear, creativity, reaction and unpredictability: a classic challenge requiring adaptive responses.

NCLS Research was established to do rigorous academic research to inform churches wanting to engage the challenges around them. It has carried out a National Church Life Survey every five years since 1991 involving both attenders and those in key roles in each participating church. Each cycle involves between 6,000-10,000 leaders and 500,000 church attenders from all denominations across Australia (and in 2001 from New Zealand, England and the US). This provided a great opportunity to do large-scale research into leadership in a particular type of not-for-profit organisation with some unique characteristics but also in other ways typical of voluntary community organisations generally.

In the mid 1990s there were requests to explore seemingly high levels of burnout among clergy and its causes. The result was research into areas such as healthy work practices, balance and boundaries, toxic church cultures, adequate personal foundations, authenticity and models of effective leadership in complex times.

Attenders and leadership completed surveys exploring the health and vitality of their church, their connections with the wider community and the nature of leadership in that church. The resultant database includes measures of:

A. styles of leadership in each church, from the perspectives of both those in key roles and attenders.

B. the vitality and health of each church.

C. the wellbeing of leaders, levels of emotional exhaustion and satisfaction with their roles.

D. the backgrounds and personalities of those in leadership, their personal foundations and the leadership strengths they bring.[1]

This provided a great opportunity for leadership research, allowing exploration of the styles most likely to be both effective and sustainable, and those that might leave people in danger of emotional exhaustion.

The research was designed in collaboration with Australian, US and UK academics, making use of established and reliable measures, and developing new scales for the project.[2] Wherever possible, multiple measures were used to triangulate results.

For further information, go to *www.ncls.org.au*.

Effective leadership in churches: What can we say?

NCLS RESEARCH SUGGESTS that, by and large, while positive about their churches, attenders are more concerned when they look to the future, many feeling their churches need to rethink where they are heading. They either see the challenge to be faced and are uncertain or anxious about how things will turn out, or they are unwilling to face the adaptive work involved.

Some findings about effective leadership from the research include:

1. Leadership matters: how leadership is exercised is important to the likely health and vitality of churches and their futures. It is more important than the personal background, education or personality of the senior leader or the type of church.

2. There is more to leadership than the senior leader: the overall leadership culture in a church is more important than the particular contributions of the senior leader. While the senior person may be important, more critical are the leadership capacities across the whole leadership team (and beyond). Leadership is a shared experience, a collaborative endeavour.

3. Those in leadership are not always aware of the strengths they bring: they need the perspectives of others to gauge their leadership strengths, rather than relying on their own assessments.

4. Vision and direction matters, but it must be owned: NCLS research in Australia and overseas suggests a clear, owned vision for the future to which members are committed is the most powerful predictor of likely vitality and health,[3] something true in our experience of organisations more broadly. However, developing a sense of vision and direction is easier said than done: most attenders are unaware of or not committed to, the vision of their church. A clear, owned vision for the future needs to consider their context, be positive and stretching, well thought out and achievable.

5. A wide range of leadership contributions are needed: this research highlighted a range of critical leadership contributions, as detailed in Chapter 5. Leadership is multi-faceted, hence the importance of collaborative leadership as discussed in Chapter 6.

6. No one person is likely to bring them all: the various leadership contributions needed are very personality dependent as discussed in Chapter 12. No-one will possess them all in equal proportion, with some coming more naturally and effectively than others. Self-knowledge is vital. Those in positions of responsibility need to put in place teams that bring the range of leadership contributions needed.

NCLS RESEARCH DATA files used in this research:

Castle, K., (2001) [computer file], 2001 NCLS Attender Survey A. NCLS Research, Sydney.

Castle, K., (2001) [computer file], 2001 NCLS Operations Survey. Sydney, Australia: NCLS Research.

Castle, K., (2001) [computer file], 2001 NCLS Leader Survey. Sydney, Australia: NCLS Research.

Castle, K., (2006) [computer file], 2006 NCLS Attender Sample Survey H, NCLS Research, Sydney.

Castle, K., (2006) [computer file], 2006 NCLS Attender Survey A. NCLS Research, Sydney.

Castle, K., (2006) [computer file], 2006 NCLS Operations Survey. Sydney, Australia: NCLS Research.

Kaldor, P., (1996) [computer file], 1996 NCLS Attender Sample Survey I. Sydney, Australia: NCLS Research.

Kaldor, P. (1996). 1996 NCLS Operations Survey, computer file. Sydney: NCLS Research.

References

Abrahamson, E. (2000). Change without pain. *Harvard business review*, *78*(4), pp. 75-81.

Achi, Z. and Garvey Berger, J. (2015). Delighting in the possible, *McKinsey Quarterly, 2*, pp. 90-99.

Ackoff, R. (1974). *Redesigning the future: A systems approach to societal problems.* New York; John Wiley and Sons.

Adams, J & Spencer, F. (2002). *Life Changes: A guide to the Seven Changes of Personal Growth.* New York: Paraview.

Aigner, G. (2011). *Leadership beyond good intentions.* Allen and Unwin.

Aigner, G and Skelton, L. (2013). *The Australian Leadership Paradox: What it takes to lead in the Lucky Country.* Sydney: Allen and Unwin.

Alinsky, S. (1971). *Rules for radicals.* New York: Random House.

Allen, M.F. (1997). *Wake of the Invercauld: Shipwrecked in the sub-Antartic: A great granddaughter's pilgrimage.* Auckland: Exisle Publishing.

Amagoh, F. (2008). Perspectives on organisation change: System and complexity theories. *The Innovation Journal: The Public Sector Innovation Journal*, *13*(3), pp. 1–14.

Argyris, C. (1991). Teaching smart people how to learn. *Harvard Business Review 69*(3), pp.99-109.

Armstrong, H. (2012). Follow the leader: Leadership development for the future, *Institute of Executive Coaching and Leadership (IECL)*, Sydney, November 2012.

Ashton, K. (2015). *How to fly a horse: The secret history of creation, invention and discovery.* London: William Heineman.

Atwood, M., Pedler, M., Pritchard, S. and Wilkinson, D. (2003). *Leading change: A guide to whole systems working.* Bristol: Policy Press.

Avolio, B.J. and Mahtre, K.H. (2012). Authentic leadership advances in theory and research on authentic leadership. In Cameron, K.S and Spreitzer, G.M (Eds), *Oxford handbook of positive organisational scholarship* (pp. 773). New York: Oxford University Press.

Barbuto, J.E and Wheeler, D.W. (2006). Scale development and construct clarification of servant leadership. *Group and organisation management, 31*(3), pp. 300-326.

Bass, B.M. (1990). From transactional to transformational leadership: Learning to share the vision. *Organisation Dynamics, 18,* pp. 19-31.

Bass, B. M. (1998). *Transformational leadership: Industrial, military, and educational impact*. New Jersey: Lawrence Erlbaum Associates.

Bennett, N. and Lemoine, J. (2014). What VUCA Really Means for You. *Harvard Business Review, 92*(1/2), pp. 27.

Bennis, W.G. (1959). Leadership theory and administrative behavior: The problem of authority. A*dministrative Science Quarterly, 4*, pp. 259–301.

Bennis, W. (1989). *On becoming a leader*. New York: Perseus.

Bleszynski, N. (2008). *Bloodlust: the unsavoury tale of Alexander Pearce the convict cannibal*. Australia: Random House.

Bolden, R. (2011). Distributed leadership in organizations: A review of theory and research. *International Journal of Management Reviews, 13*(3), pp. 251-269.

Bonhoeffer, D. (1978). *Life together*. London: SCM Press.

Bouma, G. D. (1999). Mapping religious contours. In P.H. Ballis and G. D. Bouma (Eds.), *Religion in an age of change, (pp. 5-11)*. Melbourne: Christian Research Association.

Bowman, K. (2014). *Move your DNA: Restore your health through natural movement*. Carlsborg, WA: Propriometrics Press.

Bridges, W. (2003). *Managing transitions: Making the most of change* (2nd ed.). Cambridge: Da Capo Press.

Brown, T. and Katz, B. (2009). *Change by design: How design thinking transforms organisations and inspires innovation*. Pymble: Harper Collins.

Bryman, A. (1992). *Charisma and leadership in organisations*. London: Sage.

Buckingham, M. (2007). *Go put your strengths to work*. New York: Free Press.

Bumiller, E. (2010, April 26). We have met the enemy and he is powerpoint, *New York Times*, pp. A1

Bunting, Michael (2016). *The Mindful Leader: 7 Practices for Transforming Your Leadership, Your Organisation and Your Life*. Milton Queensland: John Wiley and Sons.

Burnes, B. (2011). Why does change fail and what can we do about it? *Journal of Change Management. 11*(4) pp. 445-450

Burns, J. M. (1978). *Leadership*. New York: Harper and Row.

Butler-Bowden, T. (2007). *50 psychology classics*. London: Nicholas Brealey Publishing.

Cabaj, M. and Weaver, L. (2016). Collective impact 3.0: An evolving framework for community change. Tamarak Institute, Community Change Series 2016, retrieved from: http://cdn2.hubspot.net/hubfs/316071/Events/CCI/2016_CCI_Toronto/CCI_Publications/Collective_Impact_3.0_FINAL_PDF.pdf

Cameron, K.S., Bright, D. and Caza, A. (2004). Exploring the Relationships between organizational virtuousness and performance *American Behavioral Scientist*, Vol. 47 No. 6, February, pp. 1-24.

Cameron, K. S. (2008). *Positive Leadership*. San Francisco: Berrett Koehler.

Cameron, K.S., and Spreitzer, G.M. (Eds.). (2012). *Oxford handbook of positive orgaisational scholarship.* New York: Oxford University Press.

Cavanagh, M. (2006), Coaching from a systematic perspective: A complex adaptive conversation. In D. R. Stober and A. M. Grant (Eds.), *Evidence based Coaching Handbook: putting best practices to work for your clients* (pp. 313-354). New Jersey: John Wiley and Sons.

Chawla, S. and Renesch, J. (Eds). (1995) *Learning organizations.* Portland, Oregon: Productivity Press.

Chaskalson, M. (2010). Mindful Leadership: Training the brain to lead. *The Listener: A journal for coaches in government, 11*, pp. 2-5.

Chatfield, R., Glenn, L., Hosler, C. and Fulsaas, K. (Eds.). (2007) *Leadership the outward bound way: Becoming a better leader in the workplace in the wilderness and in your community.* Seattle: Mountaineer Books.

Christensen, C. (1997) *The innovator's dilemma: When new technologies cause great firms to fail.* Boston Massachusetts: Harvard Business Press.

Collins, P. (2002). *Hells Gates: The terrible journey of Alexander Pearce, Van Diemen's Land Cannibal.* South Yarra: Hardie Grant.

Cox, E. (2003, January 27). Civil debate needs to recognise the role of societiy's canaries. *Sydney Morning Herald,* retrieved from http://www.smh.com.au/articles/2003/01/26/1043553953970.html

Csikszentmihalyi, M. (1990). *The psychology of optimal experience.* New York: Harper Collins.

Day, D. and Antonakis, J. (2012). Leadership: Past, Present, and Future. In D. Day and J. Antonakis (Eds.), *The Nature of Leadership.* (2nd edition., pp. 3-25). California: Sage Publications.

De Bono, E. (1970). *Lateral thinking: Creativity step by step.* New York: Harper and Row.

Demerath, N. J. (2000). The varieties of sacred experience: Finding the sacred in a secular grove. *Journal for the Scientific Study of Religion 3*, pp. 1-11.

Deutschman, A., (2004, December) The fabric of creativity: At W.L. Gore, innovation is more than skin deep. *Fast Company Magazine. Retrieved from* https://www.fastcompany.com/51733/fabric-creativity.

Drath, B. (2001). The third way: A new source of leadership. *Leadership in Action 21*(2), pp. 7-11.

Druett, J. (2007) *Island of the lost: A harrowing true story of shipwreck, death and survival on a Godforsaken island at the edge of the world.* Sydney: Allen and Unwin.

Duckworth, A. L., Steen, T. and Seligman, M. (2005). Positive Psychology in Clinical Practice. *Annual Review of Clinical Psychology 1*, pp. 629-651.

Eckersley, R. (1998). *Measuring progress: is life getting better?* Collingwood: CSIRO.

Ehrenreich, B. (2009) *Bright sided: How the relentless promotion of positive thinking has undermined America.* New York: Metropolitan Books, Henry Holt and Company, LLC.

Ely, R.J. and Rhode, D.L. (2010). Women and Leadership: Defining the Challenges in Nohria, N. and Khurana, R. (Eds.), *Handbook of Leadership Theory and Practice.* Boston: Harvard Business Press.

Eoyang, G.H. (2011). Complexity and the dynamics of organisational change. In P. Allen, S. Maguire and W. McKelvey (Eds.). *The Sage Handbook of Complexity and Management.* (pp. 319-334). London: Sage Publications.

Flieshman, E. A. and Hunt, J.G. (1973). *Current developments in the study of leadership.* Carbondale: South Illinois University Press.

Fleishman, E.A., Mumford and, M.D. and Zaccaro, S.J. et al. (1991). Taxonomic efforts in the description of leader behavior: A synthesis and functional interpretation, The Leadership Quarterly, Volume 2, Issue 4, Winter 1991, pp. 245-287.

Francis, L. J., Kaldor, P., Robbins, M. and Castle, K. (2005). Happy but exhausted? Assessing two dimensions of work-related psychological health among the clergy in Australia, England and New Zealand. *Pastoral Sciences 24,* pp. 101-120.

Francis, L. J., Kaldor, P., Shevlin, M. and Lewis, C. A. (2004). Assessing emotional exhaustion among the Australian clergy: Internal reliability and construct validity of the scale of emotional exhaustion in ministry (SEEM). *Review of Religious Research, 45,* pp. 269-277.

Francis, L J. (2005). *Faith and psychology.* London: Darton, Longman and Todd Ltd.

Freedman, J. and Combs, G. (1996). Shifting paradigms: From systems to stories. In J. Freedman and G. Combs (Eds.), *Narrative therapy: The social construction of preferred realities* (pp. 1-18). New York: Norton.

Freudenberger, H. J. and Richelson, G. (1980). *Burnout: The- cost of achievement.* Garden City, NY: Doubleday.

Freire, P. (1970) *Pedogogy of the oppressed.* New York: Continuum International Publishing.

Garvey Berger, J. and Johnston, K. (2015), *Simple habits for complex times: Powerful practices for leaders. Stanford:* Stanford University Press.

Gardner, W. L., Avolio, B. J., Luthans, F., May, D. R., & Walumbwa, F. O. (2005). Can you see the real me? A self-based model of authentic leader and follower development. *Leadership Quarterly, 16,* pp. 343-372.

George, B. (2003). *Authentic leadership: Rediscovering the secrets to creating lasting value.* San Francisco: Jossey Bass.

George, B. and Simms, P. (2007). *True North: Discover your authentic leadership.* San Francisco: Jossey-Bass.

George, B., Sims, P., McLean, N. and Mayer, D. (2007). Discovering your authentic leadership. *Harvard Business Review 129,* 85(2), pp. 129.

George, B. (2013, February 22) *Resilience through mindful leadership.* The Huffington Post. Retrieved from http://www.huffingtonpost.com/bill-george/resilience-through-mindfu_b_2932269.html

Godin, S. (2008). *Tribes: We need you to lead us.* London: Platkus Books.

Godin, S. (2010). *Lynchpin; Are you indispensable?* London: Penguin Books.

Golsby-Smith, A. (2007). *The second road of thought: how design offers strategy a new toolkit*. Journal of Business Strategy, Vol. 28 Iss: 4, pp.22 - 29.

Golsby-Smith, A. (2007). *Hold Conversations, Not Meetings.* Harvard Business Review, February 15, 2011.

Goldman, D. (2002). *Primal Leadership: Realising the power of emotional intelligence.* Cambridge: Harvard Business School Press.

Goldstein, J. A., Hazy, J. K., and Lichtenstein, B. B. (2010). *Complexity and the nexus of leadership: Leveraging nonlinear science to create ecologies of innovation.* New York: Palgrave Macmillan.

Greenleaf, R. K. (1970). The servant as leader. In L.C. Spears (Ed.). *The power of servant leadership.* San Francisco: Berret-Koehler.

Gronn, P. (2009). Leadership Configurations. *Leadership 5*(3), pp. 381-394.

Gulati, R., Casto, C. and Krontiris, C. (2014), How the Other Fukushima Plant Survived, Harvard Business Review, July-August. Reprint R1407K

Hackett, A. J. (2006). *Jump start.* New Zealand: Random House Publishers.

Hamel, G. (2010, March 18). W.L. Gore: Lessons from a management revolutionary. *Wall Street Journal.*

Hackman, R. and Wageman, R. (2007). Asking the right questions about leadership. *American Psychologist, 62*(1), pp. 43-37.

Harford, T. (2011). *Adapt: Why success always starts with failure.* Giroux, New York: Farrar Straus.

Harvey, J. (1996). *The Abilene Paradox and other meditations on management.* San Francisco: Jossey-Bass.

Heath, C. and Heath, D. (2007). *Made to stick: Why some ideas survive and others die.* New York: Random House.

Heath, C. and D. (2010). *Switch: How to change things when change is hard,* New York: Broadway Books.

Heffernan, M. (2015). Forget the pecking order at work, TEDWomen, May 2015, https://www.ted.com/talks/margaret_heffernan_why_it_s_time_to_forget_the_pecking_order_at_work [Video Podcast].

Heifetz, R. A. (1994). *Leadership without easy answers.* Cambridge, MA, USA: Harvard University Press.

Heifetz, R. A. and Linsky, M. (2002). *Leadership on the line.* Boston: Harvard Business School Press.

Heifetz R., Grashow, A. and Linsky, M. (2009), Leadership in a (Permanent) Crisis, *Harvard Business Review, 87*(7-8), pp. 62-9. (Reprint *R0907F).*

Heifetz, R. A., Linsky, M. and Grashow, A., (2009). *Practice of Adaptive Leadership: Tools and tactics for changing your organisation and the world.* Cambridge: Harvard University Press.

Heilman, M.E., Wallen, A.S., Fuchs, D. and Tamkins, M.M. (2004). Penalties for Success: Reactions to Women Who Succeed at Male Gender-Typed Tasks. *Journal of Applied Psychology*, Vol. 89, No. 3, pp. 416–427.

Heilman, M. and Simon, M. (1998). The vagaries of sex bias: Conditions regulating the undervluation, equivaluation and overvaluation of female job applicants. Organisational behaviour and human decision processes, 41, pp. 98-110.

Hersey, P. and Blanchard, K. H. (1977). *Management of Organizational Behavior: Utilizing Human Resources* (3rd ed.) New Jersey/Prentice Hall.

Hesselbein, F., Goldsmith, M. and Beckhard, R. (1996). *The Leader of the Future: New Strategies and Practices for the Next Era.* San Francisco: Jossey-Bass.

Higgs, M. and Rowland, D. (2005) All changes great and small: Exploring approaches to change and its leadership. *Journal of Change Management, 5*(2), pp. 121 –151.

Hillary, E. (2003). *High adventure: The true story of the first ascent of Everest.* New York: Oxford University Press.

Holland, H. (2008). *Dinner with Mugabe: The untold story of a freedom fighter who became a tyrant.* Johannesburg, South Africa: Penguin Books.

Holbeche, L. (2015). *The agile organisation: How to build an innovative, sustainable and resilient business.* London: Kogan Page Limited.

Hooper, A. and Potter, J. (2000). *Intelligent leadership: Creating a passion for change.* London: Random House.

Hopcraft, P. (2011) *Understanding innovation the W L Gore Way.* Retrieved from: http://innovationexcellence.com/blog/2011/09/28/understanding-innovation-the-w-l-gore-way/

Hughes, P., Black, A., Kaldor, P.J., Bellamy, J. and Castle, K. (2007) *Building stronger communities.* Sydney: University of NSW Press.

Hunt, J. (1954). *The ascent of Everest.* London: Hodder and Stoughton.

Ibarra, H. (2015) The Authenticity Paradox: Why feeling like a fake can be a sign of growth. *Harvard Business Review, 54*, pp. 52-59.

Ilies, R., Morgeson, F. P. and Nahrgang, J. D. (2005). Authentic Leadership and eudaemonic wellbeing: Understanding leader-follower outcomes. *The Leadership Quarterly* 16, pp. 373-394.

Ireland, R.D. and Hitt, M.A. (2005) Achieving and maintaining strategic competitiveness in the 21st century: the role of leadership. *Academy of Management Executive, 19*(4), pp. 65-77.

Jago, A. J. (1982). Leadership: Perspectives in Theory and Research. *Management Science, 28*(3), pp. 315-336.

Jaworski, J. (1996). *Synchronicity: The inner path of leadership.* San Francisco: Berrett-Koehler.

Kaldor, P., Bellamy, J., Powell, R., Correy, M. and Castle, K. (1997). *Shaping a future. Characteristics of vital congregations.* Adelaide: Openbook.

Kaldor, P., Black, A. and Hughes, P. (2009). *Spirit matters: How making sense of life affects well being.* Homebush: NCLS Research.

Kaldor, P., Black, A. and Hughes, P. (2012). How Australian people make sense of life and assess its ultimate significance-and the difference it might make, in Miner, M., Dowson, M. and Devenish, S.E. (2012). *Beyond well-being: Spirituality and human flourishing* (pp. 89-108). Charlotte, North Carolina: Information Age Publishing.

Kaldor, P. and Bullpitt, R. (2001). *Burnout in Church Leaders.* Adelaide: Openbook.

Kaldor, P. and McLean, J. (2009). *Lead with your Strengths.* Adelaide: Openbook.

Kantner, R. (1995) Mastering Change. In S. Chawla and J. Renesch (Eds). (1995) *Learning Organizations* (pp. 71 - 84) . Portland, Oregon: Productivity Press.

Kark, R., and Shamir, B. (2002). The dual effect of transformational leadership: Priming relational and collective selves and further effects on followers. In B. J. Avolio, and F. J. Yammarino (Eds.). *Transformational and charismatic leadership: The road ahead* (pp. 7–91). Oxford: UK7 Elsevier.

Kashdan, T., Biswas-Diener, R., and King, L. (2008). Reconsidering happiness: The costs of distinguishing between hedonics and eudaimonia. *The Journal of Positive Psychology*, 3(4), 219-233.

Katz D. and Kahn R. L. (1966). *The social psychology of orgaisations.* New York: Wiley.

Katzenbach, J. R. and Smith, D.K. (1993). *The Wisdom of Teams.* Boston MA: Harvard Business School Press.

Keegan, R. and Lahey, L. (2009). *Immunity to Change: How to overcome it and unlock the potential in yourself and your organisation.* Boston MA: Harvard Business Press.

Kellerman, B. (2008). *Followership: How followers are creating change and changing leader.* Boston: Harvard Business School.

Kellerman, B. (2012). *The End of Leadership.* New York: Harper Collins.

Khurana, R. and Nohria, N. (Eds). (2010). *Handbook of Leadership Theory and Practice.* Harvard: Harvard University Press.

Kleon, A. (2012). *Steal Like an Artist: 10 Things Nobody Told You About Being Creative.* New York: Workman Publishing.

Kotler, P., Brown, L., Adam, S. and Armstrong, G. (2001). *Marketing* (5th edition). Australia: Prentice Hall.

Kouzes, J. M. and Posner, B.Z. (1987, 2002, 2007). *The leadership challenge.* San Francisco: Jossey-Bass.

Kouzes, J. M. and Posner, B. Z. (1993). *Credibility: How leaders gain and lose it. Why people demand it.* San Francisco: Jossey-Bass.

Kouzes, J. M. and Posner, B. Z. (2004). *Christian reflections on the leadership challenge.* San Francisco: Jossey-Bass.

Kouzes, J. M. and Posner, B. Z. (2010). *The truth about leadership: The no-fads, heart-of-thematter facts you need to know.* San Francisco, CA: Jossey-Bass

Krakauer, J. (1997). *Into thin air: A personal account of the Everest disaster.* London: McMillan.

Kretzmann, J. and J. McKnight (1993). Building communities from the inside out. Chicago, ACTA publications.

Kubler-Ross, E. (1973). *On death and dying.* Abingdon, Oxford: Routledge.

Kurtz, C.F. and Snowden, D.J., (2003) The new dynamics of strategy: Sense-making in a complex and complicated world. I*BM Systems Journal, 42*(3).

Lad, L. J. and Luechauer, D. (1998). On the path to servant-leadership. In L.C. Spears (Ed.) *Insights on leadership: Service, stewardship, spirit and servant-leadership, pp. 54-67*. New York: John Wiley.

Landsberg, M. (2003). *The tools of leadership: Vision inspiration and momentum*. London: Profile.

Larman, C. (2004). *Agile and iterative development: A manager's guide*. Addison-Wesley Professional.

Learmonth, E. and Tabakoff, J. (2013). *No mercy: True stories of disaster, survival and brutality*. Melbourne: Text Publishing.

Leithwood, K. and Mascall, B. (2008). Collective leadership effects on student achievement. *Educational Administration Quarterly, 44*(4), pp. 529-561.

Lencioni, P. (2002). *The five dysfunctions of a team*. San Francisco: Jossey-Bass.

Lewin, K. (1947). *Frontiers in group dynamics*. Human Relations, 1(1), 5-41.

Lewin, K. (1951). *Field theory in social science*. New York: Harper & Row.

Lewis, S. (2011) *Positive psychology at work: How positive leadership and appreciative inquiry create inspiring organizations*. Chichester: Wiley-Blackwell.

Liden, R. C., Wayne, S. J., Zhao, H. and Henderson, D. (2008). Servant leadership: Development of a multidimensional measure and multi-level assessment. *The Leadership Quarterly 19*, pp. 161-177.

Limerick, D. and Cunnington, B. (1993). *Managing the New Organisation: A blueprint for network and strategic alliances*. Chatswood New South Wales: Business and Professional Publishing.

Linley, A. (2008). *Average to A+: Realising strengths in yourself and others*. Coventry: CAPP Press.

Lipman-Bluman, J. (2005) *The allure of toxic leaders: why we follow destructive bosses and corrupt politicians-and how we can survive them*. New York: Oxford University Press.

Lummis, C. D. (1982). The Radicalism of Democracy, *Democracy*, 2, pp. 9-16, as quoted in Sydney Alliance Resources.

Luthans, F., Youssef, C. M., and Avolio, B. J. (2006). *Psychological capital: Developing the human competitive edge*. New York: Oxford University Press.

Luthans, F. and Avolio, B. J. (2003). Authentic leadership development. In K. S. Cameron, J.E. Dutton and R. E. Quinn (Eds.), *Positive Organisational Scholarship* (pp. 241-258). San Francisco: Berrett-Koehler.

MacGregor Burns, J. (1978). *Leadership*. New York: Harper and Row.

Machiavelli, N. (1505). *The Prince* (Translated by W. K. Marriott 1908). London: EP Dutton & Company: New York.

Marion, R. and Uhl-Bien, M. (2001). Leadership in complex organizations, *The Leadership Quarterly 12* (2001), pp. 389–418.

Markus. A. (2013). *Mapping Social Cohesion*, Caulfield East: Monash University, available at www.scanlonfoundation.org.au/docs/2013_SocC_report_final.pdf (accessed 5/5/14).

Maslach, C. (1976). Burned out. *Human Behaviour, 5(9), pp.* 16-22.

McAuley, I. (2002). Leading questions. *Dissent, 9,* pp. 17-19.

McCashen, W. (2004). *Communities of Hope: a strengths-based resource for building community.* Bendigo: St Luke's Innovative Resources.

McCashen, W. (2005). *The strengths approach: a strengths-based resource for sharing power and creating change.* Bendigo: St Luke's Innovative Resources.

McCroskey, J. C. (1977). Oral communication apprehension: A summary of recent theory and research. *Human Communications Research 4*, pp. 78-96.

McGregor, D. (1960). *The human side of enterprise.* New York: McGraw-Hill.

Meadows, D.H., Wright, D. (2008). *Thinking in systems: A primer.* White River Junction, VT: Chelsea Green Publishing Company.

Meadows, D.H. (2009) Dancing With Systems. In Ramage, M. and Shipp, K. (Eds.) *Systems Thinkers.* Milton Keynes: Springer London, Open University, Milton Keynes.

Meyerson, D. E. (2003). *Tempered radicals: How everyday leaders inspire change at work.* Boston: Harvard Business School Press.

Michalko, M. (2001) *Cracking creativity: The secrets of creative genius.* Berkeley, CA: Ten Speed Press.

Miner, M., Dowson, M. and Devenish, S.E. (2012). *Beyond well-being: Spirituality and human flourishing.* Charlotte, North Carolina: Information Age Publishing.

Miner, M., Sterland, S. and Dowson, M. (2006). Coping with ministry: Development of a multidimensional measure of internal orientation to the demands of ministry. *Review of Religious Research 48*(1), pp. 212-230.

Moller, C. (1992). *Employeeship: Mobilizing everybody's energy to win.* San Francisco: Time Manager International.

Morgan, A. (2000). *What is narrative therapy? An easy to read introduction.* Adelaide: Dulwich Centre.

Moxon, P. (1993). *Building a better team: A handbook for managers and facilitators.* Aldershot: Gower.

Myers, I. B. (1998). *Introduction to type: A guide to understanding your results on the Myers-Briggs Type Indicator.* Oxford: Oxford Psychologists Press.

Nadler, D. A. and Tushman, M.L. (1990). Beyond the charismatic leader: leadership and organisational change. *California Management Review 32,* pp. 77-97.

Nohria, N. and Khurana, R. (2010). *Handbook of Leadership Theory and Practice.* Boston: Harvard Business Press.

Northouse, P. G. (1997). *Leadership: Theory and practice.* Thousand Oaks: Sage Publications.

O'Regan, C. (2014, November). *What we really want from our leaders* [Audio podcast]. Retrieved from "In the Balance" BBC World Service.

Oriah Mountain Dreamer, (1999). *The Invitation.* San Francisco: Harper.

Ortberg, J. C. (1998). Taking Care of Busyness: How to minister at a healthy pace. *Christianity Today/Leadership Journal* (Fall edition). Retrieved from http://www.christianitytoday.com/pastors/1998/fall/8l4028.html

Orwell, G. (1968). *Selected Writings.* Heinemann Educational Books. The essay was originally published as 'Shooting an elephant' in New Quarterly in 1936, and is available online at http://www.online-literature.com/orwell/887/.

Page, D. and Wong, P. T. (2000). A conceptual framework for measuring servant leadership. In S. Adjibolooso (Ed.). *The human factor in shaping the course of history and development* (pp. 69-110). Washington: American University Press.

Pearce, C. L. and Conger, J. A. (2002). *Shared leadership: reframing the hows and whys of leadership.* New York: Sage publications.

Pearce, C. L., Manz, C.C., Sims, Jr., Henry, P. (2009). Where do we go from here? Is shared leadership the key to team success? *Organisational Dynamics 38*(3), pp. 234-238.

Pearce, C. L. and Sims, H. P. (2001). Shared Leadership: Toward a multilevel theory of leadership. *Advances in Interdisciplinary Studies of Work Teams 7*, pp 15-19.

Peddler, M., Burgoyne, J. and Boydell, T. (2010). *A managers guide to leadership: an action learning approach.* Maidenhead, Berkshire: McGraw Hill Publishing Company.

Peters, T. (1997). Creating the Curious Corporation. In D.S. Purgh (Ed.) *Organisational Theory: Selected Readings* (pp. 560-557.). Hammondsworth, England: The Penguin Group.

Peterson, C., Maier, S.F. and Seligman, E.P. (1993). *Learned Helplessness.* New York, Oxford University Press.

Peterson, C. and Seligman, E.P. (2004). *Character Strengths and Virtues.* New York: Oxford University Press.

Pollard, I. (2009). *Investing in your life: Your biggest investment opportunities are not necessarily financial.* Milton Queensland: Wiley.

Pugh, D. S. (1997). *Organisational theory: Selected readings.* Hammondsworth, England: Penguin Group.

Putnam, R. D. (2000). *Bowling Alone: The Collapse and Revival of American Community.* New York: Simon and Schuster.

Rao, J. and Weintraub, J. (2012) W. L. Gore—Culture of Innovation, Babson College, Massachusetts (1/4/ 2012), and Harvard Business Review case studies (Reprint BAB698).

Raynal, Francois, 1880, Wrecked on a Reef, or Twenty Months on the Auckland Islands, T. Nelson and Sons, Edinburgh. Digital publication by: Christiane Mortelier.

Read, S. and Sarasvathy, S., Dew, N., Wiltbank, R. and Ohlsson, A. (2010). *Effectual Entrepreneurship.* New York: Routledge.

Ready, D. A. and Conger, J.A. (2003). Why leadership development efforts fail. *MIT Sloan Management Review 44*(3), pp. 83 - 88.

Reynolds, C. W. (1987) Flocks, herds and schools: a distributed behavioural model. *Computer Graphics, 21*(4), pp.25–34.

Rittel, H. W. J. W. and Webber M. (1973). Dilemmas in a general theory of planning. *Policy Sciences 4*, pp. 155-169.

Rokeach, M. (1973) *The nature of human values.* New York: Free Press.

Rolls, J. (1990). The transformational leader: The wellspring of the learning organisation. S. Chowra and Renesch. J (Eds.) *In Learning Organisations: Developing Cultures for Tomorrow's Workplace* (Pp. 101 - 110). Portland: Productivity Press.

Ryan, S. (1990). Learning Communities: An Alternative to the expert model. In S. Chawla and J. Renesch (Eds.) *In Learning Organisations: Developing Cultures for Tomorrow's Workplace* (pp 279- 292). Portland: Productivity Press.

Satir, V. (1983). *Conjoint family therapy.* Palo Alto, CA: Science and Behavior Books.

Satir, V. (1988). *The new peoplemaking.* Palo Alto, CA: Science and Behavior Books.

Sawyer, K. (2007) *Group Genius: The Creative Power of Collaboration.* New York: Basic books, Perseus.

Sawyer, K. (2012) *Explaining creativity: The science of human innovation.* Oxford New York: Oxford University Press.

Sawyer, K. (2013) *Zig Zag: The surprising path to greater creativity.* San Francisco: Jossey-Bass and Wiley.

Schein, E. H. (1996) Leadership and Organisational Culture. In Hesselbein, F., Goldsmith, M. and Beckhard, R. (Eds.) *The Leader of the Future: New visions, strategies and practices for the next era* (pp. 59-70). San Francisco: Jossey-Bass.

Schein, E. (2010). *Organisational culture and leadership.* San Francisco: John Wiley and Sons.

Schwartz, S. (1994). Are there universal aspects in the structure and contents of human values? *Journal of Social Issues 50*(4), pp. 19-45.

Sendjaya, S. (2015). *Personal and organizational excellence through servant leadership: learning to serve, serving to lead, leading to transform:* Switzerland: Springer international publishing.

Sendjaya, S., Sarros, J.C. and Santora, J.C. (2008). Defining and Measuring Servant Leadership Behaviour in Organizations. *Journal of Management Studies, 45*(2): March.

Seligman, M. E. P. (1991). *Helplessness.* New York: Freeman.

Seligman, M. E. P. (2002). *Authentic happiness: Using positive psychology to realise your potential for lasting fulfilment.* Sydney: Random House.

Seligman, M. E. P. (2011). *Flourish: A visionary new understanding of happiness and well-being.* New York: Griffen Free Press.

Seligman, M. E. P. and Csikszentmihalyi, M. (2000). Positive Psychology: An introduction. *American Psychologist 55*(1), pp. 5-14.

Senge, P. M. (1990). *The Fifth Discipline: The art and practice of the learning organisation.* New York: Doubleday.

Senge, P. M., Roberts, C., Ross, R., Smith, B. and A. Kliener (1994). *The fifth discipline fieldbook.* New York: Doubleday.

Setili, A. (2014) *The agility advantage: How to identify and act on opportunities in a fast-changing world.* San Francisco: John Wiley and Sons, Inc. Jossey-Bass.

Shamir, B. and Eilam, G. (2005). What's your story: Life stories approach to authentic leadership development. *The Leadership Quarterly 16*(3), pp. 395-417.

Shamir, B., House, R. J., and Arthur, M. B. (1993). The motivational effects of charismatic leadership: A self-concept based theory. *Organisation Science 4*, pp. 577-594.

Shaw, G. B. (1921). *Back to methuselah - a metabiological pentateuch*. Hicks Press, available online.

Shipton, E. (1999). *The six mountain travel books*. London: Baton Wick.

Sims, P. (2011). *Little bets: How breakthrough ideas emerge from small discoveries*. London: Random House Business Books.

Sinclair, A. (2007). *Leadership for the disillusioned*. Crows Nest: Allen and Unwin.

Smeaton, T. and Pedotto, A. (2003). Name those assets: An assets-based approach in community capacity building. Paper presented to Building Family and Community Strengths 3rd Australian Conference. *Science 4,* pp. 577-594.

Smith, K. and Berg, D. (1997). *Paradoxes of group life understanding conflict, paralysis and movement in group dynamics*. San Francisco: Jossey-Bass.

Snow, L. K. (2004). *The Power of Asset Mapping*. Washington: Alban Institute.

Snowden, D. J. and Boone, M. E. (2007). A leader's framework for decision making., *Harvard Business Review 85*(11), pp. 68.

Spears, L. C. (1998). *Robert Greenleaf: The power of servant leadership*. San Francisco: Berret-Koehler.

Spears, L. C. (1997). Introduction: Tracing the growing impact of Servant Leadership. In L.C. Spears (Ed.) *Insights on Leadership: Service, Stewardship, Spirit and Servant-Leadership* (pp. 1-14). New York: John Wiley.

Spillane, J. P. (2006) *Distributed Leadership*. San Francisco: John Wiley and Sons and Jossey-Bass.

Spillane, J.P., Halverson, R. and Diamond, J. B. (2001, April). Investigating school leadership practice: A distributed perspective. *Educational Researcher, 30*(3), pp. 23-28.

Stace, D. and Dunphy, D. (1999). Beyond the Boundaries: Leading and Recreating the Successful Enterprise. Sydney, McGraw Hill.

Stogdill, R. M. (1974). *Handbook of leadership: A survey of theory and research*. New York: Free Press.

Strom, M., (2014). *Lead with Wisdom: How Wisdom Transforms Good Leaders into Great Leaders*. Milton, Queensland: John Wiley and sons.

Strom, M. (2013). *Grounded questions. Rich stories. Deep change*. TEDxPlainpalais, March 26. https://www.youtube.com/watch?v=tEISLatc57I.

Swenson, R. A. (1998). *The Overload Syndrome*. Colorado Spring: NavPress.

Swenson, R. A. M. D. (2004). *Margin: Restoring emotional, physical, financial and time reserves to overloaded lives* (Revised edition). Colorado Spring: NavPress.

Styhre, A. (2002). Non-linear change in organisations: Organisational change management informed by complexity theory. *Leadership and Organisation Development Journal, 23*(6), pp. 343-351.

Tacey, D. (2003). *The Spirituality Revolution - The emergence of contemporary spirituality.* Sydney: Harper Collins.

Tenzing, T. (2001). *Tenzing Norgay and the sherpas of Everest.* Camden: Ragged Mountain Press/McGraw-Hill.

Thomas, M. A. (2006). *Gurus on leadership.* London: Thorogood books.

Tichy, N. and Devanna, M.A. (1986). *The Transformational Leader.* New York: Wiley.

Todnem, R. (2005) Organisation change management: A critical review. *Journal of Change Management, 5*(4), pp. 369-380.

Tuckman, B. W. and Jenson, M.A.C. (1997). Stages of small group development. *Group and Organisational Studies 2*(2), pp. 4.

Uhl-Bien, M. and Marion, R. (Eds.) (2008). *Complexity leadership, Part 1: Conceptual foundations.* Charlotte, NC: Information Age Publishing.

Uhl-Bien, M. and Marion, R. (2009). Complexity leadership in bureaucratic forms of organizing: A meso model. *The Leadership Quarterly 20,* pp. 631–650.

Uhl-Bien, M., Marion, R. and McKelvey, W. (2007, August) Complexity Leadership Theory: Shifting leadership from the industrial age to the knowledge era. *The Leadership Quarterly 18*(4), pp. 298-318.

Ungenmerr-Baumann, M.-R. (2002). *Dadirri.* Emmaus Productions. Retrieved from: http://www.miriamrosefoundation.org.au/.

Useem, M. (1998). *The leadership moment.* New York: Random House.

Vaill, P. B. (1989). *Managing as a performing art.* San Francisco: Jossey-Bass.

Vaill, P. B. (1996). *Learning as a way of being: Strategies for survival in a world of permanent white water.* San Francisco: Jossey-Bass.

Vaill, P. B. (1998). *Spirited leading and learning: Process wisdom for a new age.* San Francisco: Jossey-Bass.

Valles, C. G. (1986). *The art of choosing.* New York: Doubleday.

Vella-Broderick, D. (2011). Positive Psychology: Reflecting on the past and projecting into the future. *InPsych: The Bulletin of the Australian Psychological Society Ltd, 33*(2), pp. 10-13.

Walumbwa, F. O., Luthans, F., Avey, J. B. and Oke, A. (2009). Authentically Leading groups: The mediating role of collective psychological capital and trust. *Journal of Organisational Behaviour, 32,* pp4-24.

Walumbwa, F. O., Avolio, B. J., Gardner, W. L., Wernsing, T.S. and Peterson, S.J (2008). Authentic leadership: Development and validation of a theory-based measure. *Journal of Management 34*(1), pp. 89-126.

Watson, A. and Bossley, J. (1995). Taking the sweat out of communication anxiety. *Personnel Journal,* pp. 111-119.

Wayne, S. J., Shore, L.M. and Liden, R.C. (1997). Perceived organisational support and leader/member exchange: A social exchange perspective. *Academy of Management Journal 40,* pp. 82-111.

Wersky, D. G. (2003). *Educational partnerships.* Paper presented to Sydney Leadership, Sydney, February.

Wessel, M. and Christensen, C. M. (2012) Surviving disruption: It's not enough to know that a threat is coming. You need to know whether it's coming right for you, *Harvard Business Review, 90*(12), pp. 56-64.

Wheatley, M. J. (2002, April). It's An Interconnected World. *Shambhala Sun,* retrieved from http://margaretwheatley.com/articles/interconnected.html.

Wheatley, M. J. (2007). F*inding our way: leadership for an uncertain time.* San Francisco: Berrett-Koehler Publishers.

Williams, Dean, (2005). *Real Leadership: Helping People and Organizations Face Their Toughest Challenges.* San Francisco: Berrett-Koehler.

Williams, L. (2011). *Think the unthinkable to spark transformation in your business.* New Jersey: Pearson Education.

Wolfe, T. (1970). *Radical Chic and Mau-mauing the Flak Catchers.* New York: Farrar, Straus and Giroux.

Worley, C. G., Williams, T. D., Lawler III, E. E. (2014a). *The agility factor: Building adaptable organisations for superior performance.* San Francisco: Jossey-Bass and John Wiley and Sons.

Worley, C. G., Williams, T. D., Lawler III, E. E. (2014b). *Assessing organisational agility: Creating diagnostic profiles to guide transformation* (J-B Short Format Series). San Francisco: Jossey-Bass and John Wiley and Sons.

Wright, W. C. (2005) *Don't step on the rope! Reflections on leadership relationships and teamwork.* Milton Keynes: Paternoster.

Wright, W. C. (2000). *Relational Leadership.* Milton Keynes: Paternoster Press.

Wright, W. C. (2005). *Reflections on leadership relationships and teamwork.* Milton Keynes: Paternoster Press.

Yukl, G. A. (1989). *Leadership in organisations* (2nd ed.). Englewood NJ: Prentice Hall.

Yukl, G. A. (1989). Managerial Leadership: a review of theory and research. *Journal of Management 15*(2), pp. 251-289.

Zackman, M. Z. and Johnson, C. E. (2004). *Leadership a communication perspective.* Long Grove: Waveland Press.

Zaleznik, A. (1992). Managers and leaders: Are they different? *Harvard Business Review on Leadership 61*, pp. 126-135.

Notes

Introduction
[1] Vaill 1998, 165.
[2] E.g. Aigner 2011, 3.
[3] Wheatley 2007, 116.

Part 1 The Challenges we face

Chapter 1 The times we are in
[1] BBC program: From Our Own Correspondent, June 2014 "Dilemma for the US".
[2] From CNN International 2/5/2003: http://edition.cnn.com/2003/US/05/01/bush.transcript.
[3] For application in human organisations, see Reynolds 1987 (as quoted in Higgs and Rowland 2005), 123. See also the Cynefin framework: Kurtz and Snowden 2004 and Snowden and Boone 2007. Sometimes the label Obvious is used instead of Simple.
[4] Cavanagh 2006, 315.
[5] Garvey-Berger and Johnson 2015, location 853.
[6] Cavanagh 2006, 315.
[7] Kanter in Chawla and Renesch 1995, 71.
[8] Bumiller 2010.
[9] Christensen 1997; Wessel and Christensen 2012.
[10] Christensen 1997; Wessel and Christensen 2012.
[11] Hughes, Black, Kaldor, Bellamy, and Castle 2007, 88.
[12] Harford 2011, 8.
[13] Aigner 2011, 45.
[14] Harford 2011, 8.
[15] Harford 2011, 239.
[16] An idea shared with me by colleague John McLean.
[17] Quoted in Thomas 2006.
[18] MacGregor Burns 1978.
[19] Northouse 1997.
[20] E.g. Burns 1978 and Bass 1990.
[21] Kaldor et al. 1997.

Chapter 2 Responding to complexity
[1] See for instance Heifetz 1994, Heifetz and Linsky 2002.
[2] Writing in the 1970s about urban planning, Horst Rittel and Melvin Webber used the term 'wicked problems' (Rittel and Webber 1973). Grass roots activist movements of the 1960s

questioned the ability of social planners to know what is 'best' for communities, what the problems were and how to resolve them.

3 Heifetz 1994.

4 Heifetz 1994. We also wish to acknowledge the contributions of Paul Porteous and Robbie MacPherson to the development of this section.

5 Heifetz 1994; Heifetz and Linsky 2002; Heifetz, Linsky and Grashow 2009.

6 As told in Ashton 2015, 71.

7 Harvey 1996.

8 Pollard 2009.

9 Heifetz 1994, 70.

Chapter 3 Beyond superheroes

1 Bennis 1959, 259.

2 Hooper and Potter 2000, 53.

3 Bryman 1992, as quoted in Northouse 1997, 4.

4 As quoted in Tichy and Devanna 1986.

5 Tichy and Devanna 1986, 90.

6 O'Regan 2014.

7 Quoted in Kellerman 2012, 4.

8 Personal experience. See also example in Chawla and Renesch 1995, 235.

9 Aigner and Skelton 2013, 14.

10 Wheatley 2007, 64.

11 Heilman, Wallen, Fuchs and Tamkins 2004.

12 Ely and Rhode 2010, Location 4780.

13 Ely and Rhode 2010, Location 4767.

14 See for instance: https://www.yahoo.com/music/how-gospel-great-mahalia-jackson-gave-wing-to-108223937471.html.

Epilogue Surviving shipwrecks: Looking deeply at the challenges we face

1 Learmonth and Tabakoff 2013, 109; Allen 1997, 54.

2 Allen 1997, 57.

3 Allen 1997, 57.

4 Allen 1997, 59.

Part 2 Rethinking Leadership for Complex Times

1 Burns, J. M. (1978). Leadership. New York, Harper and Row.

2 Fleishman 1991, as quoted in Northouse 1997, 2.

3 Allen 1997, 81.

4 An Auckland Islands shipwreck in 1864, drawn from Harper's Weekly May 16 1868 and reproduced on line in various places including Wikipedia.

5 Learmonth and Tabakoff 2013, 109; Allen 1997, 54.

6 Allen 1997 171, 204 and 174 respectively.

Chapter 4 Separating 'leadership' from 'leaders'

1 A term used by Heifetz and Linsky 2002.

2 Orwell 1968.

[3] Kellerman 2012, 20.

[4] Hughes, Black, Kaldor, Bellamy and Castle, 2007.

[5] Kellerman 2012, 22.

[6] Aigner and Skelton 2013, 198.

[7] Lummis 1982.

[8] Alinsky 1971.

[9] Thomas 2006.

[10] Heifetz 1994.

[11] Aigner 2011, 22.

[12] Aigner 2011, 21.

[13] Aigner and Skelton 2013, 16.

[14] Chatfield, Glenn, Hosler, and Fulsaas 2007.

[15] Aigner and Skelton 2013, 140.

[16] Kouzes and Posner 1993, 185.

[17] Material about Robert Mugabe from Holland 2008.

[18] Bonhoeffer 1978.

[19] As quoted in Spears 1998, 1.

[20] Greenleaf 1970.

[21] Peter Vaill in Spears 1998, xi.

[22] Shamir and Eilam 2005, 397.

[23] See for instance Sendjaya 2008 and 2015, and Barbuto and Wheeler 2006.

[24] E.g. Liden, Wayne, Zhao, and Henderson 2008, 161. Many writers have endorsed its importance: Ken Blanchard, Steven Covey, Peter Drucker, Kouzes and Posner, Max Dupree and Peter Senge (Spears 1998).

[25] Hunt, 1953, 40.

[26] Hillary 2003, 118.

[27] See for instance: Shamir, House and Arthur 1993; Wayne, Shaw and Liden 1997 or Liden et al 2008.

[28] Personal communications.

[29] Aigner and Skelton, 2013, 21.

[30] http://www.ted.com/talks/margaret_heffernan_why_it_s_time_to_forget_the_pecking_order_at_work.

[31] E.g. Kouzes and Posner 2002, 21.

Chapter 5 The leadership mosaic

[1] See, for instance, Hersey and Blanchard 1977.

[2] Hughes, Black, Kaldor, Bellamy and Castle 2007; Putnam 2000.

[3] Kaldor and McLean 2009, Chapter 5.

[4] See for instance Strom 2013.

[5] Stephanie Ryan in in Chawla and Renesch 1995, 295.

[6] For background, see Northouse 1997.

[7] Kaldor et al. 1997.

[8] Vaill 1998.

[9] Heifetz and Linsky 2002.

[10] Kaldor and McLean 2009, Chapter 5.

[11] Hackett 2006, 178.

[12] Hackett 2006, 108, 109.

[13] Hackett 2006, 178.

[14] Uhl-Bien and Marion 2009, 643.

[15] As quoted in Chatfield et al 2007, 101.

[16] Edgar Schein in Tichy and Devanna 1986.

[17] Heifetz, Linsky and Grashow 2009, 149 and Heifetz and Linsky 2002, 108.

[18] Freire 1970, 77.

[19] Chatfield et al. 2007.

[20] Heifetz 1994.

[21] Useem 1998, Chapter 2.

[22] Drawn from Gulati, Casto and Krontiris 2014.

[23] Kouzes and Posner 2007, 20.

Chapter 6 Leadership: It's a collective effort

[1] Heifetz, Grashow and Linsky 2009, 6.

[2] Katz and Kahn 1966.

[3] Schein 1996, 68.

[4] Gronn 2009.

[5] Spillane, Halverson and Diamond, 2001, 23.

[6] See for instance Bolden 2011, 257 or Pearce and Conger 2002.

[7] Leithwood and Mascall 2008.

[8] Katy Bowman 2014, quoted on "In the Balance" BBC World Service November 2014.

[9] Drawn from Setili 2014, location 2358.

[10] This discussion draws on a range of sources including Moxon 1993.

[11] Lencioni, 2002 195.

[12] See for instance Katzenbach and Smith 1993.

[13] http://www.greatthoughtstreasury.com/author/simon-sinek?page=21.

[14] Cameron 2008, 3.

[15] Cameron, Bright and Caza 2004.

[16] For more detailed exploration see Cameron 2008 or Lewis 2011.

[17] Aigner and Skelton 2013, 91.

[18] See for instance Cabaj and Weaver 2016.

[19] Aigner and Skelton 2013, 89.

[20] Aigner and Skelton 2013, 93-95.

[21] Ireland and Hitt 2005, 65.

[22] Armstrong 2012.

[23] Drath 2001.

Epilogue Surviving shipwrecks: Leadership in complexity

[1] The story here as told by Learmonth and Tabakoff, 2013, 126.

[2] Learmonth and Tabakoff 2013, 147.

[3] Learmonth and Tabakoff 2013, Location 1667.

[4] Drawings from Raynal 1880.

[5] Learmonth and Tabakoff 2013, Location 3535.

[6] Allen 1997, 161.

[7] Allen 1997, 115.

[8] Smith's report, contained in Allen 1997, 242; See also Learmonth and Tabakoff, 2013, Location 1472.

Part 3 Developing Agility with Complex Change

1 As quoted in Kellerman 2012, vii.

Chapter 7 Rethinking change

1 E.g. Brynan 1992.
2 Concepts developed by Kurt Lewin (1947 and 1951), as quoted in Higgs and Rowland 2005, 122.
3 Sawyer 2007, Location 451.
4 Worley, Williams and Lawler 2014a, section 14.
5 Uhl-Bien and Marion 2008, 13.
6 This illustration is drawn from Lewis 2011, 26.
7 Lady Elliott Island Education Centre.
8 Chawla and Renesch 1995, 15.
9 McGregor, 1960
10 Senge 1990, 3.
11 E.g. Argyris 1991.
12 Senge 1990 and Chawla and Renesch 1995.
13 Worley, Williams and Lawler 2014b, Location 171.
14 Worley, Williams and Lawler 2014a, Location 224.
15 Worley, Williams and Lawler 2014a, Location 923.
16 Marion and Uhl-Bien 2001.
17 Holbeche 2015, Section 1517.
18 Wall Street Journal March 18,2010.
19 Hamel 2010.
20 Rao 2012, 11.
21 See for instance Godin 2010, 44- 47.
22 Todnem 2005.

Chapter 8 Moving through personal uncertainty

1 Satir 1983 and 1988, Kubler-Ross 1973.
2 Bridges 2003, 5.
3 Adams and Spencer 2002.
4 Bridges 2003, 40.
5 To use a term coined by Chip and Dan Heath 2007, 127.
6 Tichy & Devanna 1986, 27.
7 Aigner and Skelton 2013, 160, quoting Heifetz, Linsky and Grashow 2009.
8 Quoted in Learmonth and Tabakoff 2013, 30.
9 Learmonth and Tabakoff, 2013, 30.
10 Jill McMahon quoted in Learmonth and Tabakoff, 2013, 23.
11 Learmonth and Tabakoff, 2013, 22.
12 Learmonth and Tabakoff, 2013, 23.
13 Learmonth and Tabakoff, 2013, 37.

Chapter 9 Navigating in unknown territory

1 As quoted in Harford 2011, 1.
2 Quoted in Sims 2011, 1.
3 Achi and Garvey Berger 2015, 2.

⁴ E.g. Transformational leadership theorists, Kouzes and Posner, and Ron Heifetz.

⁵ Kouzes and Posner 2004, 22.

⁶ Heifetz, Grashow and Linsky 2009, 6.

⁷ Fullan 2013.

⁸ Quoted in Sims 2011, 36.

⁹ Edward De Bono 1970, Chapter 2, as quoted in Butler-Bowden 2007, 39.

¹⁰ Kouzes and Posner 2003, 173 on.

¹¹ E.g. Saras Sarasvathy, quoted in Sims 2011, 10. See also Read and Sarasvathy 2010.

¹² Achi and Garvey Berger 2015, 2.

¹³ Rodeo Stampede, as awarded by Google and Apple in games of the year awards, December 2016.

¹⁴ Albert Einstein, quoted in interview by G. S. Viereck, 1929. See http://einstein.biz.

¹⁵ Harford 2011, 232.

¹⁶ Https://alpackarafts.com/about.

¹⁷ Sawyer 2013, Chapter 8, Location 3495.

¹⁸ Ashton 2015, 69.

¹⁹ Quoted in Harford 2011, 236.

²⁰ Sawyer 2013, Chapter 5, Location 2252. The Inklings writers group was also drawn from here.

²¹ Csikszentmihalyi 1990, 4.

²² Heath and Heath 2007, 50.

²³ Achi and Garvey Berger 2015, 6.

²⁴ Higgs and Rowland 2005, 124.

²⁵ Garvey-Berger and Johnson 2015, location 1654.

²⁶ As quoted in Sawyer 2013, Chapter 5, Location 2252.

²⁷ As told by Peter Day about aid workers Simon and Jane Berry on BBC Worldwide program "From our own correspondent" July 18 2013.

²⁸ As told in Ashton 2015, 45.

Chapter 10 Engaging unpredictable situations

¹ Meadows and Wright 2008, Meadows 2009.

² The discussion here is drawn from a wide range of sources and sometimes conflicting accounts of this tragedy.

³ Krakauer 1997, 6.

⁴ Marshmallow Challenge website and Ashton 2015, 216.

⁵ Wheatley 2007, 127.

⁶ Quoted in interview with Scott London 2008: http://www.scottlondon.com/interviews/wheatley.html.

⁷ Quoted in Hunt 1954, 50.

⁸ Hunt 1954, 56.

⁹ Sawyer 2013, Chapter 1, Location 533.

¹⁰ As quoted in Moller 1992.

¹¹ Worley 2014a, Chapter 2.

¹² Aigner and Skelton 2013, 159.

¹³ E.g. Holbeche 2015, Location 1379.

¹⁴ As quoted in Thomas 2006, 161.

¹⁵ Larman 2004.

Chapter 11 Embedding agile practices

[1] http://www.viviangreene.com
[2] Uhl-Bien and Marion 2009, 634.
[3] Deutschman 2004, 3.
[4] Aigner and Skelton 2013, 159.
[5] Senge 1990, 227.
[6] Heath and Heath 2010, 85.
[7] Rao 2012, 10.
[8] Hamel 2010, 2.
[9] Rao 2012, 1.
[10] Hamel 2010, 4.
[11] Heath and Heath 2010, 127.

Part 4 Contributing Leadership that makes a Difference

[1] A metaphor contributed by Susan Kaldor.

Chapter 12 Discovering our leadership strengths

[1] Linley 2008, 48.
[2] See for instance Frances 2005, 96.
[3] Commonly attributed to Oscar Wilde.
[4] As quoted in Buckingham 2007, 3.
[5] Seligman, M.E.P., & Csikszentmihalyi, M. (2000). Positive Psychology: An introduction. American Psychologist, 55(1), 5-14.
[6] See for instance Ehrenreich 2009.
[7] Buckingham 2007, 20.
[8] Buckingham 2007, 9.

Chapter 13 Living out leadership

[1] Kouzes and Posner: http://www.youtube.com/watch?v=yiAtoO61C_w, talking about Kouzes and Posner 2010, Chapter 8.
[2] Allen 1997, 119.
[3] Allen 1997, 152; Learmonth and Tabakoff, 2013, Location 2647.
[4] As quoted in Thomas 2006, 160.
[5] Kouzes and Posner 1987, 18.
[6] George and Simms 2007, 206.
[7] Miner, Sterland and Dowson 2006; Kaldor and McLean 2009, 191.
[8] Kaldor and McLean 2009, 196.
[9] See for instance Hughes, Black, Kaldor, Bellamy and Castle 2007, 88.
[10] Avolio and Mhatre 2012, 773.
[11] Markus 2013.
[12] George, Sims, McLean, and Mayer 2007, 1.
[13] Definitions and meanings drawn from several sources including Oxford, Cambridge, Macmillan and Collins dictionaries.
[14] George and Simms 2007, xxxiii.
[15] See, for instance, Walumbwa, Luthans, Avey and Oke 2009, 4 and Walumbwa, Avolio, Gardner, Wernsing and Peterson 2008, 89.

16 Ilies, Morgeson and Nahrgang 2005, 373-394.
17 Cox 2003 and Gardner, Avolio, Luthans, May and Walumbwa 2005, 343.
18 Davidson (2001) referenced in McDonald, P. (2009) Neurological Correlates to Authentic Leadership, Working Paper, Feb 2009, Victoria Management School.
19 Walumbwa, Avolio, Gardner, Wernsing and Peterson 2008, 89.
20 Chatfield, Glenn, Hosler and Fulsaas 2007,163.
21 As quoted in Ortberg 1998.
22 Kaldor and Bullpitt 2001, 9 and Kaldor and McLean 2009, 175.
23 Aigner 2011, 60.
24 Maslach 1976.
25 Freudenburger and Richelson 1980.
26 Kaldor and Bullpitt 2001, 105.
27 Swenson 1998, 59.
28 From Ortberg 1998.

Chapter 14 Building our personal foundations

1 Speech in Detroit, 23 June 1963.
2 American social psychologist Milton Rokeach (1973) distinguished between *terminal* and *instrumental* values.
3 Kouzes and Posner 1987, 52
4 As quoted in George 2003, 19.
5 Nelson Mandela: Speech at his trial in Pretoria, 20 April 1964.
6 Bunting 2016, location 1742.
7 George and Simms 2007, xxiii.
8 A term used by US psychologists Daniel Gilbert and Timothy Wilson as quoted in Sydney Morning Herald October 28 2006, 29.
9 See for instance Seligman 2002, 48 and 52 or Eckersley 1998. Peter's research is contained in Kaldor, Black and Hughes 2009.
10 Seligman 2002, 260.
11 Martin Seligman at presentation in Sydney, 2006.
12 Kaldor, Black and Hughes 2009, 89 and143; Kaldor, Black, and Hughes 2012, 99.
13 Bouma 1999, 9; Tacey 2003, 45.
14 Demerath, 2000, 1.
15 The following is a brief summary of some key results from the *Spirituality and Wellbeing* project developed by Edith Cowan University and NCLS Research between 2000 and 2005. See Kaldor, Black, and Hughes 2009, 142 and 2012, 98 for further detail.
16 Quoted in Vardey 1995.
17 Kaldor and McLean 2009, 201.
18 Kaldor and Bullpitt 2009.
19 See for instance Whetham and Whetham 2000.
20 Oriah (Mountain Dreamer), 1999.

Chapter 15 Self-awareness: the lifelong journey

1 Pollard, 2009, xvii and 335.
2 Story drawn from various reports, including Today Tonight 25/08/08: https://www.youtube.com/watch?v=0wqRAJrl0eA
3 Aigner 2011, 56.